DANIELLE WALKER'S

eat what you love

DANIELLE WALKER'S

eat what you love

everyday comfort
food you crave

———————

gluten-free, dairy-free,
and paleo recipes

PHOTOGRAPHS BY AUBRIE PICK

TEN SPEED PRESS
California | New York

CONTENTS

INTRODUCTION

When it comes to comfort food, our favorite recipes are usually ones that we first enjoyed when we were children. When we eat those same dishes as adults, not only do they taste just as good, but they also remind us of a time when life was a little more effortless and innocent. It's the food that makes us feel good, cared for, and satisfied. I can trace my fondest food memories back to my elementary school days. I loved watching my grandmothers cooking away in their kitchens, bringing their children and grandchildren together around the table. And my mom always managed to fix a mostly home-cooked dinner every night, even though she was busy working part-time and raising me and my two siblings. While "dinner" sometimes meant opening a box or combining a few packages of ingredients in a pan on the stove, I cooked with my mom frequently.

The first recipe I mastered was my grandmother's shepherd's pie, which my mom taught me how to make. Even though my Grandma Bonnie's version included canned cream soup and fried onions, a tub of sour cream, and a pile of cheese, I re-created a slightly more authentic, real-foods version for my family to keep the tradition going (see page 250). In order to be helpful, my siblings and I were often on dinner duty, and that shepherd's pie, as well as French dip sandwiches (see page 217), were my specialties. We used processed deli meat and a package of powdered au jus for those original sandwiches, but hey, at least it wasn't takeout!

My husband, Ryan, has such delicious memories of his Grandmother Betty's beef stew and mashed potatoes that I ended up creating a new version of it for this book (see page 175). Maybe you learned how to make a traditional Key lime pie from your dad, or have a favorite aunt who treated you to her famous pineapple upside-down cake whenever she visited. There's definitely a whole generation of us who were comforted by creamy one-pot casseroles that bubbled as they came out of the oven on chilly nights.

Just as you don't want to forget the people who introduced you to your favorite recipes, you also don't want to forget what those foods tasted like, even if your diet doesn't allow you to enjoy them today. Whether you're a parent trying to get your kids to eat healthier or an adult who still wants to indulge in your childhood favorites while also focusing on your health, there's one thing we all have in common: we want hearty, delicious food that warms the soul and reminds us of our youth.

I think that's why I get so many requests for classic comfort food, such as Chicken 'n' Dumplings Soup (page 173), Mini Corn Dogs (page 259), and creamy casseroles made from canned creamed soups, like Poppy Seed Chicken (page 247). I also get frequent requests for one-pot and slow-cooker meals, make-ahead and freezer foods, packed lunches, and hearty soups and salads that are easy to throw together on busy weeknights, when feeding your tribe a healthful dinner can feel like a chore. As a busy mom to Asher, Easton, and Kezia, I rely on these types of meals frequently, so I get it!

While my last cookbook, *Celebrations*, included a lot of nostalgic dishes like cinnamon rolls, green bean casserole, birthday cakes, and Christmas fudge, I still had a mile-long list of recipes that I had promised to develop. I won't stop publishing recipes until each and every one of you has grain-free renditions of your most beloved dishes that you can slide into your stained and tattered recipe journal in between your grandmother's handwritten index cards.

As with my previous cookbooks, many of these recipes are inspired by recipes developed in my family's kitchens, including my mother's, my grandmothers', my great-grandmothers', and even my husband's grandmother's. They may have spoiled us with sugary cereals and Pop-Tarts when we visited, but these ladies were also masters of homemade comfort food. Many of my Granny Sarella's recipes may already be beloved in your kitchen. (If you haven't yet, check out Granny Sarella's meat sauce from my first cookbook, *Against All Grain*, or her biscotti and panettone recipes from *Celebrations*.) In the same way, I hope Betty's Beef Stew, inspired by

Nanny, Ryan's grandmother, becomes a staple weeknight meal. I bet the Sausage-Spinach Skillet Lasagna (page 220) or Chicken Divan (page 256), fashioned after hot dishes my mom made on cold winter nights in Colorado, will be added to your regular dinner rotation. And I hope your old potluck dessert favorites, such as Banana Pudding (page 303) or Apple Crisp (page 289), can be reintroduced to your repertoire.

If the recipes you loved from childhood don't fit into your lifestyle any longer because you have food allergies or have to follow a special diet, dinnertime can be especially frustrating. You may envision a life filled with bland chicken and steamed broccoli, and suddenly you're a little short of breath. If you are newly diagnosed with celiac, a dairy allergy, gluten intolerance, or an autoimmune disease, or just want to eat healthier a few nights a week, you may feel confused and hopeless when it comes to food.

Can this really be a sustainable lifestyle for you or your family? The short answer is yes! Flip through this book and inhale deeply. You *can* still find comfort in the foods you eat, and enjoy them with your friends and family, despite your restrictions. The recipes in this book will show you that you can enjoy life, feel great, and relish in delicious and decadent food that leaves you feeling satisfied rather than deprived.

Happy cooking!

ESTABLISHING YOUR SUPPORT SYSTEM

Who is around *your* table? Do they accept your food lifestyle, or are they a bit hesitant? One of the biggest hurdles we all face when going grain-free is getting our loved ones on board. Maybe your husband doesn't buy into your choice and thinks everything will taste bad, or you're worried your kids will melt down because you stripped away their beloved chicken nuggets. Or you might have elderly, set-in-their-ways parents who don't want to attempt a dietary change, or friends who think you're crazy for turning down the bread basket and asking the server a bunch of questions when you're at a restaurant together. I wish I could tell you to forget about them and to continue on your path to health alone, but it's difficult to sustain a big lifestyle change without a community around your table for moral support and accountability. Plus, part of the joy of comforting food is sharing it with those we love.

For me, that supportive person was my husband, Ryan, who is healthy as a horse, has no diagnosed illnesses, rarely gets sick, and, when he *does* get sick, recovers from any illness three times quicker than I do. This was all true when he ate a standard American diet, but is even more so now that he's following a paleo-style diet in solidarity with me. At first, I had a really difficult time committing and adjusting to this way of eating, both mentally and physically. It seemed to be an impossible shift to make in the midst of being diagnosed with a lifelong debilitating disease, and I wasn't sure the change was worth it, or if it would even work. After a few months of dabbling with the new diet and falling off the wagon more often

than not, my kind and supportive husband looked at me and said, "Do I need to do this with you so you will stick to it?" With tears in my eyes, I said, "Yes, I think that would help. Thank you."

So we embarked on the journey together, and for the first time, I thought I might actually be able to sustain the change. I no longer made him a side of rice or served his hamburger on a roll while I ate mine on a piece of lettuce. I didn't buy bread, chips, or ice cream anymore to eliminate the chance of taking "just one bite" of his.

Our house became a safe place, and Ryan stood by my side. When we went out and I was tempted to eat something I shouldn't, Ryan would lovingly remind me of the consequences of that decision. He was so adamant about helping me stay on track that he endured many dirty looks from other women when they heard him say, "Dani, that's not on your diet," and assumed he was a controlling spouse who wanted his wife to stay trim. We ultimately came up with a silly code word to use in public so he didn't appear to be a monster husband.

In the beginning, Ryan still occasionally ate a normal diet when he was at work, then would come home and tell me he felt a bit off. He eventually realized that he was likely gluten-intolerant but had never known it. Symptoms that he never knew he had—like brain fog, achy joints, and minor digestive problems—started to disappear. He hates it when I mention this when I speak in public, but he used to spend a lot more time in the bathroom than he does now that he's mostly dairy- and grain-free!

I frequently hear from people with ill loved ones searching for ways in which they can help. In my experience, what is most impactful is helping people see the correlation between their symptoms and what they are putting in their mouths. Help them realize on their own that they need to make a change and encourage them to do it for themselves rather than to appease someone else. Children, especially, need to feel ownership over the change and cannot just be forced into it.

If you are trying to change your family's eating habits for the sake of one of your children, it is incredibly helpful if the entire family is on board. It's really difficult to tell a child, who likely already feels ostracized because of an illness, disability, or disease, that they have to eat a plate of veggies and protein while their siblings eat mac and cheese or sugary cereals. And it's incredibly difficult for kids and adults alike to make good decisions when all the food they aren't able to eat stares back at them from the pantry and refrigerator every day. Explain how the foods being eliminated have been causing them harm. Once a child knows that food A hurts their tummy, food B makes their skin itchy, or food C makes them hyper and get in trouble at school, it is a little easier for them to want to make good decisions and to do it for themselves rather than be ordered to do it.

If you're hoping to convince someone close to you that your new way of eating is actually pretty tasty, the friendliest way to encourage them is to make a meal or a treat and invite them over. Don't start the meal by saying, "Hey, this is gluten-free, dairy-free, legume-free, refined sugar-free, and free of anything else that used to give you joy." When we hear those types of disclaimers, we convince ourselves that we will not enjoy said healthful food because it's neither comforting nor indulgent.

Rather, let the food be the star. Only after people have thoroughly enjoyed the meal and feel satiated can you drop the "-free" bombs. Indulgent foods and healthful foods *can* coexist, and it has been my mission since I created my blog to give people just that: healthful food that allows you to eat well *and* feel great. So re-create some of their favorite dishes and help them see that they can still experience the comfort and nostalgia that comes with food.

If you don't need to follow a special diet out of necessity but want to make your guests feel welcome and cared for, use the recipes in this book to help achieve that goal. Of all of the stories I have heard about how my recipes have affected people's lives, the ones that really stand out are those in which a loving parent, spouse, grandparent, or friend picks up a copy of my book so they have an arsenal of recipes for when their loved one with special dietary restrictions visits. It is my hope that each of you has a person in your life that cares so deeply about you that they go out of their way to make you feel welcome. That is what gathering around the table is all about after all, and it is food that so often brings us together.

INGREDIENT GLOSSARY AND SUBSTITUTIONS

After you make the mental commitment to change your diet, the next step is to get your kitchen prepared. Start reading recipes and familiarizing yourself with some of the new ingredients that will replace old staples like all-purpose flour, sugar, and dairy milk. You might also take this opportunity to purge your kitchen of processed foods and donate anything on your new "no list" of foods to neighbors or people in need.

Because the commercial products available are ever-changing, my favorite brands change from time to time too. Find the most current list of my favorite products and an ingredient glossary on my website, againstallgrain.com/ingredients. I have also listed some of my favorite brands in Resources (page 319).

Following are descriptions of ingredients I commonly use in my kitchen and notes on some possible substitutions. Whether you have allergies or cannot find a particular ingredient called for in a recipe, the chart on pages 10–11 will help you understand what, and how much, you can swap for what.

Important note: The recipes in this book were only tested using the ingredients as called for, so if you make a substitution that isn't suggested, you run the risk that the final product will be different from what was intended or is pictured. Also, I don't suggest swapping out more than one ingredient at a time.

EGGS

I use eggs as leaveners and binders in my baked goods. The egg substitutes (see page 10) can be used in baking recipes that call for 2 eggs or fewer. Beware that egg substitutes do not make baked goods rise as high, so the texture will be more dense and moist.

AQUAFABA: This is the common name for the cooking liquid of beans and legumes such as chickpeas. Chickpeas have the least amount of lectins and phytates, which can disrupt digestion, so their liquid is best. Use either canned or home-cooked chickpeas. The liquid should have the same consistency as egg whites. If it is watery, reduce it over medium heat in a pan on the stove to get a slightly thicker consistency. While the Paleo Diet omits legumes, this is still a great egg substitute for grain-free folks who cannot tolerate eggs but can tolerate legumes on occasion. Read more at aquafaba.com.

DUCK EGGS: If you have an allergy to chicken eggs, you may be able to use duck eggs because the protein structure is slightly different. The only way to know for sure is to experiment, but if you have a serious allergy, please do this only under the advice and care of your allergist or medical practitioner. Some egg allergies can also be caused by the feed given to the bird, not the egg itself. Try to source eggs from pasture-raised birds that freely forage, or at least switch to non-GMO, soy- and corn-free eggs.

Duck eggs are quite a bit larger than chicken eggs, so weigh the duck eggs before using and adjust the amount you add accordingly. A standard chicken egg is around 50 grams.

FATS

I use minimally processed fats such as avocado oil, ghee, and coconut oil, and avoid using seed oils or other highly processed oils that oxidize easily, such as canola and soybean oils. Try to find organic and unrefined (or virgin) oils and pasture-raised versions of animal fats if possible.

COOKING FATS: Coconut oil, ghee, extra-virgin olive oil, avocado oil, or animal fats such as tallow, lard, and duck fat can be used interchangeably.

PALM SHORTENING: It gives a cakelike texture to baked goods, has a high melting point, and is fairly solid at room temperature. Pastured lard, grass-fed butter, or ghee are the best alternatives. See Resources (page 319) for sustainable, eco-friendly brands.

FLOURS

Grain-free flours are a little more difficult to substitute, because they each have different properties. There isn't an exact science or formula, which is why I spend so much time experimenting to create foolproof recipes. I included a general guideline for swapping flours (see chart on page 10), but unfortunately, whenever you make flour substitutions, the end results will be different from what was intended.

ALMOND FLOUR: The finer the grind of almond flour, the better your baked goods will turn out. I suggest purchasing blanched and finely ground almond flour from my trusted brands for the best results (see Resources, page 319) and to avoid

moist products that sink in the center or have a grainy texture. If you're a frequent baker, store a pound of almond flour in an airtight container at room temperature and refrigerate the rest for up to 1 month or freeze for up to 6 months.

ARROWROOT: Usually found in powdered form, arrowroot gives breads and cakes the elasticity often missing from grain-free baked goods because of the lack of the gluten protein. It gives a nice crunch to crackers and is a great gluten-free ingredient for baking or thickening if you have tree-nut allergies. When combined with coconut flour, arrowroot creates a wonderful nut-free crumb for baked goods.

When I was at the beginning of my health journey, I did not tolerate it well, so I abstained. After a few years of healing my gut, I found that I was able to add it into my diet slowly without any ill effects. Tapioca starch, from the cassava root, can be evenly substituted for arrowroot, but can be more difficult to digest. Use whatever works best for your body. You can also substitute coconut flour, but the result will be more cakelike.

COCONUT FLOUR: This flour is a very unique and incredibly absorbent flour, so I don't recommend substituting it in recipes that use nut flours unless you're ready for a little trial and error. If you want to experiment, use the substitutions (see chart on page 10) for recipes that call for ¼ cup or less. It is also helpful if the recipe incorporates a starch such as arrowroot, which will work with the coconut flour to give a baked item structure.

When using coconut flour, let the batter or dough rest for a few minutes before deciding whether or not to add a little more liquid. Different brands of coconut flour vary in absorbency, so find a brand you like (I use Tropical Traditions) and stick with it so you have consistent results.

GARBANZO BEAN FLOUR: This is relatively inexpensive, lower in calories and carbohydrates than standard flours, and loaded with protein and folate. Otherwise known as chickpea flour, it is an ingredient I use to keep savory dishes free from tree nuts and coconut. If you have a sensitive digestive system, seek out sprouted garbanzo bean flour. Sprouting beans before they are dried and ground makes the flour easier to digest by breaking down the complex sugars and allows the vitamins, enzymes, and minerals to be more easily absorbed. Chickpeas and garbanzo beans are not Specific Carbohydrate Diet (SCD)–friendly, but if they are soaked and sprouted and you tolerate them, they can be acceptable in paleo-style diets.

LEAVENING AGENTS

I use the following leavening agents most frequently in my recipes. Remember that baking soda and baking powder cause different reactions and cannot be evenly exchanged.

BAKING POWDER: This is a ready-made combination of baking soda and an acid, usually cream of tartar, and it often includes a starch. Since many store-bought baking powders contain grain-based starches, I make my own (see page 312) or look for Hain brand, which uses potato starch instead of cornstarch. To give your dishes optimal texture, make sure your baking powder is fresh and not expired.

BAKING SODA: Typically, baking soda is called for in recipes that also include acidic ingredients like honey, maple syrup, lemon juice, and vinegar.

When the baking soda reacts with the acid in these ingredients, it becomes a leavening agent, which helps dough to rise. Baking soda also causes baked goods to be darker and crisper than those that don't contain it.

YEAST: I don't use this ingredient often because part of its magic is only possible with gluten as a counterpart. However, there are a few recipes in this book that require yeast to mimic the taste of the conventional version, so I use a certified gluten-free active dry yeast (such as Bob's Red Mill) to provide authentic flavor and a little rise. These recipes can be made without the yeast by using the substitutions in the chart on page 11, but the flavor and rise won't be the same. So, is yeast paleo? If you don't have an allergy or intolerance to yeast, and you are not suffering from a candida overgrowth, my research says it is harmless and can fit within a paleo lifestyle.

MILKS

Dairy-free milks are fairly easy to swap among recipes, but when cashew or coconut milk is used to thicken sauces or make whipped cream, I do not recommend a substitution. If you have a nut allergy but can tolerate dairy, I have given dairy options on the chart on page 11.

ALMOND MILK: This thin nut milk can be used as a substitute for 2 percent or nonfat dairy milk. See page 308 for my homemade recipe, or purchase a version that is unsweetened and unflavored, and free of carrageenan at your grocery store. Almond milk is easily substituted for other dairy-free milks too; just keep in mind that cashew and coconut milk have a higher fat content and thicker texture.

CASHEW MILK: This can often be substituted for coconut milk or grass-fed heavy cream because it has a similar consistency and fat content. Cashew milk will not work, however, for recipes using only the cream from the can of coconut milk or for whipped cream (see page 93). Thick homemade cashew milk is used to thicken some of the sauces, desserts, and soups in this book. I do not advise substituting with coconut milk or using store-bought cashew milk in those recipes.

COCONUT MILK: I use full-fat coconut milk in recipes that are tree nut–free. Unless I specifically call for the coconut fat from the top of a can of coconut milk, or use coconut milk for its authentic taste, my homemade Cashew Milk (page 310) can be used interchangeably.

NUT BUTTERS

Almond butter, cashew butter, and sunflower seed butter can all be used interchangeably.

SUNFLOWER SEED BUTTER: When using this in place of almond or cashew butter in recipes that also call for baking soda, some baked goods may turn green when the baking soda reacts to the chlorophyll in the sunflower seed butter. To avoid this, add 1 teaspoon freshly squeezed lemon juice or raw apple cider vinegar and decrease the baking soda by half.

INGREDIENT SUBSTITUTIONS CHART

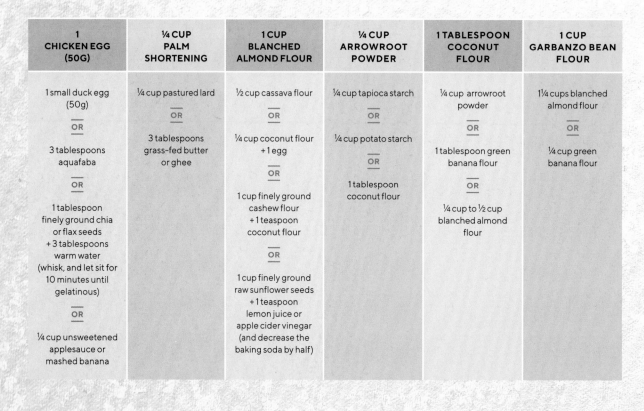

1 CHICKEN EGG (50G)	¼ CUP PALM SHORTENING	1 CUP BLANCHED ALMOND FLOUR	¼ CUP ARROWROOT POWDER	1 TABLESPOON COCONUT FLOUR	1 CUP GARBANZO BEAN FLOUR
1 small duck egg (50g)	¼ cup pastured lard	½ cup cassava flour	¼ cup tapioca starch	¼ cup arrowroot powder	1¼ cups blanched almond flour
OR	OR	OR	OR	OR	OR
3 tablespoons aquafaba	3 tablespoons grass-fed butter or ghee	¼ cup coconut flour + 1 egg	¼ cup potato starch	1 tablespoon green banana flour	¼ cup green banana flour
OR		OR	OR	OR	
1 tablespoon finely ground chia or flax seeds + 3 tablespoons warm water (whisk, and let sit for 10 minutes until gelatinous)		1 cup finely ground cashew flour + 1 teaspoon coconut flour	1 tablespoon coconut flour	¼ cup to ½ cup blanched almond flour	
OR		OR			
¼ cup unsweetened applesauce or mashed banana		1 cup finely ground raw sunflower seeds + 1 teaspoon lemon juice or apple cider vinegar (and decrease the baking soda by half)			

SWEETENERS

I use the following unrefined sweeteners in my recipes.

COCONUT SUGAR: This is also known as coconut crystals or palm sugar, and is produced from the sap of the flower buds of the coconut palm tree. It is dark in color and fairly coarse, and works really well as a brown sugar substitute.

HONEY: I use light-colored raw honey in my baking recipes for both a mild flavor and color.

MAPLE SUGAR: This can often be substituted in a 1:1 ratio for coconut sugar, but it will give the dish a deeper amber color and a less-sweet flavor. Also see againstallgrain.com/maple-sugar to find out how to make your own.

MAPLE SYRUP: Look for pure maple syrup that does not have any added ingredients. I prefer to use a dark amber syrup for its rich flavor.

Honey and maple syrup may be substituted 1:1, but the taste and color will vary.

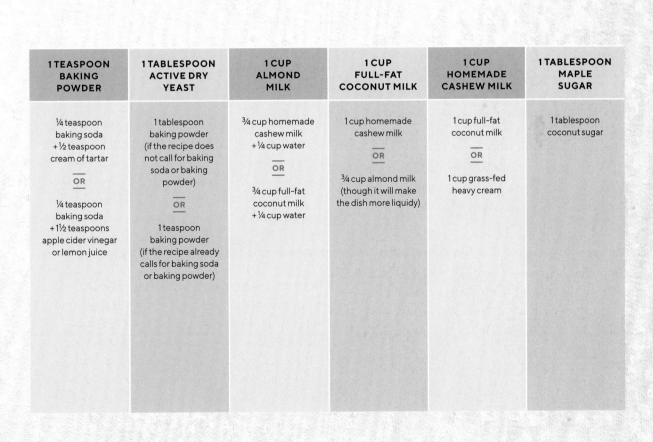

1 TEASPOON BAKING POWDER	1 TABLESPOON ACTIVE DRY YEAST	1 CUP ALMOND MILK	1 CUP FULL-FAT COCONUT MILK	1 CUP HOMEMADE CASHEW MILK	1 TABLESPOON MAPLE SUGAR
¼ teaspoon baking soda + ½ teaspoon cream of tartar OR ¼ teaspoon baking soda + 1½ teaspoons apple cider vinegar or lemon juice	1 tablespoon baking powder (if the recipe does not call for baking soda or baking powder) OR 1 teaspoon baking powder (if the recipe already calls for baking soda or baking powder)	¾ cup homemade cashew milk + ¼ cup water OR ¾ cup full-fat coconut milk + ¼ cup water	1 cup homemade cashew milk OR ¾ cup almond milk (though it will make the dish more liquidy)	1 cup full-fat coconut milk OR 1 cup grass-fed heavy cream	1 tablespoon coconut sugar

MEAL PLANNING

In addition to having a community to support your journey on this lifestyle, planning well is essential for most people to stay the course. In the past, takeout or frozen foods from the grocery store could have been your fallback if you did not plan your dinners for the week, but most of those options aren't available once you have gone grain- and dairy-free. Meal planning for the week (or month, if you're ambitious!) will become your single most valuable tool. It will help keep you and your family sane and eating well, and it can even benefit the budget.

When my oldest son was an infant, I learned quickly that waiting until 5 p.m. to prepare dinner was a recipe for disaster. As much as I wanted to nap during his nap time, or binge-watch my favorite TV show, I realized that prepping some of the ingredients or knocking out a few of the cooking steps during the day would help to ensure that I had dinner ready and wasn't reaching for the phone to order takeout or ask Ryan to pick up food on his way home from work. Planning ahead also took some of the stress out of it all, especially when the "witching hour" hit and meltdowns (of both the baby and me!) were ever present.

For me, going into the week without a plan leaves me frantic when trying to figure out what to eat around dinnertime. Not having a plan also causes me to make mistakes at the grocery store. I go in needing just a couple of things, but my cart ends up filled with more indulgent or processed items than necessary.

Sit down at the beginning of the week and use the meal plans that follow to ensure you are never in this predicament. Do your grocery shopping once a week to make your cooking more efficient, and minimize the number of impulse food items you buy.

Prep all of the vegetables you will use for the week, then pack them up in glass containers or resealable plastic bags and store them in the refrigerator to shave off time when you start cooking. Chop frequently used ingredients like onions and garlic all at once so they'll always be close at hand. They will keep in the refrigerator for about a week. This saves on cleanup and teary eyes!

Devote one day a week or month to a prep day, and make some of the refrigerator and pantry staples or a few of the meals from Chapter 7: Make It Ahead. I make salad dressings, condiments, and nut milks. And also batch-cook my Grain-Free Wraps (page 313) or Nut-Free Lunchbox Bread (page 48), as well as Pressure Cooker Chicken (page 315), so I can utilize them throughout the week. It isn't always feasible for a busy person to make *all* of these items from scratch, so I have also listed my favorite store-bought versions with most of the recipes in Basics.

Not only does being organized save time and make meal preparation simple, but it can also save you money. Meal planning helps decrease waste by ensuring that you have a plan for everything you purchase. You won't end up with a half-used wilted bunch of parsley at the end of the week, or a moldy jar of tomato puree lurking in the back of the fridge. I have constructed these meal plans so the most perishable items are used at the beginning of the week and leftover ingredients are used during the latter part of the week.

On the next page are four weeks of meal plans (including lunch). These are designed to offer variety and minimize waste and stress. I left one day open each week so you can eat leftovers, or for special occasions and dining out. Check out againstallgrain.com/meal-plans for even more.

If you're not using the meal plans I have provided for you, here are a few of my meal planning tips:

1. Shop and prep on the weekend.

2. Avoid shopping twice in one week by freezing fresh fish and poultry the day you buy it. The night before you want to cook it, defrost it in the refrigerator.

3. Check your calendar to see what's on your agenda for the week. Will you be home by 5 p.m. and have time to cook a more complex recipe? Or are you going to be running kids around to extracurricular activities and get home right at the dinner hour? You don't want to plan for six meals and only end up making three of them, so try your best to buy only what you will actually use at the beginning of each week.

4. Ask your family what they're in the mood to eat. Letting your kids or spouse flag recipes they are interested in gives them ownership over dinnertime and may result in fewer battles at the dinner table. I also try to throw in a couple of new recipes with fresh flavors that I personally want to try.

5. Next, gather all your recipes for the week, write the titles down in a blank calendar, read through them, and figure out what you already have in your kitchen. Then make your grocery list.

RECIPE ICONS

The following simple icons, found at the tops of the recipes, will help you navigate the ingredients and cooking methods. At a glance, you will know whether a recipe fits within your particular dietary restrictions, or whether you can make the dish in a single pot or pan, a slow cooker, or an electric pressure cooker.

EF Egg-free.

NF Tree nut–free, not including coconut.

NSF Nightshade-free, including tomatoes, tomatillos, eggplant, white potatoes, and sweet and hot peppers.

SCD These recipes contain only ingredients that are allowed on the Specific Carbohydrate Diet. Often they are acceptable for the Gut Psychology Syndrome (GAPS) diet as well, since many of the rules overlap.

These recipes are prepared in a single pot or sheet pan, a slow cooker, or an electric pressure cooker.

MEAL PLANS

Find the printable grocery lists for these meal plans, plus even more meal plans, at againstallgrain.com/eat-what-you-love.

PREP DAY

- Pressure Cooker Chicken (page 315)
- Açai Berry-Chia Pudding Parfaits (page 43)
- Breakfast "Hamburgers" (page 233)
- Chocolate-Zucchini Muffins (page 234)

- Smoothie Packets (page 240)
- 6 to 12 hard-boiled eggs
- Wash lettuce leaves (see page 142)

WEEK 1	DAY 1	DAY 2	DAY 3	DAY 4	DAY 5	DAY 6
BREAKFAST	Açai Berry-Chia Pudding Parfaits and hard-boiled egg	Breakfast "Hamburgers" and Berry Sorbet Smoothie	Açai Berry-Chia Pudding Parfaits and leftover sweet potatoes reheated with ghee	Chocolate-Zucchini Muffins, hard-boiled egg, and fruit	Breakfast "Hamburgers" with eggs and fruit	Lemon Ricotta Pancakes (page 23; double recipe and freeze for Week 2)
LUNCH	Club AAGwich (page 59)	Day 1 dinner leftovers	Thai Chicken AAGwich (page 58)	BBQ Chicken Salad with Peach Power Slaw (page 68)	Day 4 dinner leftovers	Day 5 dinner leftovers
DINNER	Thai Crunch Salad with Steak (page 146)	Pulled Pork with Slaw (page 206) and Pressure Cooker Sweet Potatoes (page 316)	Chicken Piccata with Artichokes and Spinach (page 185)	Betty's Beef Stew (page 175) and Roasted Garlic Mashed Cauliflower (see page 250)	Fish Sticks with Fries and Tartar Sauce (page 260; double recipe and freeze for Week 4) and White Wine Garlic Spinach and Mushrooms (page 133)	Chicken Potpie (page 253; double recipe and freeze for Week 4)

PREP DAY

- Pressure Cooker Chicken (page 315)
- Healing Chicken Soup (page 167)
- Nut-Free Lunchbox Bread (page 48)
- Honey-Mustard Chicken (page 243)
- Crustless Quiche to Go (page 24)
- 6 to 12 hard-boiled eggs
- Wash lettuce cups (see page 142)

WEEK 2	DAY 1	DAY 2	DAY 3	DAY 4	DAY 5	DAY 6
BREAKFAST	Healing Chicken Soup	Crustless Quiche to Go	Creamy Blueberry Peach Smoothie, eggs, and bacon or sausage	Crustless Quiche to Go	Lemon Ricotta Pancakes (from freezer)	Everything Bagels (page 40), smoked salmon, Ricotta Cheese (page 316), and sliced raw vegetables
LUNCH	Dill Chicken Salad (page 64; save leftovers for Day 3) in lettuce cups	Day 1 breakfast leftovers	Dill Chicken Salad leftovers on toasted Nut-Free Lunchbox Bread	Grilled Shrimp Summer Harvest Salad (page 155; use leftover honey-mustard chicken instead of shrimp)	Buffalo Chicken AAGwich (page 59; use leftover Pressure Cooker Chicken)	Day 5 dinner leftovers
DINNER	Honey-Mustard Chicken (save leftovers for Day 4) with Roasted Beets and Carrots with Citrus Vinaigrette (page 121)	Thai Yellow Curry (page 194) with Basic Cauli Rice (page 309; save half for Day 4)	Honey-Mustard Sheet-Pan Salmon (page 213)	Beef and Broccoli (page 182) with Basic Cauli Rice (left over from Day 2)	Pesto Power Meatballs (page 244) and Pesto Squash Noodles (page 138)	Chicken 'n' Dumplings Soup (page 173) and a green salad

PREP DAY

- Morning Glory Muffins (page 238)
- Açai Berry-Chia Pudding Parfaits (page 43)
- 6 to 12 hard-boiled eggs
- Wash lettuce cups (see page 142)

WEEK 3	DAY 1	DAY 2	DAY 3	DAY 4	DAY 5	DAY 6
BREAKFAST	Morning Glory Muffins, Chocolate Mint Smoothie, and hard-boiled egg or fruit	Açai Berry-Chia Pudding Parfaits and Millionaire's Bacon (page 36; double recipe for Day 4)	Green Pina Colada Smoothie and hard-boiled egg	Açai Berry-Chia Pudding Parfaits	Crispy Nut-Free Waffles (page 237; freeze leftovers for Week 4)	Biscuits and Sausage Gravy (page 26; save leftovers for Week 4)
LUNCH	Deviled Egg Salad Sandwich (page 54; save leftover egg salad for Day 3)	Chef's Salad (page 156)	Deviled Egg Salad leftovers in lettuce cups	Millionaire's AB&J (page 53)	Day 4 dinner leftovers	Chicken Caesar AAGwich (page 58)
DINNER	Sheet-Pan Teriyaki Salmon with Broccoli and Asparagus (page 224)	Sheet-Pan Steak Fajitas (page 223)	Tomato Soup with Zesty Croutons (page 164) and Grilled Chicken Caesar (page 151)	Shrimp Fried Rice (page 193)	Indian Butter Chicken (page 203)	Moroccan Chicken Sheet-Pan Supper (page 210)

PREP DAY

- Crustless Quiche to Go (page 24)
- Pressure Cooker Chicken (page 315)
- Breakfast "Hamburgers" (page 233)
- Pizza Crusts (page 265)
- Wash lettuce cups (see page 142)

WEEK 4	DAY 1	DAY 2	DAY 3	DAY 4	DAY 5	DAY 6
BREAKFAST	Breakfast "Hamburgers" with eggs and fruit	Biscuits and Sausage Gravy leftovers (or use leftover biscuits for a breakfast sandwich)	Crustless Quiche to Go	Crispy Nut-Free Waffles (from freezer)	Crustless Quiche to Go	Shrimp and Grits with Bacon Collards (page 30)
LUNCH	Dill Chicken Salad (page 64; save leftovers for Day 3) in lettuce cups	Day 1 dinner leftovers	Dill Chicken Salad leftovers in lettuce cups	California Hand Rolls (page 60)	Day 4 dinner leftovers	Italian Chopped Salad with Red Wine Vinaigrette (from Day 4)
DINNER	Shepherd's Pie (page 250)	Pizza Night with toppings of your choice	Fish Sticks with Fries and Tartar Sauce (from freezer) with a green salad	Creamy Broccoli Soup (page 163) and Italian Chopped Salad with Red Wine Vinaigrette (page 148; double recipe for Day 6)	Chicken Parmesan with Roasted Spaghetti Squash (page 214)	Chicken Potpie (from freezer)

CHAPTER 1

BREAKFAST

LEMON RICOTTA PANCAKES

Serves 4 to 6 • Ricotta is a slightly sweet fresh cheese that's most commonly found in Italian dishes like lasagna, pizza, and other pasta entrées. My dairy-free version of ricotta lends a light and delicate texture to these melt-in-your-mouth pancakes, while the lemon adds a refreshing twist. The pancakes are delicious served with maple syrup and fresh blueberries (as pictured), but the sweet blueberry sauce pairs so well with the tart lemon, you won't want to skip it.

To make the blueberry syrup, in a saucepan, combine the blueberries, maple syrup, half of the lemon zest, and 1 teaspoon of the lemon juice. Bring to a boil over medium-high heat, then turn the heat to low and simmer for 15 minutes. Pour the mixture into a blender and blend on low speed for 15 seconds, until very smooth.

To make the pancakes, meanwhile, in the bowl of a stand mixer fitted with the whisk attachment, or using an electric handheld mixer, beat the egg whites with a pinch of salt on medium-high speed until they hold stiff peaks, 3 to 5 minutes. Set aside.

Combine the egg yolks, the remaining lemon juice from the blueberry syrup, the almond milk, ghee, vanilla, vinegar, ricotta, cashew flour, coconut flour, arrowroot, maple sugar, baking powder, and ¼ teaspoon salt in a food processor. Process on high speed for 30 seconds, until smooth. Transfer the mixture to a large bowl, and stir one-third of the egg whites into the batter to lighten it. Gently fold in the remaining egg whites and the remaining lemon zest from the blueberry syrup, being careful not to deflate the whites.

Lightly grease a griddle or large skillet with palm shortening and place it over medium heat. Spoon about ¼ cup of batter onto the hot pan for each pancake. Cook for 3 to 4 minutes, or until bubbles appear on the surface and the edges release easily. Flip and continue to cook for 2 to 3 minutes more, until the pancakes are firm and lightly browned. Keep the pancakes warm in a 200°F oven or covered on a plate. Repeat until all of the pancake batter is used. Serve warm, drizzled with the blueberry syrup.

BLUEBERRY SYRUP

2 cups frozen blueberries

½ cup pure maple syrup

Finely grated zest and juice of 1 lemon

PANCAKES

4 eggs, separated

Fine sea salt

½ cup Almond Milk (page 308)

¼ cup melted ghee

1 teaspoon pure vanilla extract

¼ teaspoon apple cider vinegar

1 cup Ricotta Cheese (page 316), or any store-bought dairy-free ricotta (see Tidbits)

1 cup cashew flour

3 tablespoons coconut flour

2 tablespoons arrowroot powder

¼ cup pure maple sugar

1 teaspoon Grain-Free Baking Powder (page 312)

Tidbits: If you don't want to make your own ricotta, Kite Hill makes a great dairy-free version that is sold in health food stores.

CRUSTLESS QUICHE TO GO

Makes 12 • These are perfect for breakfast on a busy morning. I keep a dozen in the freezer so I can pull them out and heat them quickly in the toaster oven for breakfast, or put them in Asher's lunchbox. I like to put them in a warmed thermos so they stay hot, but he also doesn't mind eating them thawed. My favorite sweet potato for this is the Hannah variety, which has white flesh and leans more toward savory than sweet. To ensure the ingredients are paleo-friendly, I use sugar-free bacon and the sausage mix from my Breakfast "Hamburgers." Feel free to substitute your favorite greens for the chard, such as spinach or collard greens.

12 eggs

¼ cup Almond Milk (page 308)

¼ cup full-fat coconut milk

¾ teaspoon fine sea salt

¼ teaspoon freshly ground black pepper

3 ounces chopped cooked bacon

3 ounces crumbled cooked breakfast sausage or Breakfast "Hamburgers" (page 233)

1 cup packed stemmed and chopped Swiss chard

1 cup peeled shredded sweet potato

¼ cup finely chopped fresh chives

Preheat the oven to 350°F. Place a 12-cup silicone muffin pan on a rimmed baking sheet and lightly grease the cups with ghee.

In a large bowl, beat the eggs with the almond milk, coconut milk, salt, and pepper. In a separate bowl, combine the bacon, sausage, chard, sweet potato, and chives. Divide the bacon mixture among the 12 cups, filling each one halfway full, and press down on the mixture slightly. Pour the egg mixture over the top, filling the cups two-thirds full. Bake for 20 minutes, until the centers are just set and a toothpick inserted into the center of a quiche comes out clean. Allow the quiches to cool in the pan for 20 minutes, then release them onto a cooling rack. Serve immediately, or let them cool to room temperature before storing.

Store the quiches in an airtight container in the refrigerator for 3 days. To reheat, place the quiches on a baking sheet and heat for 5 to 7 minutes in a 400°F oven until heated through.

Freeze the quiches in a single layer on a rimmed baking sheet tightly covered with plastic wrap, for 4 hours. Transfer the frozen quiches to an airtight container and store in the freezer for 3 months. Defrost the quiches overnight in the refrigerator before reheating.

Tidbits: To make this NF, substitute full-fat coconut milk for the almond milk. To comply with SCD, omit the sweet potato and substitute shredded butternut squash or celeriac.

BISCUITS AND SAUSAGE GRAVY

Serves 6 • Biscuits and gravy is a true classic, but truth be told, it wasn't really on my radar until I started getting requests for a gluten-free rendition. A while back, I had a chance to taste a real Southern version at a Nashville restaurant—now I understand what all the fuss is about. To be sure, my recipe does this favorite justice. I served it to two of my friends from the South—Annie, who hails from Atlanta, and Angie from Nashville—and it passed their test. I hope all of you biscuit-and-sausage-gravy fans love this grain- and dairy-free version too.

BISCUITS

3½ cups blanched almond flour, sifted

⅓ cup coconut flour, sifted, plus more for rolling out the dough

2 eggs

¼ cup Almond Milk (page 308)

1 tablespoon light-colored raw honey

2 teaspoons apple cider vinegar

1 teaspoon baking soda

½ teaspoon fine sea salt

⅓ cup palm shortening or 5 tablespoons ghee

1 egg yolk, mixed with 1 tablespoon full-fat coconut milk, for wash

SAUSAGE GRAVY

1 pound ground pork

1 tablespoon pure maple syrup

1 teaspoon coconut sugar

½ teaspoon ground sage

¼ teaspoon garlic powder

¼ teaspoon onion powder

¼ teaspoon ground cinnamon

To make the biscuits, preheat the oven to 350°F. Line a baking sheet with parchment paper.

Combine the almond flour, coconut flour, eggs, almond milk, honey, vinegar, baking soda, and salt in the bowl of a stand mixer fitted with the beater attachment, or use an electric handheld mixer. Mix on medium speed until a loose dough forms. Switch to a dough hook or use a pastry cutter to blend in the palm shortening, leaving pea-size bits of shortening visible in the dough. Lightly sprinkle some coconut flour on a sheet of parchment paper. Turn the dough out onto the floured surface. Gather it into a ball and form it into a 7-inch-wide disk that's about 2 inches thick, using your palms to gently flatten the top.

Use a 3-inch round biscuit cutter to cut out four biscuits. Gather the dough scraps into a ball, form into a disk again, and cut out the remaining two biscuits. (Alternatively, shape six biscuits from the dough by hand.) Place the biscuits on the prepared baking sheet and brush them with the egg wash.

Bake for 18 minutes, rotating the sheet once midway through baking, until the biscuits are golden brown. Allow the biscuits to cool slightly on a wire rack before serving.

To make the sausage gravy, meanwhile, in a large bowl, combine the pork, maple syrup, coconut sugar, ground sage, garlic powder, onion powder, cinnamon, nutmeg, 1¾ teaspoons salt, and ⅛ teaspoon pepper and mix well with your hands. Place the pork sausage mixture in a large saucepan over medium-high heat and cook, breaking up the pieces with a wooden spoon until browned and no longer pink, about 10 minutes. Add the cashew milk and simmer for 30 seconds, stirring constantly, until thickened. Remove the pan from the heat. Stir in the fresh sage and up to 2 tablespoons water if the gravy needs thinning. Season with salt and pepper to taste.

Cut each biscuit in half. Place two halves on each plate and spoon the sausage gravy over the top. Sprinkle with pepper and chives and serve.

Tidbits: To comply with SCD, substitute 1 tablespoon light-colored raw honey for the maple syrup and coconut sugar in the sausage gravy.

¼ teaspoon ground nutmeg

Fine sea salt and freshly ground black pepper

3 cups Cashew Milk (page 310)

1 tablespoon chopped fresh sage

Chopped fresh chives, for garnish

BANANA-CHOCOLATE-HAZELNUT FRENCH TOAST

Serves 4 to 6 • French toast is one of my guilty pleasures. Before I stopped eating regular bread, I used to make French toast with a crusty French bread, and I always ordered the stuffed French toast when I saw it on a brunch menu. If you have it, use leftover banana bread in this recipe, but because that doesn't exist in our house, I end up baking a loaf especially for this recipe and hiding it from Ryan and the boys! The sweet and nutty chocolate-hazelnut mixture that gets spread onto the bread along with extra bananas makes this the ultimate breakfast treat for an indulgent weekend or special celebration.

In a shallow bowl or pie plate, whisk together the eggs, coconut milk, almond milk, cinnamon, nutmeg, and vanilla until combined.

Heat a large skillet over medium heat. Add 1 teaspoon of the ghee and spread it around the skillet as it melts.

Working in batches, dip each side of a banana bread slice into the egg mixture and move it around gently until well coated. Place the coated bread pieces into the skillet and cook until golden brown, about 2 minutes per side. Repeat until all of the bread slices are cooked, adding ghee to the pan, a teaspoon at a time, as needed.

Transfer the French toast to plates and slather each piece with the chocolate hazelnut spread. Top with a few slices of banana and serve.

2 eggs

¼ cup full-fat coconut milk

¼ cup Almond Milk (page 308)

1 teaspoon ground cinnamon

½ teaspoon ground nutmeg

½ teaspoon pure vanilla extract

2 tablespoons ghee

8 slices Banana Bread (page 39), each ¼ inch thick

½ cup Chocolate Hazelnut Spread (page 307), at room temperature

1 banana, cut into ¼-inch slices

SHRIMP AND GRITS WITH BACON COLLARDS

Serves 6 • There are seemingly endless varieties of shrimp and grits recipes: some add mushrooms or bell peppers, others include bacon or sausage. And I've seen grits with cheese and without. I decided to keep this recipe fairly simple—adding just bacon, herbs, and a side of sautéed collards—but the simplicity means you can freely add vegetables of your choice as well. Rather than cornmeal, which is typically used for grits, I use ground almonds here to keep this grain-free. Look for almond *meal* rather than almond *flour*, as the coarser texture makes this feel more like traditional grits. Find it in the bulk bins at your local supermarket.

GRITS

2 cups Cashew Milk (page 310)

½ cup Chicken Bone Broth (page 310)

1½ cups coarse almond meal

Fine sea salt and freshly ground black pepper

1 tablespoon melted ghee or extra-virgin olive oil

SHRIMP

6 slices thick-cut bacon, chopped

1 pound collard greens, ribs and stems removed, cut into 2-inch strips

3 cloves garlic, minced

Fine sea salt and freshly ground black pepper

2 pounds large raw shrimp (about 30 pieces), peeled and deveined, with tails on

2 tablespoons ghee or extra-virgin olive oil

To make the grits, in a saucepan over high heat, combine the cashew milk and bone broth and bring to a boil. Turn the heat to medium and whisk in the almond meal. Bring the mixture to a simmer and cook for 10 to 12 minutes, whisking constantly to prevent clumping, until the mixture has thickened. Season with 1 teaspoon salt and ¼ teaspoon pepper, and stir in the ghee. Keep warm over low heat.

To make the shrimp, cook the bacon in a large saucepan over medium heat, stirring occasionally, until crisp, about 10 minutes. Transfer the bacon to a plate using a slotted spoon and reserve the fat in the pan.

Return the pan to medium-high heat. Add the collard greens and sauté until slightly softened, 4 to 5 minutes. Stir in half of the garlic and cook until fragrant, about 30 seconds. Season with salt and pepper to taste. Transfer the collards to a plate and cover to keep warm.

Season the shrimp generously with salt and pepper. Return the skillet to medium-high heat and add the ghee. Working in batches, add the shrimp to the pan in a single layer and cook until bright pink, about 1 minute per side. Using a slotted spoon, transfer the shrimp to a plate. Add the remaining garlic to the saucepan and

CONTINUED

1 cup Chicken Bone Broth
(page 310)

2 tablespoons freshly squeezed
lemon juice

¾ teaspoon hot pepper sauce
(such as Frank's)

2 tablespoons chopped fresh
flat-leaf parsley, for garnish

4 green onions, tender green
and white parts only, thinly
sliced, for garnish

cook, stirring constantly, until golden, about 1 minute. Increase
the heat to high, add the bone broth, and scrape any browned bits
from the bottom of the pan. Bring the broth to a boil, then return
the shrimp and bacon to the pan and add the lemon juice and hot
sauce. Cook, stirring frequently, until the sauce thickens, about
1 minute.

Divide the grits among six bowls. Top each with four or five shrimp
and pour some of the sauce over the top. Place some collards on
the side of each bowl. Garnish each bowl with parsley and green
onions and serve.

Tidbits: Like cheesy grits? Stir in ½ cup grated Cheddar and
½ cup grated Parmesan at the end of cooking. To make a dairy-free
version, add 2 tablespoons nutritional yeast for a cheesy flavor.

To make this NSF, omit the hot sauce.

CHOCOLATE SPRINKLE DOUGHNUTS

Makes 16 • These are really more of a dessert—not breakfast—but when I asked Ryan to name the first breakfast comfort food that came to mind, he said "doughnuts." And I have to agree. When I was growing up, it was a rare treat to get doughnuts for breakfast, but I have fond memories of visiting my grandparents and going to their favorite doughnut spot, World's Fair, for breakfast. (I also remember saving my offering money at church and giving it to the doughnut basket instead!) These chocolate-covered cake doughnuts with a chocolate glaze and sprinkles are such a treat! We make them for special occasions or a lazy weekend morning.

Preheat a doughnut maker. If using a doughnut pan, preheat the oven to 350°F and grease the pan liberally with palm shortening.

In a blender, combine the eggs, coconut milk, oil, maple syrup, vinegar, vanilla, cocoa powder, coconut sugar, coconut flour, arrowroot, baking soda, and salt and blend on high speed for 30 seconds, until well incorporated. Let the batter rest for 2 minutes, then blend again on high for 15 seconds. Scoop the batter into a large resealable plastic bag, seal the top, and snip one of the bottom corners to make a piping bag. Pipe the batter into the doughnut mold or pan, filling it completely. Cook until the doughnut machine indicator light goes off, about 5 minutes, or bake for 15 to 17 minutes in the oven, until a toothpick inserted into the center of a doughnut comes out clean. Remove the doughnuts from the mold or pan and cool on a wire rack.

To make the glaze, bring 1 inch of water in a saucepan to a simmer. Place the chocolate, maple syrup, and coconut oil in a heatproof bowl and set it over the simmering water, creating a double boiler. Turn the heat to medium-low and stir the mixture frequently until the chocolate melts and the mixture is smooth. Turn off the heat, remove the bowl from the pan, and stir in 1 tablespoon water.

3 eggs, at room temperature

½ cup full-fat coconut milk

⅓ cup melted expeller-pressed coconut oil or ghee

¼ cup pure maple syrup

½ teaspoon apple cider vinegar

1 teaspoon pure vanilla extract

½ cup unsweetened cocoa powder

½ cup coconut sugar

6 tablespoons coconut flour

¼ cup arrowroot powder

¾ teaspoon baking soda

¼ teaspoon fine sea salt

GLAZE

3 ounces dark chocolate (85 percent cacao), chopped

1½ tablespoons pure maple syrup

1 tablespoon expeller-pressed coconut oil (see Tidbits)

½ cup Rainbow Sprinkles (page 304); see Tidbits

CONTINUED

Pour the sprinkles into a shallow dish. Dip the tops of the cooled doughnuts in the warm glaze and twist gently as you remove them from the bowl to allow excess glaze to drip off. Place the doughnuts on a wire rack to set for 10 minutes, then dip the tops of the doughnuts a second time. Immediately dip the tops in the sprinkles. Serve immediately, or chill in the refrigerator for 1 hour to harden the chocolate.

Store the doughnuts in an airtight container in the refrigerator for 2 weeks, or freeze the doughnuts in an airtight container, with a square of parchment paper placed between each row of doughnuts, for 4 months. Defrost at room temperature for 1 hour.

Tidbits: I use expeller-pressed coconut oil so the glaze doesn't taste too coconutty, but virgin coconut oil would work as well.

While making your own sprinkles is fun and ensures they are free of artificial dyes, refined sugar, and cornstarch, India Tree makes some dye-free sprinkles that would work well here.

MILLIONAIRE'S BACON

Serves 4 • I will never forget the first time I had Millionaire's Bacon. Ryan and I escaped to San Francisco for a little anniversary getaway and stumbled across a popular brunch place that had it on the menu. I was always the kid who hated when the maple syrup from my pancakes would run onto my bacon, so I tried it hesitantly, only to fall in love immediately. Traditional recipes use brown sugar, but I use unrefined maple sugar and coconut sugar here to give it that accidental, but delectable, pancakes-and-bacon flavor.

8 ounces thick-cut bacon (about 8 slices)

2 tablespoons maple sugar

2 tablespoons coconut sugar

½ teaspoon chili powder

¼ teaspoon ground cinnamon

⅛ teaspoon fine sea salt

⅛ teaspoon red pepper flakes

Preheat the oven to 400°F. Line a large rimmed baking sheet with parchment paper and place a wire rack on top. Arrange the bacon in a single layer on the rack, so that the slices are nestled together with no space between them.

In a small bowl, combine both sugars, the chili powder, cinnamon, salt, and red pepper flakes. Sprinkle the mixture over the bacon, covering each slice completely.

Bake, rotating the sheet halfway through baking, until the sugar is melted and the bacon is brown and shiny, 20 to 25 minutes. Let cool on the rack for about 5 minutes. Loosen the slices from the rack with a spatula and continue to cool for 5 minutes longer, until the bacon is crisp. Serve warm.

BANANA BREAD

Makes 1 loaf • The banana bread recipe in my first cookbook, *Against All Grain*, is a major fan favorite, but I constantly get requests for a nut-free version. For those of you who have tree-nut allergies, this one's for you! My family loves the flavor of this loaf so much that I typically don't add anything to the mix, but some dark chocolate chips or walnuts would be delicious additions.

Preheat the oven to 350°F. Lightly grease the short sides of a 10 by 4½-inch loaf pan with ghee or coconut oil. Line the bottom and long sides of the pan with parchment paper so the ends hang over the sides.

In a stand mixer fitted with the beater attachment, or using an electric handheld mixer, beat the eggs, honey, coconut sugar, palm shortening, and vanilla on medium speed for 30 seconds. Scrape down the sides of the bowl, then add the coconut flour, arrowroot, baking powder, baking soda, and salt. Beat on high for 30 seconds, until smooth. Add the mashed banana and beat on medium-low speed until just incorporated.

Pour the batter into the prepared loaf pan and gently smooth the top with a spatula. Place the pan in the oven and bake for 50 to 55 minutes, until a toothpick inserted into the center of the loaf comes out clean. Cool in the pan for 20 minutes, then gently lift the parchment flaps to remove the loaf from the pan. Cool completely on a wire rack, about 4 hours.

To store, once the loaf is fully cooled, wrap it in a piece of parchment paper and seal it in a resealable plastic bag or wrap it again tightly in plastic wrap. It will keep in the refrigerator for 10 days. To serve, cut the loaf into ¼-inch-thick slices.

Freeze slices of bread in a single layer on a rimmed baking sheet, tightly covered with plastic wrap, for 4 hours. Transfer the frozen slices to an airtight container and store in the freezer for 3 months. Defrost in the refrigerator overnight, or defrost from frozen in a 300°F oven for 10 minutes.

6 eggs, at room temperature

3 tablespoons light-colored raw honey

2 tablespoons coconut sugar

¼ cup palm shortening or ghee

1½ teaspoons pure vanilla extract

½ cup plus 2 tablespoons coconut flour

½ cup arrowroot powder

1½ teaspoons Grain-Free Baking Powder (page 312)

¾ teaspoon baking soda

¼ teaspoon fine sea salt

1½ cups mashed overripe banana (about 4 bananas)

EVERYTHING BAGELS

Makes 6 • My first job was at a bagel shop, and the smell of a good yeast dough *still* makes my mouth water. There are many paleo re-creations of bagel recipes out there, but most of them leave out the yeast and wind up tasting like dense muffins to me. I hunted around the back corners of my pantry to find a little packet of active dry yeast to try in this recipe. The yeast was the missing link and is what gives these bagels an authentic taste. My dairy-free Ricotta Cheese (page 316) tastes great smeared across these, or pick up a tub of Kite Hill dairy-free cream cheese at your grocery store.

½ cup full-fat coconut milk

2 tablespoons finely ground golden flaxseeds

1 tablespoon light-colored raw honey

1½ tablespoons gluten-free active dry yeast (see Tidbits)

4 eggs

¼ cup melted ghee or virgin coconut oil

1 teaspoon apple cider vinegar

1½ cups arrowroot powder

⅓ cup coconut flour

1½ teaspoons Grain-Free Baking Powder (page 312)

1 teaspoon fine sea salt

EVERYTHING SEASONING

1 teaspoon poppy seeds

1 teaspoon dried minced garlic

1 teaspoon dried minced onion

½ teaspoon white sesame seeds

½ teaspoon black sesame seeds

½ teaspoon coarse sea salt

Pour the coconut milk into a small saucepan and heat it over low heat to 110°F. Place the warmed coconut milk, the flaxseeds, honey, and yeast in the bowl of a stand mixer fitted with the beater attachment and mix on low speed to combine. Let the mixture sit for 4 to 5 minutes, until it begins to foam.

Add the eggs, ghee, and vinegar to the bowl and mix on medium speed to combine. Add the arrowroot, coconut flour, baking powder, and salt and mix again until fully incorporated. Cover the bowl with a kitchen towel and let it sit for 1 hour at room temperature.

To make the everything seasoning, combine all of the ingredients in a small bowl and stir to combine.

Preheat the oven to 350°F. Scoop the batter into a 3½-inch silicone doughnut pan (see Tidbits), filling each cavity two-thirds full. Sprinkle the tops with the seasoning and bake for 20 to 25 minutes, until the bagels are golden brown and a toothpick inserted into the center comes out clean. Cool the bagels in the pan on a wire rack for 20 minutes, then remove them from the pan and cool completely on the rack.

Store in an airtight container in the refrigerator for 1 week, or in the freezer for 6 months.

Tidbits: To make bagel shop–size bagels, check out the silicone pan I use at againstallgrain.com/bagels.

To omit the yeast, add another 1 teaspoon grain-free baking powder, and bake immediately. The texture will be a little denser and the bagels will not rise as high.

AÇAI BERRY–CHIA PUDDING PARFAITS

Makes 6 • I ate these parfaits constantly right after our daughter Kezia was born. I would wake up to two growing boys looking for a breakfast of their own, plus a baby eager to nurse, and having these healthful puddings ready to go in the fridge made it easy to nourish myself while I tended to the kids. If you're hurrying out the door for school drop-off or running late for the office, these ready-made breakfasts will save the day. Collagen peptides add extra protein and are also soothing to the gut, and açai has incredible antioxidant properties, so this is not your average chia pudding.

In a blender, combine ¼ cup of the almond milk, the strawberries, banana, collagen peptides, almond butter, açai powder, and mint and blend on high speed, adding more almond milk, if needed, a little bit at a time, until the consistency is a bit thicker than a smoothie.

In a large bowl, whisk together the coconut milk, the remaining 1½ cups almond milk, the chia seeds, vanilla, and cinnamon. Let the mixture sit for 5 to 10 minutes, until the chia seeds have started to expand, then whisk again to prevent clumping.

Distribute the açai mixture among six clean ½-pint (8-ounce) jars and top with the chia mixture, dividing it evenly. Cover and chill in the fridge for about 3 hours, overnight, or up to 5 days. Add your desired toppings right before serving.

Tidbits: To make this NF, use coconut milk in place of the almond milk and sunflower seed butter instead of the almond butter.

I usually add grass-fed collagen peptides powder, such as Vital Proteins brand, to my smoothies to promote healthy immune and digestive systems.

1¾ cups Almond Milk (page 308; see Tidbits), plus more as needed for blending

1 cup frozen strawberries

1 ripe banana

2 tablespoons unflavored collagen peptides powder (optional; see Tidbits)

1 tablespoon unsweetened almond butter

1 tablespoon açai powder

4 fresh mint leaves

1 (13.5-ounce) can full-fat coconut milk

¾ cup white chia seeds

½ teaspoon pure vanilla extract

½ teaspoon ground cinnamon

Toasted unsweetened coconut flakes, bee pollen, chopped nuts, fresh mint leaves, fresh berries, and chopped kiwi, for topping (optional)

CHAPTER 2
PACKED LUNCHES

Packing lunches doesn't have to be complicated. My biggest secrets for lunch-to-go success are utilizing leftovers and stocking my freezer with items from Chapter 7: Make It Ahead. If I'm prepping vegetables at dinnertime, I cut up some extras and store them in the refrigerator so that I always have something nutritious to pack as a side dish as I try to get out the door in the morning. Whether I make a batch of my favorite meatballs to pack throughout the week, or make dinner and repurpose the leftovers, a little preplanning goes a long way.

A lunchbox with bento box compartments is perfect for packing a variety of foods, whether you're taking leftovers to the office or packing your child's school lunch. The boxes are a bit of an investment, but I've been using ours for many years now and have not had to replace them, plus I was able to cut down on purchasing and wasting paper and plastic bags. When I'm packing cold food, I put the entire box in the fridge to chill overnight and put a frozen ice pack inside before leaving the house.

A thermos is great for packing a hot lunch and leftovers. I fill it with boiling water and let it sit for five minutes, then dump out the water before adding the food. This additional step keeps the food extra warm. Packing last night's chili (see page 170) or Beef and Broccoli (page 182) and knowing you or your children can have a warm lunch gives you something to look forward to during your morning.

NUT-FREE LUNCHBOX BREAD

Makes 24 slices • Like many kids these days, Asher is currently attending a nut-free elementary school, so my previous bread recipes are no longer useful for his packed lunches. This nut-free sandwich bread is one of only three recipes in this book that utilize yeast, an ingredient you don't see very often in the AAG kitchen (see page 9). It's not essential, but oh my word, does it deliver an authentic, bready taste.

¾ cup full-fat coconut milk

¼ cup finely ground golden flaxseeds

1½ tablespoons light-colored raw honey

2 tablespoons gluten-free active dry yeast (see Tidbits)

6 eggs, separated

¼ cup extra-virgin olive oil or melted coconut oil

1½ teaspoons apple cider vinegar

2 cups arrowroot powder

¾ cup coconut flour

¾ teaspoon baking soda

1¾ teaspoons fine sea salt

1½ teaspoons cream of tartar

Pour the coconut milk into a small saucepan and heat it over low heat to 110°F. Place the warmed coconut milk, the flaxseeds, honey, and yeast in a large bowl and whisk gently to combine. Let the mixture sit for 4 to 5 minutes, until it begins to foam.

Add the egg yolks, oil, and vinegar and mix well with a rubber spatula to combine. Add the arrowroot, coconut flour, baking soda, and salt and mix again until fully incorporated, stopping to scrape down the sides and along the bottom of the bowl. Cover the bowl with a kitchen towel and let it sit for 1 hour at room temperature.

Meanwhile, preheat the oven to 350°F. Lightly grease the short sides of a 10 by 4½-inch loaf pan with ghee or coconut oil. Line the bottom and long sides of the pan with parchment paper so the ends hang over the sides.

Once the batter has rested for an hour, in the bowl of a stand mixer fitted with the whisk attachment, or using an electric handheld mixer, beat the egg whites with the cream of tartar on medium-high speed until stiff peaks form, 2 to 3 minutes. Add half of the whipped egg whites to the batter and mix vigorously with a rubber spatula until fully incorporated. Scrape down the sides and along the bottom of the bowl. Gently fold in the remaining egg whites with the spatula until there are no visible streaks of white, being careful to not deflate the whites.

CONTINUED

Scoop the batter into the prepared loaf pan and bake for 40 to 45 minutes, until the crust is browned and a toothpick inserted into the center of the loaf comes out clean. Cool in the pan for 20 minutes, then gently lift the parchment flaps to remove the loaf from the pan. Cool completely on a wire rack before slicing, about 2 hours.

Store the bread, tightly wrapped, at room temperature for 4 days, or in the refrigerator for 2 weeks.

Freeze slices of bread in an airtight container, with parchment paper placed between each slice, for 4 months. To defrost, let the slices sit at room temperature for 15 minutes before toasting, or defrost in the refrigerator overnight to serve them untoasted.

Tidbits: To omit the yeast, add 1 teaspoon Grain-Free Baking Powder (page 312) and bake immediately. The texture will be a little denser and the loaf will not rise as high.

MILLIONAIRE'S AB&J

Serves 2 • While there's no need to alter the perfection that is a classic peanut butter and jelly, sometimes it's fun to put a new twist on a childhood classic while still paying homage to the traditional flavors. In this rendition, the sweet and spicy flavors of bacon meld perfectly with the tangy jam and salty nut butter. I promise you will relish in every bite.

Preheat a skillet over medium-low heat.

Spread each piece of bread with 1 tablespoon almond butter, then spread 1 tablespoon jam on 2 of the slices. Lay 3 strips of bacon over the jam and top with the remaining 2 slices of bread, almond butter side down. Brush the tops well with some of the ghee, then place both sandwiches in the skillet, ghee side down. Brush the top sides with the remaining ghee.

Cook for 45 to 60 seconds, until the bottoms are golden brown. Flip the sandwiches and grill again for 45 to 60 seconds, until the other sides are golden brown. Remove from the skillet and cut in half on a diagonal.

Pack It: Cover the sandwich tightly in plastic wrap or place it in a bento compartment. Store at room temperature for 2 hours, packed in a lunchbox with an ice pack for 4 hours, or in the refrigerator for 1 day.

Tidbits: My favorite store-bought jam is St. Dalfour. It is unsweetened and contains pectin from fruit rather than corn.

To make this NF, use sunflower seed butter in place of the almond butter.

4 slices Nut-Free Lunchbox Bread (page 48)

4 tablespoons unsweetened almond butter or sunflower seed butter

2 tablespoons unsweetened raspberry jam

6 slices Millionaire's Bacon (page 36)

2 teaspoons melted ghee

DEVILED EGG SALAD SANDWICH

Serves 6 • My dad made egg salad sandwiches often when I was growing up, but I never cared for them much. I did, and will always, love deviled eggs, however. Instead of the abundant mayo and black olives that my dad throws into his recipe, I put only a little mayo, along with mustard, paprika, chives, and bacon into mine. My favorite way to hard-boil eggs is in an electric pressure cooker because the shells practically fall off, but you can use whatever method you like. Asher likes hard-boiled egg whites for breakfast (I cannot get the boy to eat the yolks, for the life of me!), so I always cook a few extra for him while I prepare the eggs for this sandwich. To learn my favorite method for making hard-boiled eggs that peel like a dream, see againstallgrain.com/pressure-cooker-hard-boiled-eggs.

8 hard-boiled eggs

½ cup Mayonnaise (page 314)

1 teaspoon Dijon mustard

2 slices cooked bacon, chopped

1 tablespoon chopped fresh chives

¼ teaspoon sweet paprika

Fine sea salt and freshly ground black pepper

8 slices Nut-Free Lunchbox Bread (page 48) or 4 Sandwich Rolls (page 317)

½ cup watercress or 1 head lettuce, leaves separated

Peel and chop the eggs and place them in a bowl. Stir in the mayonnaise, mustard, bacon, chives, and paprika. Season with salt and pepper to taste.

Toast the bread and make sandwiches with the egg salad and watercress.

Pack It: Cover the sandwich tightly in plastic wrap or place it in a bento compartment. Store at room temperature for 2 hours, packed in a lunchbox with an ice pack for 4 hours, or in the refrigerator for 1 day.

Tidbits: To comply with SCD, substitute your favorite SCD-friendly bread for the lunchbox bread.

eat what you love

AAGWICH

Makes 1 wrap • I was first inspired to make this wrap when I was craving a deli meat sandwich so badly that I started wrapping sandwich fillings in lettuce instead of bread, like a burrito. This holds together better than a lettuce cup and there's something really satisfying about biting into it. I started sharing the ones I made Ryan for work every morning on Instagram and people went crazy for them. (If you want more ideas, search the hashtag #aagwich to see tons of lettuce-wrapped sandwiches.)

Here's the overall method along with eight filling combinations to get started. After that, feel free to be creative and play with whatever fillings you prefer. You could also wrap all these fillings in Grain-Free Wraps (page 313), or sandwich them between slices of Nut-Free Lunchbox Bread (page 48) or Sandwich Rolls (page 317). You'll need two 14-inch-long pieces of parchment paper.

8 large leaves green-leaf lettuce, romaine, or Swiss chard

Fillings and Sauces (see next page)

Lay a piece of parchment paper on a cutting board. Piece together 2 lettuce leaves lengthwise, overlapping the root ends a bit, and place them toward the bottom right corner of the parchment. Begin layering the remaining lettuce pieces in the same way, slightly overlapping each piece, working toward the center of the parchment rectangle.

Pile the fillings in the center, leaving a 2-inch border of uncovered lettuce, then spread your desired sauces over the toppings. Wrap the ends of the lettuce closest to you over the toppings, rolling it into a burrito shape, then use one hand to pull the lower right corner of the parchment over the rolled lettuce. Tuck the parchment under the lettuce roll and pull tightly with your other hand to eliminate slack in the paper. Continue rolling the lettuce wrap tightly, then stop midway through and fold in the ends of the parchment paper. Continue rolling, pulling the paper taut. Cut the wrap in half, then roll it again in the second piece of parchment paper.

CONTINUED

FILLINGS AND SAUCES

CHICKEN CAESAR: 1 cup cubed cooked chicken, 3 slices tomato, 2 teaspoons Parmesan Cheese (page 315), and 2 tablespoons Caesar Dressing (page 151).

THAI CHICKEN: 1 cup shredded cooked chicken, ¼ cup sliced cucumber, ¼ cup grated carrots, 1 sliced radish, and 2 tablespoons Thai Dressing (page 147).

PHILLY CHEESESTEAK: 1 cup shredded leftover French Dip beef (see page 217), ¼ cup Ricotta Cheese (page 316), ½ cup combined sautéed thinly sliced yellow onions and thinly sliced green bell peppers, and 2 tablespoons Mayonnaise (page 314) mixed with ¼ teaspoon minced garlic.

TURKEY CRANBERRY: ¼ cup Ricotta Cheese (page 316) or 2 tablespoons Mayonnaise (page 314), 8 slices turkey, ¼ cup baby spinach, and 1 tablespoon fruit juice–sweetened dried cranberries (such as Eden Organics).

MEDITERRANEAN VEGETERRANEAN: ¼ cup Cauliflower Hummus (page 94), ¼ cup baby spinach, 4 strips red bell pepper, 2 slices avocado, 6 thin slices red onion, 1 tablespoon chopped fresh mint leaves, and 2 teaspoons toasted pine nuts.

REUBEN: 8 slices deli corned beef, ¼ cup Ricotta Cheese (page 316), ¼ cup drained sauerkraut, 2 tablespoons Mayonnaise (page 314) mixed with 1 teaspoon Ketchup (page 313), ½ teaspoon chopped pickles, ½ teaspoon prepared horseradish, ¼ teaspoon caraway seeds, and salt and pepper to taste.

BUFFALO CHICKEN: 1 cup shredded cooked chicken, 1 thinly sliced celery stalk, 2 tablespoons grated carrots, 2 tablespoons hot pepper sauce (such as Frank's) mixed with 2 teaspoons melted ghee, ½ teaspoon apple cider vinegar, and salt and pepper to taste.

CLUB: 8 slices deli turkey or ½ cup shredded cooked chicken, 2 slices cooked bacon, 2 slices tomato, 2 slices avocado, 2 slices dill pickle, and 2 tablespoons Mayonnaise (page 314) mixed with 1 tablespoon Pesto (page 244).

Pack It: After rolling each wrap, cover it tightly with plastic wrap and fold up the ends to secure. Store at room temperature for 2 hours, packed in a lunchbox with an ice pack for 4 hours, or in the refrigerator for 1 day.

CALIFORNIA HAND ROLLS

Serves 4 to 6 • I love ordering sushi hand rolls without the rice from our local Japanese restaurant. I can't afford to order takeout every day though, so I started making these at home and they remain a favorite quick lunch. There's honey in the sauce to make the American-style mayonnaise taste more like Kewpie, a Japanese mayo used at most sushi restaurants, but feel free to omit it if you're avoiding added sweeteners. If you do go out to eat and want to order this, be sure to ask if the restaurant uses real crabmeat. If you see *krab* (with a "k") on the menu, it is artificial and contains wheat.

DIPPING SAUCE

½ cup coconut aminos

3 tablespoons unseasoned rice vinegar or apple cider vinegar

2 tablespoons peeled and minced fresh ginger

2 tablespoons chopped green onion, tender green and white parts only

2 teaspoons grated fresh horseradish root

2 cloves garlic, minced

1 teaspoon sesame oil

ROLLS

2 cups cooked crabmeat (about 1 pound), picked through for shells

¼ cup Mayonnaise (page 314)

1 teaspoon light-colored raw honey

1 teaspoon unseasoned rice vinegar or apple cider vinegar

½ teaspoon fine sea salt

½ teaspoon dry mustard powder

To make the dipping sauce, in a small bowl, whisk together the coconut aminos, vinegar, ginger, green onion, horseradish, garlic, and oil. Cover and refrigerate until you are ready to serve.

To make the rolls, in a separate bowl, mix together the crabmeat, mayonnaise, honey, vinegar, salt, and mustard powder until well combined.

Working with dry hands, lay a nori sheet half, shiny side down, on a cutting board or flat surface. Place 2 tablespoons of the crab mixture, two avocado slices, a few cucumber and red bell pepper sticks, and a pinch of microgreens diagonally on the right side of the sheet so they point toward the bottom right corner of the nori. (Don't overfill your roll.)

Fold the top right corner of the nori over the filling ingredients, then pick the roll up and wrap the left side of the nori tightly around the fillings to form a cone shape, leaving a small triangular flap. Moisten the flap of nori with a bit of water and press it to seal the cone. Repeat until all of the nori and fillings are used. Serve immediately (so the nori doesn't get soggy) with the dipping sauce on the side.

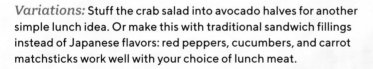

Variations: Stuff the crab salad into avocado halves for another simple lunch idea. Or make this with traditional sandwich fillings instead of Japanese flavors: red peppers, cucumbers, and carrot matchsticks work well with your choice of lunch meat.

Pack It: Pack the nori strips, filling, and dipping sauce separately. Roll them right before serving.

Tidbits: To make this NSF, omit the red bell pepper.

8 standard-size sheets toasted nori, cut in half crosswise

3 large ripe avocados, pitted, peeled, and thinly sliced

2 Persian cucumbers, peeled, seeded, and julienned

1 red bell pepper, seeded and julienned (optional)

½ cup microgreens

MEATBALL SUB

Serves 4 • This Italian-style sandwich is filled with zesty meatballs, marinara sauce, and dairy-free cheeses. The key to making this sub a quick lunch option is to use leftovers. Having many of the staple items ready to go from a previous dinner speeds things up, but you could also take some shortcuts by purchasing the rolls and ricotta cheese.

Preheat the broiler with a rack placed about 3 inches from the heating element.

Combine the meatballs and the sauce in a small saucepan and cook over medium heat for 5 to 7 minutes, until warmed through.

Cut each roll in half and spread both halves with ghee. Toast the rolls under the broiler for 1 minute, until golden brown. Spread the bottom half of each roll with 2 tablespoons ricotta cheese and top with 3 or 4 meatballs. Sprinkle Parmesan over the top, then place the second half of the roll on top.

Pack It: Wrap the sandwich tightly in aluminum foil. Store at room temperature for 2 hours, packed in a lunchbox with an ice pack for 4 hours, or in the refrigerator for 1 day. Alternatively, pack the hot meatballs with the sauce and cheese in a heated thermos, and keep the roll on the side until ready to serve.

12 to 16 Pesto Power Meatballs (page 244), defrosted if frozen

¾ cup marinara sauce

4 Sandwich Rolls (page 317)

2 tablespoons ghee

½ cup Ricotta Cheese (page 316), or any store-bought dairy-free ricotta

2 tablespoons Parmesan Cheese (page 315)

DILL CHICKEN SALAD

Serves 6 to 8 • This chicken salad is one of my favorite recipes to batch-cook on the weekend and use for lunches all week long. If you use cooked chicken, this comes together quickly and easily. To avoid lunchtime boredom, change up the way you serve this salad each day: put it in Grain-Free Wraps (page 313) with some lettuce and avocado, sandwich it between two slices of toasted Nut-Free Lunchbox Bread (page 48), use some of my Dippers (page 98), or simply serve it inside lettuce cups. You could also throw in some sliced grapes or add 1 to 2 tablespoons of curry powder midway through the week to keep things interesting.

1 cup Mayonnaise (page 314)

¼ cup full-fat coconut milk

2 teaspoons freshly squeezed lemon juice

1 teaspoon brine from a jar of pickles

1 tablespoon chopped fresh dill

Fine sea salt and freshly ground black pepper

4 cups cubed Pressure Cooker Chicken (page 315), or other chopped cooked chicken (see Tidbits)

2 apples (such as Fuji or Pink Lady), diced

2 celery stalks, thinly sliced

½ cup diced cucumber

¼ cup currants or raisins

¼ cup chopped pecans, toasted (see Tidbits)

2 tablespoons chopped fresh chives

In a large bowl, whisk together the mayonnaise, coconut milk, lemon juice, pickle brine, and dill. Season with salt and pepper to taste. Stir in the chicken, apples, celery, cucumber, currants, pecans, and chives. Cover and refrigerate for at least 30 minutes or up to 5 days.

Pack It: If making a sandwich, cover it tightly with plastic wrap or place it in a bento compartment. Store at room temperature for 2 hours, packed in a lunchbox with an ice pack for 4 hours, or in the refrigerator for 1 day.

Tidbits: If you don't have any cooked chicken on hand, poach some chicken breasts or thighs. Bring a pot of water to a boil over high heat. Add 2 pounds boneless, skinless chicken breasts or thighs and season the water generously with salt and pepper. Cover the pot, turn the heat to medium-low, and poach for 5 minutes. Remove the pot from the heat and let it stand for 10 to 12 minutes, until a thermometer inserted into the chicken reads 165°F. Remove the chicken from the water and let it cool completely before chopping into cubes.

To make this NF, omit the pecans.

SEVEN-LAYER BEAN DIP CUPS

Makes 6 • In the old days, if bean dip was ever served at a potluck or football watching party, you could usually find me standing next to it. Not only did I have an affinity for crunchy, salty tortilla chips, but I could also never turn down the layers of beans, guacamole, veggies, and tangy sour cream. Making the dip in individual lidded jars is a great way to keep the dip looking nice, and the jars are easy to pack for lunch. Most of the layers come from homemade recipes in this book, but you could also buy any of these items at the store if you like.

To make the taco seasoning, combine all of the ingredients in a small bowl. Store the seasoning in an airtight container at room temperature for 6 months.

To make the dip cups, in a small bowl, mix together the sour cream and 1½ tablespoons of the taco seasoning. (Reserve the remaining taco seasoning for another use.) Scoop about ¼ cup refried beans into each of six 8-ounce lidded jars and spread into an even layer using the back of a spoon. Add 3 tablespoons guacamole followed by 2½ tablespoons of the seasoned sour cream to each jar, smoothing each layer as you go. Sprinkle the tomatoes evenly over the top, followed by the lettuce, black olives, and green onions. Secure the lids on the jars and store in the refrigerator until ready to serve, or for up to 3 days.

Serve with plantain chips, jicama sticks, and carrots sticks for dipping.

Pack it: Store at room temperature for 2 hours, packed in a lunchbox with an ice pack for 4 hours, or in the refrigerator for 1 day.

Tidbits: Green Valley Organics makes a good lactose-free sour cream, if you can tolerate dairy.

TACO SEASONING

1½ tablespoons chili powder

1½ teaspoons fine sea salt

1½ teaspoons ground cumin

1½ teaspoons dried oregano

1 teaspoon onion powder

1 teaspoon ground coriander

1 teaspoon sweet paprika

½ teaspoon cayenne pepper

⅛ teaspoon freshly ground black pepper

DIP CUPS

1 cup Dairy-Free Sour Cream (page 311; see Tidbits)

1½ cups Refried "Beans" (page 122)

1 cup plus 2 tablespoons Guacamole (page 95)

2 large Roma tomatoes, diced

1 cup shredded romaine lettuce

½ cup sliced black olives

3 green onions, tender green and white parts only, chopped

Plantain Chips (page 98), sliced jicama, and carrot sticks, for serving

BARBECUE CHICKEN SALAD WITH PEACH POWER SLAW

Serves 4 • This tangy barbecue chicken salad and power slaw is packed with protein and fiber. I use precooked chicken so I can assemble this salad before heading to bed, or make it quickly in the morning before running out the door. You can speed things up even more by using a store-bought rotisserie chicken and paleo-friendly barbecue sauce. These fillings can also work well in an AAGwich-style lettuce wrap (see page 57).

6 cups thinly sliced lacinato (Tuscan) kale

6 teaspoons extra-virgin olive oil

8 teaspoons freshly squeezed lemon juice

1 cup thinly sliced radishes

2 carrots, peeled and julienned

½ cup julienned jicama

2 yellow peaches, pitted and thinly sliced

3 tablespoons raw sunflower seeds

4 small pitted dates

2 tablespoons chopped fresh cilantro

½ teaspoon fine sea salt

Freshly ground black pepper

3 cups shredded Pressure Cooker Chicken (page 315), or any other cooked chicken

¾ cup BBQ Sauce (page 309), or any paleo-friendly barbecue sauce

2 avocados, pitted, peeled, and sliced

In a large bowl, toss together the kale, 2 teaspoons of the oil, and 2 teaspoons of the lemon juice. Add the radishes, carrots, jicama, peaches, and sunflower seeds and toss to combine. Set aside to allow the greens to wilt slightly.

In a blender or food processor, combine the dates, the remaining 4 teaspoons oil, the remaining 6 teaspoons lemon juice, the cilantro, salt, and pepper to taste. Blend or process on medium-low speed for 10 seconds, until smooth. Pour the dressing over the slaw and toss to combine. Divide the slaw evenly among four bowls.

In the same bowl used to mix the slaw, toss together the chicken and BBQ sauce until well combined. Divide the chicken evenly among the four bowls and top with the avocado slices and a sprinkling of pepper.

Pack It: Store at room temperature for 2 hours, packed in a lunchbox with an ice pack for 4 hours, or in the refrigerator for 1 day.

CHICKEN GYRO WRAP

Serves 4 • A staple of Greek cuisine, gyro meat is usually slow-cooked on a vertical rotisserie and served in a flatbread-like pita. Sadly, the meat itself often has wheat flour added to it, not to mention the pita. Not one to settle for missing out on this traditional favorite, I used leftover cooked chicken tossed in its own seasonings to help this wrap come together quickly. Stuffed with fresh veggies and finished with a cool and tangy cucumber yogurt sauce, this fresh take on the classic will leave you wanting for nothing.

In a bowl, toss together the chicken, oil, vinegar, oregano, and a pinch of salt and pepper. Divide the chicken evenly among the wraps, then top each with the cucumber, onion, tomato, and lettuce. Drizzle 1 tablespoon tzatziki sauce over the top of the filling in each wrap, then roll the wraps up to close.

Pack It: After rolling each wrap, cover it tightly with plastic wrap and fold up the ends to secure. Store at room temperature for 2 hours, packed in a lunchbox with an ice pack for 4 hours, or in the refrigerator for 1 day.

Tidbits: To comply with SCD, substitute lettuce cups for the wraps.

2 cups shredded Pressure Cooker Chicken (page 315), or any other cooked chicken

2 tablespoons extra-virgin olive oil

2 teaspoons red wine vinegar

2 teaspoons dried oregano

Fine sea salt and freshly ground black pepper

4 Grain-Free Wraps (page 313), or large iceberg lettuce cups (see Tidbits)

½ English cucumber, halved lengthwise and sliced into thin half-moons

¼ red onion, thinly sliced

1 tomato, thinly sliced

1 cup shredded romaine lettuce

¼ cup Tzatziki Sauce (page 95)

PIZZA POCKETS

Makes about 6 • When I was growing up, one of my favorite after-school snacks was a Hot Pocket, the microwavable frozen-dough sandwiches. My favorite flavors were ham and Cheddar, and pizza. These are really like miniature calzones, the stuffed pizzas popular in Italy. My version is good for an on-the-go meal and is an easy, freezable lunch idea. Calzones are the perfect vehicles for using up leftover odds and ends in the fridge; the flavor combinations are endless.

DOUGH

¾ cup full-fat coconut milk, warmed

1 teaspoon freshly squeezed lemon juice

1 tablespoon finely ground golden flaxseeds

1 egg white

2 cups blanched almond flour

2 cups arrowroot powder

1 teaspoon Grain-Free Baking Powder (page 312)

½ teaspoon fine sea salt

1 to 2 teaspoons ice water

1 egg yolk, mixed with 1 tablespoon full-fat coconut milk, for wash

FILLING

¾ cup Ricotta Cheese (page 316), or any store-bought dairy-free ricotta

¾ cup pizza sauce

1 egg

2 tablespoons chopped fresh basil

¼ teaspoon fine sea salt

6 ounces salami, chopped

6 ounces mild Italian sausage, cooked and crumbled

To make the dough, in the bowl of a stand mixer fitted with the whisk attachment, whisk together the warmed coconut milk, lemon juice, and flaxseeds. Let rest for 2 minutes. Switch to the beater attachment or use a handheld electric mixer to beat in the egg white until incorporated. Add the almond flour, arrowroot, baking powder, and salt and beat on medium speed until a dough forms. Add 1 teaspoon ice water and knead it into the dough by hand. Divide the dough into two equal pieces.

Preheat the oven to 375°F and line a baking sheet with parchment paper.

Place one piece of dough between two sheets of parchment paper and roll into a ⅛-inch-thick circle. Remove the top parchment and trim the edges to make a 9 by 5-inch rectangle. Cut the rectangle into three 3 by 5-inch rectangles. Repeat with the remaining piece of dough, then gather the scraps from both and reroll and cut six more rectangles, for a total of twelve rectangles. If the dough dries out, knead the remaining 1 teaspoon ice water into the dough before rolling. Transfer six of the rectangles to the baking sheet.

To make the filling, in a small bowl, mix together the ricotta, pizza sauce, egg, basil, and salt. Spread the mixture in the center of each piece of dough, leaving a ½-inch border. Place 1 ounce each of salami and sausage on top.

Brush the inside edges of the dough with the egg wash, then cover each of the filled rectangles with a piece of dough to make six pockets. Use a fork to crimp the edges and seal them shut. Brush

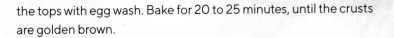

the tops with egg wash. Bake for 20 to 25 minutes, until the crusts are golden brown.

Let the pockets cool on the baking sheet. Wrap each cooled pocket with a double layer of plastic wrap. Store the pockets in an airtight container or resealable plastic bag in the fridge for 5 days. To reheat, bake at 350°F for 10 minutes, until heated through.

Store in the freezer for 3 months. Bake from frozen at 400°F for 20 minutes, until heated through.

Variations: Following are some additional ideas for fillings.

Pressure Cooker Chicken (page 315), BBQ Sauce (page 309), fresh chopped cilantro, red onion, and Ricotta Cheese (page 316)

Pressure Cooker Chicken (page 315), hot pepper sauce (such as Frank's), and Ricotta Cheese (page 316)

Breakfast "Hamburgers" (page 233) or other crumbled sausage, and scrambled eggs

French Dip beef (see page 217), sautéed green bell peppers and onions, Mayonnaise (page 314), and Ricotta Cheese (page 316)

Pack It: Place reheated pockets in a warmed thermos, or pack wrapped pockets from the fridge and reheat right before eating.

Tidbits: To make a dough that complies with SCD, see the variation in Cinnamon Sugar Toaster Tarts (page 105).

CHAPTER 3

SNACKS

Snacking can be difficult on a grain-free diet, for kids and adults alike. Of course, fruits and vegetables are always quick and nutritious snacks, but sometimes we all hanker for something that feels a little bit indulgent. You might recognize the recipes that follow as being inspired by the snacks you knew and loved growing up.

When I'm really short on time and want a snack made from ingredients I trust, I search out the store-bought snacks below. Most of these can be found in health food stores or ordered in bulk online or through againstallgrain.com/shop.

- Chocolate treats: Alter Eco, Eating Evolved, Hu Kitchen

- Coconut oil chips: Terra plantain chips, Jackson's Honest sweet potato chips

- Dried fruits and fruit strips: Made in Nature, Eden Organics, Peeled Snacks, Barnana, Veggie-Go's

- Freeze-dried fruits: Little Duck Organics, Nature's All, Karen's Naturals

- Meat sticks and jerky: The New Primal, Chomps, Epic Bar

- Snack and protein bars: RXBar, Larabar

- Seaweed snacks: SeaSnax

A lot of the recipes in this chapter can be made in batches and stored in the pantry or refrigerator for a good amount of time. Plan on a snack-making marathon once a month or so, and you'll always have a variety of items on hand when you feel a snack attack coming on.

BUTTERSCOTCH SNACK PACKS

Serves 4 • Ryan's favorite childhood dessert was butterscotch pudding. He asked me to attempt to re-create it for years, and I finally mustered up the courage to try a version of his beloved original for this book. Despite its name, butterscotch pudding doesn't typically contain scotch (much to Ryan's chagrin, as a whiskey-loving guy). I've heard the name came about because the butter is scorched. I use ghee to keep this lactose- and casein-free, but if you tolerate butter, I would use unsalted grass-fed butter for a truly authentic-tasting butterscotch pudding. For an egg-free version, check out againstallgrain.com/egg-free-butterscotch-pudding.

3 tablespoons ghee or unsalted grass-fed butter

½ cup coconut sugar

¼ cup pure maple syrup

1 vanilla bean, halved lengthwise and seeds scraped out

½ cup full-fat coconut milk

3 egg yolks

2½ tablespoons arrowroot powder

¼ teaspoon fine sea salt

1½ cups Cashew Milk (page 310), warmed (see Tidbits)

1 teaspoon pure vanilla extract

Whipped Cream (page 93; optional), for serving

Shaved dark chocolate (optional), for serving

Melt the ghee in a saucepan over medium-high heat. Add the coconut sugar, maple syrup, and the vanilla bean pod and seeds and cook for 2 to 3 minutes, whisking frequently, until bubbling. Don't let the mixture smoke or burn. Whisk in the coconut milk and cook for 2 minutes more, until thickened slightly. Remove the pan from the heat.

In a small bowl, whisk the egg yolks, arrowroot, and salt into the warmed cashew milk, then whisk the egg mixture into the pan. Return the pan to the stove over medium-high heat and cook for 3 to 4 minutes more, whisking constantly, until the mixture thickens and a path is left when a spoon is drawn through the pudding.

Remove the pan from the heat, discard the vanilla bean pod, and stir in the vanilla extract. Divide the pudding among four 8-ounce jars and press plastic wrap directly on top of the pudding surfaces. Refrigerate for 2 hours, until set and fully chilled.

Store the set pudding in an airtight container in the refrigerator for 3 days.

Serve topped with whipped cream and chocolate shavings.

Variation: To make chocolate pudding, omit the vanilla bean. After removing the pudding from the heat, whisk 2 ounces chopped unsweetened chocolate into the mixture, then stir in the vanilla extract until smooth.

Tidbits: If you use store-bought cashew milk, add 1 tablespoon unflavored powdered gelatin to the pot when you add the coconut milk.

ANIMAL CRACKERS

Makes 36 • Remember the animal crackers packed in a box with a circus scene on the outside? There was a little string attached that you could use to carry the box like a purse, and you had to open some waxy white paper to get to the cookies inside. Those were always a favorite treat of mine growing up. This version, like the original, is mildly sweet and crunchy, and it's so fun to make at home using cookie cutters of your favorite zoo animals.

In the bowl of a stand mixer fitted with the beater attachment, or using an electric handheld mixer, combine the arrowroot, coconut flour, coconut oil, maple sugar, vanilla, salt, baking powder, and nutmeg and beat on medium speed until combined. Add the eggs and beat on medium-high speed until the eggs are fully incorporated and a loose dough forms.

Using your hands, form the dough into a ball. Divide the dough in half. Place each piece of dough between two sheets of parchment paper and roll into an 8-inch round that's about ¼ inch thick. Stack the dough rounds on a baking sheet with the parchment separating them and chill in the freezer for no longer than 30 minutes.

Preheat the oven to 325°F. Line a separate baking sheet with parchment paper.

Remove one dough round from the freezer. Using cookie cutters, cut out animal shapes and place each cracker on the prepared baking sheet. Gather and reroll the scraps to cut out more shapes. Bake for 10 minutes, until the edges are golden. Cool the crackers completely on a wire rack. Repeat with the remaining dough round.

Store the crackers in an airtight container at room temperature for 1 week, or in the refrigerator for 3 weeks.

¾ cup arrowroot powder

½ cup plus 1 teaspoon coconut flour

½ cup expeller-pressed coconut oil

½ cup maple sugar

½ teaspoon pure vanilla extract

½ teaspoon fine sea salt

½ teaspoon Grain-Free Baking Powder (page 312)

⅛ teaspoon ground nutmeg

2 eggs

CHOCOLATE MILK

Serves 4 • When I was a kid, we just added chocolate syrup to a glass of milk for an instant chocolate milk treat. Making it dairy-free, however, poses a challenge. I pack this chocolate milk (see photo on page 82) in a reusable canteen for Asher to take to school as an occasional treat. It's nice for him to have something yummy and dairy-free to sip when the rest of the kids are drinking their boxed milks or juices. And to be honest, when there are leftovers in the fridge, I find myself sipping on it straight from the bottle throughout the day. This also makes a delicious and easy hot cocoa when warmed up.

2 cups (about 300g) whole raw cashews (see Tidbits, page 310)

5 ounces pitted Deglet Noor dates (about 12 small dates)

6 tablespoons raw cacao powder

½ teaspoon pure vanilla extract

¼ teaspoon fine sea salt

Bring a kettle of water to a boil. Place the cashews in a bowl and add enough boiling water to cover. Soak for 4 hours, then drain, rinse, and drain again.

Combine the cashews and dates in a high-speed blender with the cacao powder, vanilla, and salt. Pour in 6 cups water and blend on high speed for 2 minutes, until very smooth and creamy. If using a conventional blender, scrape down the sides of the blender if needed and blend again until smooth and creamy.

Transfer the mixture to an airtight container and refrigerate for 1 hour, or for up to 5 days. Shake the container and serve cold.

SUNFLOWER SEED BUTTER CRUNCH BARS

Makes 24 • These no-bake crunch bars (see photo on page 87, bottom) are really simple to make. The candied pecans give the bars a satisfying crunch, but can easily be made nut-free by removing the pecans if you want to send them to school with your little ones.

Preheat the oven to 350°F. Line a baking sheet with parchment paper.

In a bowl, combine the pecans, 3 tablespoons maple syrup, and a pinch of salt. Stir to coat the nuts evenly, then spread in a single layer on the prepared baking sheet. Bake for 15 minutes, until the syrup is bubbling.

Meanwhile, very lightly grease the short sides of an 8 by 11-inch baking pan with coconut oil. Line the bottom and long sides of the pan with parchment paper so the ends hang over the sides.

In a saucepan, bring 2 inches of water to a simmer. Place the chocolate and 2 teaspoons oil in a heatproof bowl and set it over the simmering water, creating a double boiler. Be sure not to let the bowl touch the water. Turn the heat to medium and stir the mixture frequently until the chocolate melts and is fully combined with the oil, about 3 minutes. Turn off the heat and remove the bowl from the pan.

In a bowl, stir together the sunflower seed butter, the remaining ⅔ cup maple syrup, the arrowroot, coconut flour, cacao butter, vanilla, and ½ teaspoon salt. Stir in the candied pecans, then press the mixture into the prepared pan. Pour the melted chocolate mixture over the sunflower butter mixture to cover, using a spatula to smooth the top. Cover with plastic wrap, then chill in the refrigerator for 1 hour, until set.

Gently lift the parchment flaps to remove the slab from the pan. Use a sharp knife to cut the bars into 24 squares and serve.

Store in an airtight container in the refrigerator for 2 weeks. Let the bars sit at room temperature for 15 minutes before serving.

1 cup finely chopped pecans

⅔ cup plus 3 tablespoons pure maple syrup

Fine sea salt

1 cup chopped dark chocolate (80 percent cacao)

2 teaspoons virgin coconut oil

1 cup unsweetened sunflower seed butter

½ cup arrowroot powder

6 tablespoons coconut flour

¼ cup melted raw cacao butter

½ teaspoon pure vanilla extract

Tidbits: To make this NF, omit the pecans.

ENERGY BALLS

Makes 12 • I created these chocolate balls of energy for the moments when we all need a little pick-me-up. They pack a protein punch from the sunflower seed butter, flaxseeds, and cacao powder, and the dose of collagen peptides is great for improving digestion and building strong nails and hair.

½ cup golden flaxseeds

1 cup unsweetened sunflower seed butter

½ cup light-colored raw honey

15 small pitted dates

3 tablespoons raw cacao powder

2 tablespoons coconut flour

2 tablespoons unflavored collagen peptides powder or protein powder of your choice

1 teaspoon pure vanilla extract

½ cup chopped dark chocolate (80 percent cacao)

Fine sea salt

Cocoa powder or finely shredded unsweetened coconut, for rolling

Place the flaxseeds in a food processor and process until finely ground. Add the sunflower seed butter, honey, dates, cacao powder, coconut flour, collagen peptides, and vanilla and process until smooth. Stir in the chocolate and a pinch of salt. Remove the blade and chill the mixture in the fridge for 30 minutes.

Place cocoa powder or shredded coconut on a plate. Roll the chilled mixture into 1-inch balls, and roll each ball in the topping until coated.

Store in an airtight container in the fridge for 1 week, or in the freezer for 6 months. Eat straightaway; or, if you prefer, defrost at room temperature for 30 minutes before serving.

APPLE PIE APPLESAUCE

Serves 6 • My grandmother always dotted her pies and fruit crisps with squares of butter, which melted into the crust and gave it a rich flavor that complemented the fruit and spices. In this applesauce recipe, I cook apples with apple pie spices—cinnamon and allspice—and use ghee to add a creamy, buttery flavor. A mix of sweet and tart apples ensures that no added sweetener is needed. The applesauce also works great as baby food. I usually put just a touch of ghee in most of my vegetable or fruit baby purees because the fat helps babies' little bodies absorb the nutrients. The same is true for adults.

Peel, core, and slice the apples. Place the apples, ¾ cup water, and the lemon juice, ghee, cinnamon, allspice, and salt in an electric pressure cooker or a large saucepan.

If using an electric pressure cooker, secure the lid and turn the valve to pressure. Select the manual button and set it to high pressure for 5 minutes. Once the timer has sounded, let the machine release the pressure on its own; it will take about 15 minutes. (Alternatively, carefully release the pressure manually.) Remove the lid.

To make on the stovetop, cover the saucepan and cook over medium heat for 30 minutes, until the apples are fork-tender.

Using an immersion blender or conventional blender, pulse the applesauce to your desired consistency. Serve warm with cinnamon sprinkled on top, or refrigerate and enjoy chilled.

Store the applesauce in an airtight container in the refrigerator for 10 days or in an airtight container in the freezer for 6 months. Allow it to thaw overnight in the refrigerator before serving. If desired, reheat in a saucepan over medium-low heat for 8 to 10 minutes, until heated through.

Tidbits: Spoon applesauce into reusable puree pouches for a nutritious and tidy on-the-go snack for little ones.

3½ pounds assorted sweet and tart apples (such as Gala, Granny Smith, and Fuji)

2 teaspoons freshly squeezed lemon juice

2 teaspoons ghee

¼ teaspoon ground cinnamon, plus more for serving

⅛ teaspoon ground allspice

⅛ teaspoon fine sea salt

PROBIOTIC FRUIT SNACKS

These gummy fruit snacks allow you to easily add gut-healing gelatin to your diet along with probiotics. I make these two flavors frequently: Pomegranate Raspberry during the summer, when raspberries are in abundance, and Cold Buster with elderberries, when school is back in session and cold and flu season ramps up. If you don't have silicone candy molds, pour the mixture into glass baking dishes, filling them about ½ inch up the sides, then cut into squares once the gummies are chilled and set.

Makes about 72

1 cup frozen raspberries

1 cup unfiltered unsweetened apple juice

¼ cup pomegranate juice concentrate

2 teaspoons freshly squeezed lemon juice

4½ tablespoons unflavored powdered gelatin (see Tidbits)

3 tablespoons light-colored raw honey (optional)

1 (50 billion IU) dairy-free and gluten-free probiotic capsule (see Resources, page 319)

POMEGRANATE RASPBERRY

Place the raspberries, ½ cup of the apple juice, and the pomegranate juice in a blender and blend on high speed until smooth. Strain the liquid through a fine-mesh sieve into a bowl and discard the pulp. Add the lemon juice.

Sprinkle the gelatin over the raspberry juice mixture. Let the mixture sit for 5 minutes, until the gelatin has absorbed most of the liquid.

Warm the remaining ½ cup apple juice in a saucepan over medium heat until steaming but not boiling. Pour the hot juice into the gelatin mixture and whisk until the gelatin is completely dissolved. Whisk in the honey and the contents of the probiotic capsule.

Use a turkey baster or medicine dropper to fill candy molds with the mixture. Refrigerate for 3 to 4 hours, until set.

Store the fruit snacks in an airtight container in the refrigerator for 2 weeks.

COLD BUSTERS

Place the elderberries and 1 cup water in a saucepan over high heat and bring to a boil. Turn the heat to low, cover, and simmer for 1 hour. Strain the elderberry juice through a fine-mesh sieve and return the juice to the saucepan. Discard the elderberries. Add the apple, pomegranate, and lemon juices.

Sprinkle the gelatin over the mixed juice mixture. Let the mixture sit for 5 minutes, until the gelatin has absorbed most of the liquid.

Return the pan to medium heat and warm until the liquid is steaming but not boiling, then whisk until the gelatin has completely dissolved. Let the mixture cool to room temperature. Whisk in the honey and the contents of the probiotic capsule.

Use a turkey baster or medicine dropper to fill candy molds with the mixture. Refrigerate for 3 to 4 hours, until set.

Store the fruit snacks in an airtight container in the refrigerator for 2 weeks.

Tidbits: If the mixture begins to solidify before the molds are full, warm it in a saucepan over low heat until it liquefies again. I use Vital Proteins gelatin. If using Great Lakes or Knox gelatin, use 1 tablespoon less than what is called for.

Makes about 96

½ cup dried elderberries

½ cup unfiltered unsweetened apple juice

¼ cup pomegranate juice concentrate

1 teaspoon freshly squeezed lemon juice

¼ cup unflavored powdered gelatin (see Tidbits)

¼ cup light-colored raw honey

1 (50 billion IU) dairy-free and gluten-free probiotic capsule (see Resources, page 319)

DIPS...

Having a variety of dips in the refrigerator to use with snacks or to pack in lunchboxes can encourage adults and little ones alike to eat more fruits and vegetables. Use carrots, jicama, celery, or cucumber sticks as dippers for these savory sauces, and fruit or cookies for the whipped cream. I also have recipes for dippers on pages 98 and 99 and several store-bought recommendations on page 78.

NF • NSF • SCD

HERB RANCH DRESSING

Makes 2 cups • I've streamlined my famous herb ranch dressing recipe so you can make it quickly in a blender, eliminating the need for premade mayonnaise.

2 egg yolks

5 teaspoons freshly squeezed lemon juice

1 teaspoon white vinegar

¾ teaspoon fine sea salt

¼ teaspoon Dijon mustard

¾ cup avocado oil

⅓ cup full-fat coconut milk

¼ cup chopped fresh flat-leaf parsley

2 cloves garlic, crushed

2 tablespoons chopped fresh chives

2 tablespoons chopped fresh dill

½ teaspoon onion powder

Combine the egg yolks, 1 teaspoon of the lemon juice, the vinegar, salt, and mustard in a small blender or mini food processor and blend on low speed until combined. With the blender running, add the oil very slowly, a drop at a time. When the mixture starts to thicken, pour in the remaining oil in a slow, steady stream, until all of the oil has been incorporated and the mixture is thick like mayonnaise. Add the coconut milk, parsley, garlic, chives, dill, onion powder, and the remaining 4 teaspoons lemon juice and pulse a few times, until well combined. Serve immediately, or store in an airtight container in the refrigerator for 5 days.

Variation: I frequently turn this into a delicious Buffalo Ranch Dressing by adding 2 tablespoons hot pepper sauce (such as Frank's), 2 teaspoons melted ghee, and 1 teaspoon white wine vinegar.

Tidbits: If you do not have a small blender or mini food processor, an immersion blender works really well here.

WHIPPED CREAM

Makes 1½ cups • Cashews and macadamia nuts are both soft nuts that blend easily and make this dip smooth and creamy. Feel free to use either one here.

Bring a kettle of water to a boil. Place the cashews in a bowl and add enough boiling water to cover. Soak for 30 minutes, then drain, rinse, and drain again.

Combine the cashews, coconut milk, coconut oil, maple syrup, cacao butter, vanilla, and salt to taste in a high-speed blender and blend on high for 1 minute, until very smooth. If using a conventional blender, scrape down the sides of the blender and blend again until all of the cashew fragments are blended smooth. Transfer the mixture to the bowl of a stand mixer or a large glass bowl. Cover and refrigerate for at least 6 hours, or up to 5 days.

Remove the bowl with the cashew mixture from the refrigerator, and using a stand mixer fitted with the whisk attachment or an electric handheld mixer, beat the cream on medium speed for 10 seconds, until it holds soft peaks when the whisk is lifted out. Serve cold, or store, covered, in the refrigerator for 5 days.

Tidbits: To comply with SCD, substitute honey for the maple syrup.

½ cup (about 75g) whole raw cashews or macadamia nuts (see Tidbits, page 310)

¾ cup full-fat coconut milk

2 tablespoons expeller-pressed coconut oil, at room temperature

2 tablespoons pure maple syrup (see Tidbits)

1½ tablespoons melted raw cacao butter

¼ teaspoon pure vanilla extract

Fine sea salt

CAULIFLOWER HUMMUS

Makes 2 cups • Asher has loved hummus and crackers since he was a toddler. Spoon some of this into a small sauce container and pack it with a stack of Everything Crackers (page 99), Plantain Chips (page 98), or carrot sticks.

1 large head cauliflower, cut into florets

1 head garlic, top one-third cut off

¼ cup melted ghee or avocado oil

Fine sea salt and freshly ground black pepper

2 tablespoons tahini

1 tablespoon freshly squeezed lemon juice, plus more to taste

1 tablespoon extra-virgin olive oil, plus more for serving

1 tablespoon chopped fresh flat-leaf parsley, for serving (optional)

Sweet paprika, for serving (optional)

Preheat the oven to 450°F.

In a baking dish with a lid, toss together the cauliflower and garlic head with the ghee, ½ teaspoon salt, and a pinch of pepper. Cover the baking dish and roast the cauliflower and garlic for about 12 minutes, until they begin to soften. Uncover and roast for 10 minutes more, until the cauliflower is crisp-tender. Toss the florets, and roast for 10 to 12 minutes more, until the cauliflower is golden brown and completely tender.

Squeeze four large garlic cloves out of their papery skins and place them in a food processor with the cauliflower, tahini, and lemon juice. Reserve the remaining garlic for another use (see Tidbits). Blend on high speed until smooth. With the motor running on low, drizzle in the oil. Scrape down the sides of the processor as needed and blend again until smooth. Add more salt and lemon juice to taste.

Transfer the hummus to a bowl and drizzle with oil. Sprinkle with parsley or paprika if serving immediately. Otherwise, store in an airtight container in the refrigerator for 3 days and add your desired toppings just before serving.

Tidbits: Use the leftover roasted garlic as a spread for crackers or whisk it into a vinaigrette.

To make this NSF, omit the sweet paprika.

TZATZIKI SAUCE

EF • NF • NSF • SCD

Makes 1 cup • This cool cucumber sauce is a staple in Mediterranean cuisine and can be served as a dip, drizzled into a wrap (see page 71), or even used as a salad dressing.

Set a colander in the sink. Combine the cucumbers and a generous amount of salt in the colander and toss together. Let the cucumbers sweat for 15 minutes. Rinse the cucumbers and drain on paper towels.

In a bowl, whisk together the yogurt, garlic, lemon juice, oil, dill, mint, and salt and pepper to taste. Stir in the cucumbers. Season with more salt and pepper to taste. Serve immediately.

Store in an airtight container in the refrigerator for 3 days.

Tidbits: To make this NF, substitute any store-bought dairy-free yogurt, such as coconut milk yogurt.

2 Persian cucumbers, peeled, seeded, and finely chopped

Fine sea salt

¾ cup Dairy-Free Yogurt (page 312; see Tidbits)

1 clove garlic, minced

1 tablespoon freshly squeezed lemon juice

1 tablespoon extra-virgin olive oil

1 teaspoon chopped fresh dill

1 teaspoon chopped fresh mint

Freshly ground black pepper

GUACAMOLE

EF • NF • SCD

Makes 1 cup • My favorite way to make guac is in a food processor so I can skip all the chopping and mashing!

Place the onion, jalapeños, and garlic in a food processor and pulse a few times until everything is coarsely chopped. Scoop the avocados out of their peels and add to the food processor along with the lime juice, salt, and a pinch of pepper. Pulse 4 or 5 times, until everything is incorporated and the avocado is still a little chunky. If serving right away, scoop the guac into a serving bowl, stir in the cilantro, and serve.

If not serving immediately, place one of the avocado pits in with the guac in an airtight container and cover the container with a paper towel before securing the lid. Store in the refrigerator for 2 days.

¼ red onion

2 jalapeño chiles, halved and seeded

1 clove garlic, peeled

2 ripe avocados, pitted

2 teaspoons freshly squeezed lime juice

½ teaspoon fine sea salt

Freshly ground black pepper

2 tablespoons chopped fresh cilantro

...AND DIPPERS

These homemade dippers are designed to be served with the dips starting on page 92. Also see page 78 for some store-bought crunchy snacks.

EF · NF · NSF

PLANTAIN CHIPS

Makes about 8 ounces • You can often find green plantains near the bananas or coconuts in your supermarket.

1½ pounds green plantains

1 cup avocado oil

1 cup virgin coconut oil

1 teaspoon kosher salt

Peel the plantains and cut them on the diagonal into ⅛-inch ovals. Set a wire rack over a baking sheet lined with paper towels.

Combine the avocado and coconut oils in a deep sauté pan. There should be enough oil to fully cover the plantains, about 2 inches deep. Heat the oils over medium-high heat to 375°F to 400°F.

Working in batches, add the plantains to the hot oil. Fry until golden, 2 to 3 minutes. Remove the chips from the oil with a slotted spoon and transfer to the wire rack to drain. Immediately sprinkle with salt on both sides. Let the chips cool completely before serving.

Store in an airtight container at room temperature for 2 weeks.

Variation: To bake the chips, toss the plantain slices with 2 tablespoons avocado oil and 1 teaspoon kosher salt. Place the chips in a single layer—not touching—on two parchment paper-lined baking sheets. Bake at 400°F for 15 to 20 minutes, flipping once, until crispy and golden brown.

EF · NF · NSF

SOCCA CRACKERS

Makes 24 • These buttery and flaky crackers make a delicious nut-free, salty, and crunchy snack.

Preheat the oven to 325°F and line a baking sheet with parchment paper.

Place the garbanzo bean flour, palm shortening, cold water, rosemary, and salt in a food processor and process until thoroughly combined and a loose dough forms. Remove the blade and pack the dough into a ball. Place the ball between two sheets of parchment and roll into a 10-inch round that's about ⅛ inch thick.

Remove the top sheet of parchment and lightly prick the dough all over with a fork. Use a pizza cutter or sharp knife to cut the dough into 1 by 3-inch rectangles. Carefully transfer the rectangles to the prepared baking sheet.

Bake for 15 minutes, rotating the sheet once halfway through baking, until golden. Let the crackers cool completely on a wire rack. Store in an airtight container at room temperature for 2 weeks.

1¼ cups garbanzo bean flour (see page 9)

½ cup palm shortening

¼ cup cold water

1 teaspoon chopped fresh rosemary

¾ teaspoon fine sea salt

EVERYTHING CRACKERS

EF · NSF · SCD

Makes 36 • These crunchy little crackers deliver an oniony, garlicky flavor.

Preheat the oven to 325°F and line a baking sheet with parchment paper.

Place the almond flour, cold water, oil, salt, onion powder, and garlic powder in a food processor and process until thoroughly combined and a loose dough forms. Remove the blade and pack the dough into a ball. Place the ball between two sheets of parchment and roll into an 8-inch round about ⅛ inch thick.

Remove the top sheet of parchment and lightly prick the dough all over with a fork. Sprinkle with the poppy seeds and sesame seeds. Use a cookie cutter to cut out 2-inch squares. Carefully transfer the squares to the prepared baking sheet.

Bake for 15 minutes, rotating the sheet once halfway through baking, until golden. Turn the oven off and leave the crackers inside for 10 minutes more. Let the crackers cool completely on a wire rack. Store in an airtight container at room temperature for 2 weeks.

1 cup blanched almond flour

2 tablespoons cold water

1½ teaspoons extra-virgin olive oil

½ teaspoon fine sea salt

½ teaspoon onion powder or dried minced onion

¼ teaspoon garlic powder or dried minced garlic

½ teaspoon poppy seeds

½ teaspoon black or white sesame seeds

NUT-FREE GRANOLA BARS

Makes 12 • Store-bought granola bars almost always contain oats or nuts. Using a combination of seeds and coconut, these bars are both grain- and nut-free. The chocolate chips are a favorite for both me and my kids, but you could also use raisins or any other dried fruit.

Preheat the oven to 350°F. Lightly grease the short sides of a 9 by 13-inch baking dish or rimmed baking sheet with ghee or coconut oil. Line the bottom and long sides of the pan with parchment paper so the ends hang over the sides.

Whisk the warm water and chia seeds in a small bowl and set aside.

Melt the honey in a small saucepan over medium-high heat. Turn the heat to medium and simmer for 5 to 7 minutes, until a candy thermometer reads 225°F. Stir in the oil and sunflower seed butter and remove the pan from the heat. Let cool for 10 minutes.

Place the pepitas and sunflower seeds in a food processor and pulse once or twice until coarsely chopped. Add the coconut flakes, sesame seeds, vanilla, cinnamon, and salt and pulse a few times more, until coarsely chopped and incorporated. Add the chia mixture and the honey mixture and stir by hand until just combined. Immediately spread the mixture into the prepared baking dish.

Place a piece of parchment paper on top and use a flat-bottomed measuring cup to press the mixture firmly and evenly into the pan. Remove the top piece of parchment and bake for 15 minutes, until golden. Sprinkle the chocolate chips over the top. Let cool in the pan for 30 minutes, then transfer the pan to the freezer for 1 hour, until set.

Remove the pan from the freezer and lift the parchment flaps to remove the slab from the pan. Using a sharp knife, cut into 12 rectangular bars. Serve the bars chilled.

Store in an airtight container in the refrigerator for 2 weeks, or in the freezer for 6 months. Defrost in the fridge overnight.

2 tablespoons warm water

1 tablespoon chia seeds

⅓ cup light-colored raw honey

1 tablespoon virgin coconut oil

2 tablespoons unsweetened sunflower seed butter

¾ cup raw pepitas

¾ cup raw sunflower seeds

1 cup unsweetened coconut flakes

2 tablespoons sesame seeds

2 teaspoons pure vanilla extract

2 teaspoons ground cinnamon

½ teaspoon fine sea salt

¼ cup chocolate chips, raisins, or dried fruit pieces

CHEESE CRACKERS

Makes about 60 • Goldfish-style crackers rank high on my list of most requested recipes. Because this book is dairy-free (besides the use of ghee), I went rogue with this recipe and included real Cheddar and Parmesan for that truly cheesy flavor.

2 cups blanched almond flour

1 tablespoon melted ghee

4 teaspoons ice water

1 egg white

1 teaspoon fine sea salt

½ teaspoon baking soda

½ teaspoon sweet paprika

½ teaspoon dry mustard powder

1 cup shredded Cheddar cheese (see Tidbits)

½ cup grated Parmesan cheese (see Tidbits)

Flaky sea salt or kosher salt

Preheat the oven to 350°F and line a baking sheet with parchment paper.

Place the almond flour, ghee, ice water, egg white, fine sea salt, baking soda, paprika, and mustard powder in a food processor and pulse until a loose dough forms. Scrape down the sides, add the cheeses, and pulse again until well combined. Remove the blade and pack the dough into a ball. Place the ball between two sheets of parchment and roll it into an 18-inch round that's about ⅛ inch thick.

Remove the top sheet of parchment. Use a fluted pastry cutter or square cookie cutter to cut the dough into 1-inch squares. Gather the scraps and reroll to cut out more crackers. Carefully transfer the squares to the prepared baking sheet. Use the flat end of a skewer to poke a hole in the center of each cracker. Sprinkle the tops with flaky sea salt.

Bake for 12 to 15 minutes, rotating the sheet once halfway through baking, until golden around the edges. Let the crackers cool completely on a wire rack.

Store in an airtight container at room temperature for 3 weeks.

Tidbits: If you do not tolerate dairy, substitute 3 tablespoons nutritional yeast for both of the cheeses.

The thinner you roll these, the crunchier they will be. Roll them as thin as the dough will allow; just be sure you can still easily transfer them to the baking sheet.

CINNAMON SUGAR TOASTER TARTS

Makes 6 • Goodness, I was a sucker for Pop-Tarts when I was younger. I loved the cinnamon and brown sugar flavors and the strawberry one topped with sprinkles and frosting. I haven't enjoyed a toaster pastry in close to twenty years, so it was pretty fun testing this recipe and getting to experience these familiar flavors once again. If you also loved those frosted strawberry tarts, try experimenting with fillings and use my homemade Rainbow Sprinkles (page 304) on top.

To make the tart dough, place the almond flour, arrowroot, and salt in a food processor and process for 10 seconds. Add the egg whites and process again to incorporate. Add the shortening pieces, spacing them around the bowl. Pulse 3 or 4 times, just until the shortening is mixed in. Add the ice water, a tablespoon at a time, pulsing until the dough just comes together.

Remove the blade and pack the dough into a ball, then flatten it into a disk. Cover the disk in plastic wrap and chill it in the freezer for 30 minutes.

To make the filling, meanwhile, in a small bowl, mix together the coconut sugar, maple sugar, cinnamon, and coconut flour. Set aside.

Remove the dough from the freezer. Place it between two sheets of parchment paper and roll into an oval about ⅛ inch thick. Remove the top sheet of parchment and trim the edges to make a 9 by 10-inch rectangle. Use a pizza cutter or knife to cut the dough lengthwise into three 10 by 3-inch strips. Cut the strips in half to make six 3 by 5-inch rectangles. Transfer three of the rectangles to a parchment paper–lined baking sheet and place the remaining three rectangles on a baking sheet in the freezer.

Place 2 tablespoons of the filling on each of the three rectangles, leaving a ¼-inch border around the edges. Brush the edges with half of the egg wash. Remove the remaining three rectangles from the freezer and place one on top of each of the filled pieces. Use your fingertips to press down firmly on the edges to seal the dough

CONTINUED

TART DOUGH

2½ cups blanched almond flour

1¼ cups arrowroot powder

⅛ teaspoon fine sea salt

2 egg whites, chilled

¼ cup cold palm shortening, broken up into small pieces

2 to 3 tablespoons ice water

1 egg yolk, mixed with 1 tablespoon full-fat coconut milk, for wash

FILLING

¼ cup coconut sugar

¼ cup maple sugar

2 teaspoons ground cinnamon

2 teaspoons coconut flour

FROSTING

¼ cup arrowroot powder

¼ cup maple sugar

1 ounce raw cacao butter, melted

1 tablespoon egg white

¼ teaspoon pure vanilla extract

PARTY MIX

Makes 4 cups • Party mix is a tradition in many American homes. We didn't often make our own growing up, but I do remember fishing through the store-bought bags for my favorite component—the thin and crunchy rye bread toasts. I think I favored them because they had the biggest salty and spicy punch. Most mixes involve breadsticks, pretzels, rice cereal, or other grain-based snacks, so for my version, I swapped in some crunchy plantain chips, nuts, and seeds instead. You can use olive oil if you have a dairy allergy, but ghee gives this mix the traditional buttery flavor in an easily digestible manner.

¼ cup ghee

1½ tablespoons coconut aminos

1 teaspoon pure maple syrup

1 teaspoon fish sauce

¼ teaspoon freshly squeezed lime juice

1¼ teaspoons fine sea salt

¾ teaspoon garlic powder

½ teaspoon sweet paprika

¼ teaspoon onion powder

¼ teaspoon chili powder

5 ounces Plantain Chips (page 98)

1 cup whole unroasted almonds

1 cup whole raw cashews

½ cup raw sunflower seeds

½ cup pepitas

Preheat the oven to 250°F.

Melt the ghee in a saucepan over low heat. Stir in the coconut aminos, maple syrup, fish sauce, lime juice, salt, garlic powder, paprika, onion powder, and chili powder. Turn off the heat, then add the plantain chips, almonds, cashews, sunflower seeds, and pepitas and stir until evenly coated. Spread the party mix in a single layer on a large rimmed baking sheet.

Bake for 90 minutes, stirring every 20 to 30 minutes. Remove from the oven and let the baking sheet cool on a wire rack. The nuts will look slightly wet when removed from the oven but will continue to dry out as they cool.

Store the completely cooled mix in an airtight container at room temperature for 1 month.

Tidbits: If you struggle with digestive problems, try soaking and dehydrating your nuts and seeds before cooking with them. It will help to break down the outer barrier that makes them hard to digest.

BEEF JERKY

Makes 1 pound • While many children awaken on Christmas morning to stockings full of toys (or socks and underwear!), my Grandma Marge always stuffed ours with homemade treats. My favorite item to find in my stocking was her beef jerky. Most commercial beef jerky contains soy sauce, soy protein, wheat, and sugar. There are a few brands now that use healthful ingredients (see page 78), but I find that it's still easier, cheaper, and more flavorful to just make my own jerky at home. Keep it in the pantry for when you need a salty snack or are on the run and don't have time to fix lunch.

2 pounds very lean London broil or flank steak

½ cup coconut aminos

1½ teaspoons all-natural liquid smoke

1½ teaspoons chili powder

1 teaspoon fine sea salt

½ teaspoon freshly ground black pepper

½ teaspoon garlic salt

½ teaspoon onion powder

½ teaspoon smoked paprika

⅛ teaspoon cayenne pepper

Place the steak in the freezer for 2 hours to firm it up; this makes it easier to slice thinly.

Once the steak is firm, trim any visible fat using kitchen scissors or a sharp knife (any fat left on the meat will spoil after drying). Cut London broil with the grain and flank steak against the grain into ⅛-inch slices.

In a shallow dish large enough to hold all of the steak slices, whisk together the coconut aminos, liquid smoke, chili powder, salt, pepper, garlic salt, onion powder, smoked paprika, and cayenne. Add the steak, cover the dish, and marinate in the refrigerator overnight or for up to 24 hours, turning the steak occasionally to keep it evenly coated. (Alternatively, combine the steak and marinade in a resealable plastic bag.)

Remove the strips of beef from the marinade and pat them dry with paper towels.

To cook in a dehydrator, place the strips of beef on dehydrator sheets lined with parchment paper, spacing them out so they don't touch. Dehydrate the beef for 3 to 4 hours at 145°F, flipping the slices once halfway through, until they're dry to the touch.

To cook in the oven, preheat the oven to its lowest setting, usually 150°F to 170°F. Line two rimmed baking sheets with parchment paper or aluminum foil and place a heavy wire rack over each one (oven-safe cooling racks will do). Place the strips of beef on the racks, spacing them apart so they don't touch. Place the baking sheets in the oven, leaving the door open a crack to allow air to circulate. Dehydrate for 8 to 10 hours, depending on the thickness of the meat, flipping the slices halfway through, until they're dry to the touch. (If your oven has a convection mode, the fan will help to dry out the meat more quickly than a standard oven. In this case, check for dryness after 5 hours and continue dehydrating until the strips are no longer moist.)

Store the jerky in an airtight container at room temperature for 2 weeks.

Tidbits: If you have a helpful butcher, ask for the steak to be trimmed and sliced for you; then you can skip the initial freezer step.

CHAPTER 4

VEGGIES AND SIDES

People often think that a paleo-style diet is meat heavy, but in my family, we actually find it to be quite the opposite. We eat more vegetables, and a greater variety of them, than we did when we were filling half of our plates with bread, pasta, or rice.

Many of the recipes in this book contain vegetables as part of the main dish, but as a parent, I'm always looking for ways to get my kids to eat more vegetables, so I often serve a side dish as well. When I don't have a lot of extra time, steamed broccoli or carrots with sea salt or a simple dressed salad make their appearance on the dinner table. As good as these quick sides can taste, even I agree that they can get boring when eaten too frequently.

To keep our meals interesting and our diet varied, I change things up with the recipes in this chapter. They come together almost as quickly as a salad, and make a bigger—and more delicious—impression.

ROASTED LEMON-CHILE ASPARAGUS

Serves 4 to 6 • Surprisingly, asparagus was one of the first vegetables my boys liked, so I have been serving it frequently, and with different flavor profiles, ever since. Ryan and I love the mild heat from the chiles that balances the acid from the lemon juice, but I usually sprinkle the flakes on our portions after serving the kids.

Preheat the oven to 425°F.

Heat 2 tablespoons of the oil in a cast-iron skillet over medium-high heat. Add the shallot and a pinch of salt and panfry for about 30 seconds, until the slices are browned and crisp. Transfer the shallots to a plate with a slotted spoon and wipe out the pan with a paper towel.

Toss the asparagus in the pan with the remaining 2 tablespoons oil, 1 tablespoon lemon juice, the garlic, and ½ teaspoon salt. Place the skillet in the oven and roast the asparagus until just cooked through but still crisp-tender at the center, 5 to 7 minutes.

Arrange the asparagus on a platter. In a small bowl, mix together the shallot, crushed chiles, and lemon zest and sprinkle the mixture over the asparagus. Serve immediately.

Make It Ahead: Store the asparagus and shallot separately, in airtight containers in the refrigerator, for 2 days. Reheat on a baking sheet in a 400°F oven for 3 to 5 minutes, until heated through.

4 tablespoons avocado oil

1 shallot, thinly sliced

Fine sea salt

1 pound asparagus, ends trimmed

Finely grated zest and juice of 1 lemon

4 cloves garlic, minced

2 small dried red chiles, crushed into small flakes, or ½ teaspoon red pepper flakes

CUMIN ROASTED CARROTS

Serves 4 to 6 • Growing up, I disliked cooked carrots. Especially if they were glazed and sweet, or soggy from cooking in a stew or soup all day. When I started cooking on my own, I discovered that I actually adore them, as long as they are roasted until just tender with Indian-inspired seasonings like in this dish.

1 pound small carrots, scrubbed and trimmed

2 tablespoons avocado oil

2 tablespoons coconut aminos

¾ teaspoon ground cumin

¼ teaspoon ground coriander

¼ teaspoon ground ginger

¼ teaspoon fine sea salt

¼ cup chopped fresh cilantro leaves, for garnish

2 tablespoons toasted pepitas, for garnish

Preheat the oven to 400°F.

On a rimmed baking sheet, toss together the carrots with the oil, coconut aminos, cumin, coriander, ginger, and salt. Spread the carrots in a single layer and roast for 15 minutes. Flip the carrots and roast for 10 to 15 minutes more, until fork-tender. Place the carrots in a serving dish, sprinkle with the cilantro and pepitas, and serve warm.

Make It Ahead: Store the roasted carrots without the cilantro and pepitas in an airtight container in the refrigerator for 5 days. Reheat on a baking sheet in a 400°F oven for 5 to 7 minutes, until heated through, then sprinkle with the cilantro and pepitas before serving.

ROASTED BEETS AND CARROTS WITH CITRUS VINAIGRETTE

Serves 4 to 6 • Many people describe beets as earthy (a nice way of saying they taste like dirt!), but a slight sweetness comes out when they are roasted, and I think they taste delicious that way. Here I pair beets with roasted carrots, a tangy vinaigrette, smooth ricotta cheese, and a topping of pistachios and fresh mint.

Preheat the oven to 425°F.

Peel the beets and cut them into 1-inch wedges. In a bowl, toss together the beets with 1 tablespoon of the oil, half of the garlic, and a pinch each of salt and pepper. Arrange the beets in one half of a baking dish with a lid.

In the same bowl, toss together the carrots with 1 tablespoon of the oil, the remaining garlic, and a pinch each of salt and pepper. Arrange the carrots in the other half of the baking dish. Cover and roast for 35 to 40 minutes, until the vegetables are tender.

Meanwhile, in a bowl, mix together the shallot, vinegar, and a pinch of salt. Set aside for 10 minutes to let the shallot soften. Whisk in the orange zest, 1 tablespoon orange juice, and the remaining 2 tablespoons oil and season to taste with salt and pepper.

Spread the ricotta cheese on the bottom of a serving platter. Spoon the roasted vegetables on top of the ricotta and drizzle with the vinaigrette. Sprinkle the pistachios and mint over the top and serve warm.

Store leftovers in an airtight container in the fridge for 3 days. Reheat in a 425°F oven for 10 minutes.

Tidbits: Save the beet greens and sauté them like you would spinach or collard greens, or add them to one of the smoothie packets on page 240.

Purchase dairy-free ricotta cheese from Kite Hill, or if you tolerate dairy, fresh ricotta or goat cheese taste wonderful in this recipe.

To comply with SCD or make this NF, omit the pistachios.

2 pounds red beets (see Tidbits)

4 tablespoons avocado oil

3 large cloves garlic, minced

Fine sea salt and freshly ground black pepper

12 ounces small carrots, trimmed

1 tablespoon minced shallot

1 tablespoon champagne vinegar

Finely grated zest and juice of 1 orange

½ cup Ricotta Cheese (page 316; see Tidbits), or any store-bought dairy-free ricotta

¼ cup roasted chopped pistachios (see Tidbits)

2 tablespoons chopped fresh mint

REFRIED "BEANS"

Serves 4 to 6 • This dish could have more accurately been called Refried Plantains and Eggplant, but then your family probably wouldn't dare to try it, so Refried "Beans" it is. But honestly, this really does taste like the real thing, but without the digestive upset a lot of people experience after consuming beans or legumes. In my younger years, I would seek out what I'd call greasy Mexican food (as opposed to lighter, more refined California-Mexican cuisine) just to get a good plate of refried beans with my enchiladas or tacos. This gets pretty close to the beans I used to love, without including beans at all.

2 pounds green plantains

8 ounces bacon, coarsely chopped

½ cup diced yellow onion

1½ cups Chicken Bone Broth (page 310)

1 tablespoon fine sea salt

2 teaspoons ground cumin

1½ teaspoons chili powder

12 ounces eggplant, peeled and cubed

3 cloves garlic, sliced

2 teaspoons unsweetened cocoa powder (optional)

Chopped fresh cilantro, for garnish (optional)

Bring a large pot of water to a boil over high heat. Cut the ends off the plantains and slice each one into three or four segments, keeping the peels on. Add the plantains to the boiling water, turn down the heat, and simmer for 20 minutes. Drain and set aside until the plantains are cool enough to handle. Peel the plantains, discarding the peels, and place in a food processor.

In a large cast-iron skillet, cook the bacon over medium heat for 10 minutes, until the fat has rendered and the bacon is mostly crisp. Use a slotted spoon to remove the bacon; save it for another use. Reserve ¼ cup of the rendered bacon fat in a small bowl for refrying the "beans" and leave 3 tablespoons in the skillet. Pour off any remaining fat.

Return the skillet to medium heat, add the onion, and cook for 3 to 4 minutes, until softened and browned. Use a slotted spoon to transfer the onion to the food processor. Add the bone broth, salt, cumin, and chili powder and process for about 45 seconds, just until the plantains are smooth and creamy. Don't overprocess or the plantains will get gummy.

CONTINUED

Place the eggplant and garlic in the same skillet and sauté for 5 to 7 minutes, until the eggplant is softened and browned. Add a bit of the reserved bacon fat if the pan starts to look dry. Pour the eggplant mixture into the food processor. Process just until the eggplant is incorporated into the plantain mixture but still has some small pieces intact, about 20 seconds.

Return the skillet to medium-high heat and add the ¼ cup reserved bacon fat. Pour the plantain puree into the skillet and cook, stirring frequently, for 2 minutes, until all of the fat has been absorbed. Stir in the cocoa powder to add a little color and garnish with the cilantro. Serve immediately.

Store leftovers in an airtight container in the refrigerator for 3 days. Reheat in a dry skillet over medium-low heat until heated through, stirring frequently, about 5 minutes.

SEASONED FRIES

Serves 4 to 6 • I was a huge fan of frozen seasoned french fries until I started paying attention to the ingredients and saw how they affected my health. Many fries are coated in flour or cornstarch and the seasonings have surprising, undesirable ingredients as well.

In this recipe, I took inspiration from the seasoned fries at Red Robin, one of my favorite restaurants growing up. I use sweet potatoes instead of russets to make a side dish the whole family will love. While the fried version comes out more crispy and reminiscent of twice-fried restaurant fries, I've also included a baked version here. I love to serve these fries with Ketchup (page 313) or Buffalo Ranch Dressing (see Variation, page 92) on the side.

Wash the potatoes well, then cut each one lengthwise into ½-inch-thick slices. Cut each slice lengthwise again into ¼-inch sticks. Place the potatoes in a large bowl and add enough water to cover, soaking them for at least 30 minutes or up to 24 hours. (Soaking the potatoes helps remove excess starch and keeps them from turning brown before you cook them.)

To make the seasoned salt, meanwhile, combine all of the ingredients in a bowl and stir well to combine. (Store any leftover seasoned salt in an airtight jar for 6 months.)

Drain the potatoes and pat dry with paper towels. Heat the oil in a deep-fryer or a large saucepan over medium-high heat to 300°F. Add two handfuls of potatoes to the hot oil, making sure they are submerged and that there's at least 1 inch of oil above them. Parcook the potatoes until light brown, 3 to 5 minutes. Using a mesh skimmer or slotted spoon, remove the potatoes from the oil, gently shaking off any excess oil, and let them drain on a wire rack. Repeat until all of the potatoes are parcooked.

3 sweet potatoes (about 2 pounds; preferably Hannah or another white-fleshed variety), unpeeled

4 cups avocado oil or melted duck fat

SEASONED SALT

2 teaspoons fine sea salt

1 teaspoon smoked paprika

1 teaspoon garlic powder

½ teaspoon onion powder

½ teaspoon chili powder

½ teaspoon dried basil

¼ teaspoon ground cumin

¼ teaspoon ground sage

¼ teaspoon freshly ground black pepper

⅛ teaspoon dried oregano

CONTINUED

Increase the heat on the fryer or the stove slightly until the temperature of the oil reaches 350°F. Fry the potatoes again, two handfuls at a time, until golden brown, about 3 minutes. Using a mesh skimmer or slotted spoon, remove the potatoes from the oil, gently shaking off any excess oil, and place them back on the rack to drain. Repeat until all of the potatoes are fried.

Place the fries in a bowl and toss with seasoned salt to taste before serving warm.

Store the fries in an airtight container in the fridge for 3 days. To reheat, place the fries on a baking sheet under the broiler for 2 to 3 minutes, until heated through.

Variation: To bake the fries, preheat the oven to 450°F with a rack placed about 3 inches from the broiler. In a large bowl, toss together the cut potatoes and ⅓ cup melted duck fat or avocado oil until well coated. Place the fries in a single layer on two rimmed baking sheets; don't let any fries overlap. Bake one baking sheet at a time, uncovered, for 8 to 10 minutes, then flip the fries and bake for 8 to 10 minutes more, until tender and golden. Repeat with the second batch. Once all of the fries are baked, combine them on a single baking sheet. Sprinkle the top with seasoned salt to taste and toss to coat. Set the oven to broil. Broil the fries for 2 minutes, toss, and broil for 2 minutes more, until the fries are lightly browned and crispy. Serve immediately.

Tidbits: To reuse your frying oil, pour it through a fine-mesh sieve to remove any food particles and store it in an airtight container in the fridge for 2 weeks. I don't recommend using it more than once more, as it will start to darken and give your food a burned flavor. For other recipes that call for frying, check out Plantain Chips (page 98), Onion Rings (page 137), Mini Corn Dogs (page 259), Chicken Nuggets (page 262), and Fried Chicken (page 188).

CLASSIC PICKLES, TWO WAYS

Makes 1 pint • My family loves a good crunchy pickle, especially with summery barbecue. We all lean toward the salty and sour dill variety, but I have received so many requests from fans for a refined sugar–free bread-and-butter pickle that I decided to include recipes for both.

⅓ cup white wine vinegar

¼ cup apple cider vinegar

1 tablespoon light-colored raw honey

1 tablespoon fine sea salt

½ teaspoon mustard seeds

1 cup hot water

1 pound Persian or Kirby cucumbers, sliced into ¼-inch rounds

¼ cup chopped fresh dill

2 cloves garlic, minced

DILL PICKLES

In a glass bowl, combine both vinegars, the honey, salt, and mustard seeds. Pour in the hot water and stir until the honey and salt are dissolved. Let the mixture cool to room temperature.

In a separate large glass bowl, combine the cucumbers, dill, and garlic. Pour the vinegar mixture over the cucumbers and stir to combine. Place a small plate over the cucumbers to keep them submerged, then cover the bowl with plastic wrap. Refrigerate the pickles for 4 hours or overnight, stirring once or twice.

Transfer the pickles and their liquid to a clean 1-pint (16-ounce) glass jar. Secure the lid tightly, then store in the refrigerator for 1 month.

BREAD-AND-BUTTER PICKLES

In a glass bowl, toss together the cucumbers, onion, and salt and cover with the ice cubes. Let the vegetables sit for 3 hours, stirring occasionally. Rinse the mixture and drain it well.

Place the cucumber and onion mixture in a saucepan over low heat. Add the honey, vinegar, mustard seeds, coriander seeds, celery seeds, turmeric, and a pinch of red pepper flakes, stirring to combine. When the mixture reaches a low simmer, remove the saucepan from the heat. Do not let it boil.

Transfer the pickles and their liquid to a clean 1-pint (16-ounce) glass jar. Let it sit at room temperature for 2 hours, until cooled. Secure the lid tightly, then store in the refrigerator for 1 month.

Tidbits: To make this NSF, omit the red pepper flakes.

1 pound Persian or Kirby cucumbers, sliced into ¼-inch rounds

¼ white onion, thinly sliced

1½ tablespoons fine sea salt

3 to 4 cups ice cubes

⅓ cup light-colored raw honey

⅓ cup apple cider vinegar

2 teaspoons mustard seeds

1 teaspoon coriander seeds

¼ teaspoon celery seeds

¼ teaspoon ground turmeric

Red pepper flakes

SAVORY SWEET POTATO MASH

Serves 4 to 6 • I was well into my twenties before I learned to love sweet potatoes. I never enjoyed them growing up because they were always loaded with marshmallows and sugar. I love to create savory versions, like this mash with ghee, sea salt, and thyme. I use this dish as a base for Sloppy Joes (page 190) most often, but it's also a great side dish for any protein.

3 pounds Garnet sweet potatoes, peeled and cubed

½ cup Almond Milk (page 308)

1½ teaspoons fine sea salt

¾ teaspoon freshly ground black pepper

⅓ cup melted ghee

1 tablespoon finely chopped fresh thyme, plus whole leaves for garnish

Place the sweet potatoes in a large saucepan and add enough water to cover by 2 inches. Bring the potatoes to a boil over high heat, then turn the heat to medium-low and simmer until tender, about 18 minutes. Remove the potatoes from the heat, drain the water from the pan, then return the potatoes to the pan.

Add the almond milk, salt, and pepper to the potatoes and use a potato masher to mash to your desired consistency. Drizzle with the ghee, sprinkle in the chopped thyme, and stir gently until just combined. Garnish with thyme leaves and serve warm.

Store leftovers in an airtight container in the refrigerator for 3 days. Reheat in a dry skillet over medium-low heat until heated through, stirring frequently, about 5 minutes.

WHITE WINE GARLIC SPINACH AND MUSHROOMS

Serves 4 to 6 • When my dad was on dinner duty, I could always count on a side dish that was heavy on the garlic and butter—an affinity he inherited from his dad. He had three classics in his repertoire—sautéed zucchini, spinach, or mushrooms. I meshed together my two favorites—spinach and mushrooms—and created a recipe that dishes out lots of fond memories of being in the kitchen with my dad.

Heat the oil and ghee in a large skillet over medium heat. Add the garlic and cook until softened and fragrant, about 2 minutes. Add the mushrooms and turn the heat to medium-high. Season with salt and pepper and cook, stirring occasionally, until the mushrooms are cooked through and browned in spots, 8 to 10 minutes.

Add the spinach, sprinkle with a pinch of salt, and stir until wilted, about 2 minutes. If needed, add the spinach a few handfuls at a time, adding more after each batch wilts.

Add the vinegar to the pan, stirring constantly until it is absorbed, then stir in the white wine. Turn the heat to low and simmer until the wine has been almost completely absorbed. Season with salt and pepper to taste and sprinkle with the parsley. Serve warm.

2 tablespoons extra-virgin olive oil

1 tablespoon ghee

3 cloves garlic, minced

12 ounces cremini mushrooms, sliced

Fine sea salt and freshly ground black pepper

10 ounces baby spinach

1 tablespoon balsamic vinegar

½ cup dry white wine (such as Chardonnay)

1 tablespoon chopped fresh flat-leaf parsley, for garnish (optional)

CAULI COUSCOUS

Serves 4 to 6 • Cauliflower has had its fair share of starring moments in the grain-free and low-carb world over the past few years. You can transform it into pizza dough, a mashed potato stand-in, fried rice (see page 193), or even a Mediterranean couscous, as featured here. This dish is seasoned with fresh herbs, garlic, and dried cherries and goes really well with the Moroccan Chicken Sheet-Pan Supper (page 210).

1 large head cauliflower, cut into florets

2 tablespoons extra-virgin olive oil

¾ cup diced yellow onion

2 cloves garlic, minced

1 teaspoon fine sea salt

¼ teaspoon freshly ground black pepper

2 tablespoons unsweetened dried cherries

¼ cup chopped fresh basil

¼ cup chopped fresh cilantro

Finely grated zest of 1 lemon

Grate the cauliflower by running the florets through a food processor fitted with the grating attachment, or use a box grater to create couscous-size pieces. Pick out any large fragments that didn't get shredded and finely chop them by hand.

Heat the oil in a skillet over medium heat. Add the onion and garlic and sauté for 2 minutes, until fragrant. Add the cauliflower couscous, salt, and pepper and sauté for 8 to 10 minutes, until the cauliflower is tender. Stir in the cherries, basil, cilantro, and lemon zest. Serve warm.

Store leftovers in an airtight container in the refrigerator for 3 days. Reheat in a dry skillet over medium-low heat until heated through, stirring frequently, about 5 minutes.

ONION RINGS

Serves 4 to 6 • There is no side dish that says "comfort" to me more than onion rings. These are dipped in a light tempura-like batter and fried until the onions are tender. The breading stays crispy, as it should, and will take you back to the days of burger joints, when you ordered onion rings and a milkshake on the side.

Heat the palm shortening in a deep pot over medium-high heat until it reaches 350°F, then adjust the heat as needed to maintain a constant temperature. The shortening should be about 2 inches deep. Add more palm shortening if necessary.

In a wide, shallow dish, whisk together the garbanzo bean flour, arrowroot, 2 teaspoons salt, and baking powder. Add the eggs and sparkling water and stir until just combined and smooth. The batter should be a bit thicker than pancake batter.

Dip an onion ring into the batter, letting the excess drip back into the bowl, then carefully lower the ring into the hot shortening; beware of splattering. Repeat with additional rings, until the pot is full but not crowded. Fry the onion rings for about 2 minutes, turning each one occasionally with a mesh skimmer, until golden and crispy. Using the skimmer or a slotted spoon, transfer the onion rings to a paper towel–lined baking sheet and sprinkle lightly with salt. Serve immediately with a side of ketchup for dipping.

Store leftovers in an airtight container in the refrigerator for 3 days, or in the freezer for 3 months. Reheat the onion rings on a rimmed baking sheet in a 425°F oven for 5 minutes, or from frozen in a 400°F oven for 12 minutes.

Tidbits: To reuse the palm shortening for frying a second time, see Tidbits on page 127.

4 cups palm shortening, avocado oil, or lard, plus more as needed, for frying

2 cups garbanzo bean flour (see page 9)

¾ cup arrowroot powder

Fine sea salt

2 teaspoons Grain-Free Baking Powder (page 312)

4 eggs, beaten

2 cups sparkling water

3 large sweet onions, cut into ½-inch rings

Ketchup (page 313), for serving (optional)

PESTO SQUASH NOODLES

Serves 4 to 6 • Every summer, I try to find new ways to use the abundance of squash we grow in our backyard garden. It's pretty amazing how just a couple of dollars' worth of seeds can produce dozens and dozens of squash! My family never tires of this simple but flavorful dish of spiralized squash noodles. I toss the noodles in a bright pesto sauce and top them with blistered cherry tomatoes, which makes this dish wonderfully juicy and sweet.

2 large zucchini

2 large yellow squash

Fine sea salt

2 tablespoons extra-virgin olive oil

Red pepper flakes

1 cup grape or cherry tomatoes

Freshly ground black pepper

½ cup Pesto (page 244; see Tidbits)

Line a baking sheet with paper towels. Using a spiral slicer or julienne peeler, cut the zucchini and yellow squash into long noodles. Place the noodles on the prepared baking sheet and sprinkle them generously with salt.

In a Dutch oven or other heavy pot, warm the oil and a pinch of red pepper flakes over medium heat until fragrant. Once the oil is hot, add the tomatoes and a pinch of salt. Cook, stirring occasionally, until the tomatoes are browned in spots and the skins start to pop, about 3 minutes. Continue to cook, lightly crushing the tomatoes with the back of a spoon until they break down further, about 3 minutes more. Remove the pot from the heat and transfer the tomatoes to a large bowl.

Wipe out the pot, add the zucchini and yellow squash noodles, and sauté over medium heat for 5 minutes, until the noodles are crisp-tender. Use tongs to transfer the noodles to the bowl with the tomatoes, leaving the excess liquid in the pan.

Stir the pesto into the noodles and tomatoes, season to taste with salt and pepper, and serve warm.

This is best served fresh. Leftovers can be stored in an airtight container in the refrigerator for 2 days, and are best eaten chilled.

Tidbits: Substitute kale or arugula for the basil in pesto if you like. Each green has a little different flavor, and it's nice to have an alternative flavor combination every so often.

CHAPTER 5

SALADS, SOUPS, AND STEWS

Although salads and soups are commonly served as starters or side dishes, the recipes in this chapter are all substantial enough to make a meal by themselves. Ryan doesn't feel full unless I make a substantial salad full of protein and vegetables to go along with his bowl of soup, so sometimes I serve them both.

A hearty salad that is filling enough for dinner usually means a lot of time-consuming chopping right before you eat. But if you prepare your proteins, dressings, and chopped ingredients in advance, it's really easy to throw these salads together. Wash your lettuce or other greens when you get home from the grocery store. Wrap them in a slightly damp paper towel and put them back in the produce bag in which they came. Store the bag in the crisper drawer and your greens will last for five to seven days.

Aside from shrimp, which is best eaten fresh, make and cut up your proteins ahead of time and store them in the refrigerator for three to five days. I usually keep a few extra pieces of grilled Honey-Mustard Chicken (page 243), store-bought organic rotisserie chicken, or Pressure Cooker Chicken (page 315) in the fridge so I can swap them in if I don't have time to make the protein called for in a recipe. If you have some time over the weekend, make one or two salad dressings and store them in the fridge so you can throw something together even more quickly.

While I particularly enjoy a steaming hot bowl of soup or stew during the winter months, soup can be comforting all year long and has healing benefits when made with my homemade bone broth (see page 310). Occasionally I even eat soup for breakfast when I'm feeling under the weather or just need a change from my standard breakfast routine.

Most of the soups and stews in this chapter are one-pot dishes that can be made in a slow cooker or an electric pressure cooker. Chop all of the ingredients the night before. Put them in the pot of the cooker, cover tightly with plastic wrap, and store the pot in the fridge. If using a slow cooker, place the cooker pot into the machine before you leave the house, set the cook timer, and walk away for the day. If using an electric pressure cooker, remove the cooker pot from the refrigerator 30 minutes before cooking to bring the food back to room temperature, then cook according to the recipe instructions.

Invest in a slow cooker with a 6- or 7-quart capacity, a timer, and a warming function that keeps your food warm after the timer goes off. I recommend those with a pot that is wider than it is deep, as I think they cook more evenly. I use a 6-quart Instant Pot for my electric pressure cooker recipes.

SESAME-CRUSTED SEARED AHI SALAD

Serves 4 to 6 • I love how this salty dressing balances the tart grapefruit and slightly spicy radishes. Sesame-crusted ahi really makes the salad pop with fresh and light flavor, but you could easily swap in steak, shrimp, or even chicken.

In a bowl, whisk together the vinegar, coconut aminos, tahini, fish sauce, and ginger. Slowly drizzle in the oil, whisking continuously to emulsify. Place the kale and cabbage in a large bowl and drizzle ¼ cup of the dressing over the top. Toss to combine, then place the bowl in the refrigerator to allow the kale to wilt slightly.

Meanwhile, brush 2 tablespoons of the dressing over both sides of the tuna steaks. In a shallow dish, combine the sesame seeds, five spice powder, salt, and pepper and press each ahi steak into the mixture to coat on both sides.

Heat a large skillet over medium-high heat and pour in enough oil to lightly coat the pan. Add 2 crusted tuna steaks and sear until slightly pink in the center, about 2 minutes per side. Transfer the fish to a plate and repeat with the remaining tuna steaks. Let the fish rest for 5 minutes, then slice thinly on the diagonal.

Remove the kale from the fridge. Using a sharp knife, remove the skin and bitter white pith from the grapefruit. Working over the salad bowl, cut in between the membranes to release the sections. Toss the salad with the grapefruit pieces, then divide among plates, and arrange the tuna steaks, avocados, and radishes over the salads. Sprinkle each plate with cashews and a pinch of sesame seeds. Serve immediately, with the additional dressing on the side.

Store any unused dressing in an airtight container in the refrigerator for 1 week. Shake before using.

Tidbits: I use organic unseasoned rice vinegar because the seasoned version often has added sugar, corn syrup, or MSG. Rice vinegar is made by fermenting the sugars in white rice into alcohol, and then into acid. While rice itself isn't paleo, many people find that grain vinegars are tolerable because of the fermentation.

2 tablespoons unseasoned rice vinegar (see Tidbits) or apple cider vinegar

1 tablespoon coconut aminos

1 tablespoon tahini

1 teaspoon fish sauce

½ teaspoon peeled and minced fresh ginger

½ cup avocado oil, plus more for cooking

6 cups thinly sliced lacinato (Tuscan) kale, center ribs and stems removed

2 cups shredded napa cabbage

6 (6-ounce) ahi tuna steaks

½ cup sesame seeds, plus more for garnish

2 tablespoons five spice powder

1 teaspoon fine sea salt

¼ teaspoon freshly ground black pepper

1 pink grapefruit

2 avocados, pitted, peeled, and thinly sliced

2 watermelon radishes, sliced paper-thin

½ cup chopped dry-roasted, salted cashews

ITALIAN CHOPPED SALAD WITH RED WINE VINAIGRETTE

Serves 4 to 6 • On a hot summer day, or a busy night with three kids melting down, a big salad with lots of fresh, hearty ingredients is often my default meal. For this Italian-inspired chopped salad, I dice antipasto ingredients and combine them to make a substantial main course. I usually buy organic cooked beets from the market's produce section so I can just chop them up and not have to worry about roasting and peeling. This dish also comes together quickly with the use of precooked chicken.

10 cups green-leaf lettuce, romaine, or mixed baby greens

2 cups diced Pressure Cooker Chicken (page 315), or other cooked chicken (see Tidbits)

3 ounces salami, thinly sliced into ribbons

1 cup diced roasted beets

½ cup pitted green olives, halved

1 (6.5-ounce) jar artichoke hearts, drained, rinsed, and diced

1 tomato, cut into wedges

VINAIGRETTE

2 teaspoons freshly squeezed lemon juice

2 teaspoons chopped fresh basil

2 teaspoons red wine vinegar

¾ teaspoon Dijon mustard

1 clove garlic, minced

½ cup extra-virgin olive oil

Fine sea salt and freshly ground black pepper

In a large serving bowl, toss together the lettuce, chicken, salami, beets, olives, artichoke hearts, and tomato.

To make the vinaigrette, in a small bowl, whisk together the lemon juice, basil, vinegar, mustard, and garlic. Slowly drizzle in the oil, whisking continuously to emulsify. Season with salt and pepper to taste.

Drizzle ¼ cup of the dressing over the salad and toss to coat. Serve immediately, with the additional dressing on the side.

Store any unused dressing in an airtight container in the refrigerator for 1 week. Shake before using.

Tidbits: The quickest way to cook chicken for a salad is to poach it. Fill a small pot halfway with water and bring to a boil over high heat. Add 1 pound boneless, skinless chicken breasts, turn the heat to low, partially cover the pot, and simmer for 8 minutes. Remove the pot from the heat and let the chicken sit in the hot water, covered, for 15 minutes. Remove the chicken from the pot, allow it to cool, then dice or shred it.

GRILLED CHICKEN CAESAR

Serves 4 to 6 • Topped with a creamy dressing, lots of my tangy dairy-free Parmesan cheese, and garlicky croutons, a Caesar salad is always a crowd-pleaser. I've designed this one to be hearty with added chicken. Serve it as a meal or leave the chicken out and make it a side salad to accompany your favorite Italian entrée, like Chicken Parmesan with Roasted Spaghetti Squash (page 214) or Spaghetti and Meatballs (page 204).

Preheat a grill or a grill pan on the stovetop to medium-high heat.

To make the dressing, coarsely chop the garlic cloves and place them in a blender with the lemon juice, anchovy paste, egg yolks, mustard, and vinegar. Blend on high speed for 10 seconds, until smooth. With the blender running on low speed, slowly drizzle in the oil until the dressing emulsifies. Season with salt and pepper.

Place each chicken breast between two pieces of parchment paper or plastic wrap. Using a kitchen mallet or heavy skillet, pound the breasts until they're about ¼ inch thick. Place the chicken in a bowl and season generously with salt and pepper. Add 2 tablespoons of the dressing and toss the chicken to coat. Grill the chicken breasts until golden and crisp, 3 to 4 minutes per side. Transfer the chicken to a clean plate to rest.

Remove any wilted outer leaves from the romaine, then cut each head lengthwise into quarters. Brush the cut sides with 1 tablespoon of the dressing, then grill the lettuce, turning the quarters so they are slightly browned on all sides, about 5 minutes total. Chop the grilled romaine heads into large ribbons and place them in a large salad bowl.

Brush the bread slices with the oil and grill until grill marks appear, about 2 minutes per side. Cut the bread into bite-size pieces and slice the chicken breasts into thin strips. Place them in the bowl with the romaine. Toss with the remaining dressing, then sprinkle the Parmesan cheese on top. Serve immediately.

Store any unused dressing in an airtight container in the refrigerator for 1 week. Shake before using.

CAESAR DRESSING

2 cloves garlic, peeled

¼ cup freshly squeezed lemon juice

2 tablespoons anchovy paste

2 egg yolks

2 teaspoons Dijon mustard

2 teaspoons apple cider vinegar

1 cup extra-virgin olive oil or avocado oil

Fine sea salt and freshly ground black pepper

2 pounds boneless, skinless chicken breasts or thighs

Fine sea salt and freshly ground black pepper

3 heads romaine lettuce

6 slices Nut-Free Lunchbox Bread (page 48), each ½ inch thick

2 tablespoons extra-virgin olive oil or avocado oil

2 tablespoons Parmesan Cheese (page 315)

Tidbits: To make this NF, omit the Parmesan Cheese.

STEAK SALAD WITH ROASTED SWEET POTATOES AND CARAMELIZED ONIONS

Serves 4 to 6 • This is a salad for meat-and-potato eaters. It is hearty enough to call a meal, and the balsamic-coated sweet potato and caramelized onion mixture is full of flavor. To get this salad on the table in under 30 minutes and avoid having to fire up a grill, I cook thin flank steaks on the stovetop until they have a nice crust on the outside but are medium-rare and juicy on the inside. The cook time will vary depending on the thickness of your steaks, so keep a meat thermometer handy to ensure they're cooked perfectly.

8 tablespoons avocado oil

1 red onion, halved and thinly sliced into half-moons

1 sweet potato, scrubbed and cut into 1½-inch dice

2 teaspoons balsamic vinegar

Fine sea salt and freshly ground black pepper

1 tablespoon ghee

2 pounds flank steak, cut into 2 or 3 pieces

2 tablespoons red wine vinegar

1 teaspoon Dijon mustard

10 cups baby arugula

1 pint grape tomatoes, a mix of red and yellow, halved

Heat 2 tablespoons of the oil in a large skillet over medium heat. Add the onion and sauté until soft, about 7 minutes. Add the sweet potato and balsamic vinegar and sauté for 10 minutes, until the sweet potatoes are crisp-tender. Season with salt and pepper to taste, then transfer the mixture to a plate to cool.

Wipe the pan clean, return it to medium-high heat, and add the ghee. Season the steaks generously with salt and pepper, add them to the pan, and cook for 5 minutes per side, until a thermometer inserted into the thickest part of each steak reads 140°F for medium-rare. Transfer the steaks to a cutting board and let them rest for 5 minutes.

In a large bowl, whisk together the remaining 6 tablespoons oil, the vinegar, mustard, ¼ teaspoon salt, and a pinch of pepper. Add the arugula and tomatoes to the bowl and toss gently to combine.

Thinly slice the steaks diagonally against the grain. Divide the salad mixture among plates and top each with some of the caramelized onion and sweet potato mixture and a few slices of steak. Serve immediately.

GRILLED SHRIMP SUMMER HARVEST SALAD WITH BASIL VINAIGRETTE

Serves 4 to 6 • Being a California girl, I love to add fresh fruits, nuts, and a cornucopia of my favorite produce to a salad to make a light but satisfying weeknight meal. This one is piled high with avocado, stone fruit, sweet strawberries, and a juicy heirloom tomato and finished with a super-flavorful basil dressing.

To make the vinaigrette, pulse the garlic in a food processor until chopped. Add the basil and pulse until finely chopped. Add the oil, vinegar, and lemon juice and process until smooth, about 10 seconds. Season with salt and pepper to taste.

Place the shrimp in a large resealable plastic bag, add ¼ cup of the vinaigrette, and press out any excess air. Seal the bag, then shake to coat the shrimp with the dressing. Marinate the shrimp in the fridge for 30 minutes or up to 24 hours.

Preheat a grill or a grill pan on the stovetop to medium-low heat. Lightly oil the grill grates or grill pan with avocado oil. Cook the shrimp until it turns pink on the bottom, about 2 minutes. Flip and cook for 2 to 3 minutes more, until the shrimp is opaque and cooked through. Transfer the shrimp to a plate and let it cool for 10 minutes.

Place the baby greens in a large bowl. Add the avocados, nectarines, strawberries, and tomato and toss gently to combine. Sprinkle the cashews and chives over the top, then add the shrimp. Drizzle the salad with ½ cup of the dressing. Serve immediately, with the additional dressing on the side.

Store any unused dressing in an airtight container in the refrigerator for 1 week. Shake before using.

Tidbits: To make this NSF, omit the tomato. To make this NF, omit the cashews.

VINAIGRETTE

2 cloves garlic, peeled

2 cups packed fresh basil leaves, coarsely chopped

½ cup extra-virgin olive oil

2 tablespoons champagne vinegar

1½ tablespoons freshly squeezed lemon juice

Fine sea salt and freshly ground black pepper

1½ pounds large raw shrimp, peeled and deveined, with tails on

10 cups mixed baby greens

2 avocados, pitted, peeled, and sliced

2 yellow nectarines, pitted and sliced

1 cup sliced strawberries

1 heirloom tomato, cut into wedges (see Tidbits)

¼ cup chopped dry-roasted salted cashews

2 tablespoons chopped fresh chives

CHEF'S SALAD

Serves 4 to 6 • I loved a good chef's salad when I was growing up. But because it is usually doused in a creamy dressing and topped with cheese and deli meat, I haven't been able to enjoy it for a while. Until recently, I've had a hard time finding good-quality deli meats that are free of carrageenan, nitrates, and added sugar. Thankfully a lot of brands have removed many of the harmful ingredients, so now there are more options than ever. Look for the organic varieties made by Applegate, True Story, Wellshire Farms, Organic Prairie, and Diestel. In my version of a classic chef's salad, I replace the iceberg lettuce with a more nutrient-dense leaf lettuce and top it off with a delicious dairy-free ranch-style dressing.

1½ pounds Boston, Bibb, or green- or red-leaf lettuce, or a mixture

Fine sea salt and freshly ground black pepper

1 cup Herb Ranch Dressing (page 92)

4 ounces deli ham, cut into ¼-inch slices

4 ounces Pressure Cooker Chicken (page 315), or any cooked chicken, cut into 2-inch pieces

4 ounces deli roast beef, cut into ¼-inch slices

2 hard-boiled eggs, cut into wedges

2 avocados, pitted, peeled, and diced

16 cherry or grape tomatoes, halved

2 Persian cucumbers, thinly sliced on the diagonal

Tear the lettuce into bite-size pieces and place in a large serving bowl. Season with salt and pepper to taste and toss with ½ cup of the dressing. Arrange the ham, chicken, roast beef, eggs, and avocados on top of the salad, with each ingredient in its own section, like the spokes on a wheel. Scatter the tomatoes and cucumbers over the top. Season with more salt and pepper to taste. At the table, drizzle the remaining dressing over the top and toss so everyone gets a little bit of everything.

Tidbits: If you tolerate cheese, tossing in ½ cup grated Gruyère or another Swiss cheese makes this more classic.

FRENCH ONION SOUP

Serves 4 to 6 • There was a little French bistro in the neighborhood I grew up in, and my mom used to take us there on cold winter days for a fresh baguette and a bowl of onion soup. Yes, it was topped with bread and melted stringy cheese, but in this version, I sprinkle nutritional yeast on top of grain-free toast to give a similar flavor. Properly caramelizing onions takes a long time on the stovetop, and I often get impatient and increase the heat, which results in either tough or burned onions. Instead of having to babysit them, I put the slow cooker to use here and let it caramelize the onions while we sleep.

In a 5-quart slow cooker, combine the onions, 2 tablespoons of the ghee, the oil, 1 tablespoon salt, and ½ teaspoon pepper. Cover and cook overnight on low, until the onions are browned and soft.

Stir the bone broth, coconut aminos, fish sauce, vinegar, thyme, onion powder, garlic powder, bay leaves, lime juice, and cloves into the onions. Cover and continue cooking for 6 to 8 hours on low. Season with salt and pepper to taste.

Preheat the broiler with a rack placed about 3 inches from the heating element.

Melt the remaining 2 tablespoons ghee in a small saucepan over low heat. Stir in the nutritional yeast and ¼ teaspoon salt. Brush each slice of bread with the ghee mixture, then place the bread on a baking sheet. Broil for 1 to 2 minutes, until toasted on one side.

Ladle the onions and soup into oven-safe bowls and top each with a piece of toast. Serve immediately.

Store leftover soup in an airtight container in the refrigerator for 5 days, or in the freezer for 6 months. Defrost overnight in the refrigerator. Reheat in a saucepan over medium heat, stirring frequently, for 10 minutes.

Variation: If you tolerate cheese, omit the ghee-and-yeast mixture and top each slice of bread with a generous quantity of shredded Gruyère cheese. Broil as directed, until the cheese is melted.

4 large yellow onions, quartered and sliced into quarter-moons

4 tablespoons ghee

2 tablespoons extra-virgin olive oil

Fine sea salt and freshly ground black pepper

8 cups Beef Bone Broth (page 310)

⅓ cup coconut aminos

1 tablespoon fish sauce

1 tablespoon balsamic vinegar

1 tablespoon dried thyme

2 teaspoons onion powder

2 teaspoons garlic powder

3 bay leaves

1 teaspoon freshly squeezed lime juice

¼ teaspoon ground cloves

1 tablespoon nutritional yeast

4 to 6 slices Nut-Free Lunchbox Bread (page 48)

LOADED BAKED POTATO SOUP

Serves 6 • During the first major flare-ups of my autoimmune disease, when I wasn't able to eat much of anything, a loaded baked potato was one of the few things I could stomach. I've since learned that my body doesn't tolerate white potatoes (likely because they are nightshades and also due to the high starch content) or dairy well, so baked potatoes were probably a terrible food to eat while I was trying to heal. They are still one of my favorite comfort foods, so I developed this recipe using Hannah sweet potatoes, which are white fleshed and less sweet than the orange variety. This creamy soup shares some of the loaded baked potato flavors and is one of my favorites to eat during the winter months, when I'm craving a hearty bowl of soup.

6 slices thick bacon, coarsely chopped

1 yellow onion, diced

2 cloves garlic, chopped

2 pounds Hannah sweet potatoes, peeled and diced

10 ounces cauliflower, cut into florets

5½ cups Chicken Bone Broth (page 310)

1 cup Cashew Milk (page 310; see Tidbits)

3½ teaspoons fine sea salt

½ teaspoon smoked paprika

½ teaspoon apple cider vinegar

½ teaspoon freshly squeezed lemon juice

Chopped fresh chives, for serving (optional)

Dairy-Free Sour Cream (page 311) or Herb Ranch Dressing (page 92), for serving (optional)

Line a plate with paper towels. In a stockpot, cook the bacon over medium heat until the fat is rendered and the bacon is crisp, about 8 minutes. Using a slotted spoon, remove the bacon from the pot and set it on the prepared plate to drain. Pour off most of the grease, reserving about 2 tablespoons in the pot.

Return the pot to medium-high heat, add the onion and garlic, and sauté for 2 minutes, until fragrant. Add half of the sweet potatoes and all of the cauliflower and cook for 5 minutes, stirring frequently. Add the bone broth, bring it to a gentle boil, and cook for 10 minutes, until the potatoes and cauliflower are tender.

Using an immersion blender, or working in batches in a blender, blend the soup until smooth. (If using a blender, remove the cap in the blender top and place a kitchen towel over the top to allow steam from the hot liquid to release while you blend.) Return the puree to the stockpot. Add the remaining sweet potatoes, the cashew milk, salt, paprika, vinegar, and lemon juice. Bring to a boil over medium-high heat, then turn the heat to low and simmer for 12 to 15 minutes, stirring frequently, until the sweet potatoes are tender and the cashew milk has thickened the soup.

Ladle the soup into bowls and top with the reserved bacon, chives, and a dollop of sour cream. Serve immediately.

Store leftover soup in an airtight container in the refrigerator for 5 days, or in the freezer for 6 months. Defrost overnight in the refrigerator. Reheat in a saucepan over medium heat, stirring frequently, for 10 minutes.

Tidbits: If using store-bought cashew milk, decrease the bone broth to 4½ cups to help thicken the soup.

CREAMY BROCCOLI SOUP

Serves 4 to 6 • I grew up eating creamy soups from a can. Artichoke, mushroom, asparagus, broccoli—you name it. Eliminating dairy and wheat doesn't have to mean giving up comforting creamy soups though. In this recipe, I boil white sweet potatoes with the other vegetables instead of using heavy cream or a roux made with white flour. This not only thickens the soup, but it also helps to make it velvety-smooth. If you cannot find Hannah sweet potatoes or other white-fleshed varieties, you can use russet potatoes if you tolerate them. You could also use ½ cup Cashew Milk in place of the potatoes.

Melt the ghee in a large stockpot over medium heat. Add the leeks and onion and sauté for 3 to 4 minutes, stirring frequently, until they are fragrant and softened. Add the broccoli, sweet potato, celery, and garlic and continue to cook for 5 minutes more. Pour in the bone broth, add 1½ teaspoons salt and ¼ teaspoon pepper, and bring to a boil. Lower the heat and simmer for 8 to 10 minutes, until the vegetables are fork-tender and the broccoli is bright green.

Using an immersion blender, or working in batches in a blender, blend the soup until very smooth. (If using a blender, remove the cap in the blender top and place a kitchen towel over the top to allow steam from the hot liquid to release while you blend.) Return the soup to the pan and season with salt and pepper to taste. Serve hot, with a sprinkling of pepper and a drizzle of olive oil on top.

Store leftover soup in an airtight container in the refrigerator for 5 days, or in the freezer for 6 months. Defrost overnight in the refrigerator. Reheat in a saucepan over medium heat, stirring frequently, for 10 minutes.

3 tablespoons ghee or extra-virgin olive oil

2 cups chopped leeks, white and tender green parts

½ yellow onion, chopped

1 pound broccoli, cut into florets, stems peeled and chopped

1 small Hannah sweet potato or other white-fleshed variety, peeled and cut into 1-inch cubes (about ½ cup)

1 celery stalk, chopped

2 cloves garlic, minced

4 cups Chicken Bone Broth (page 310)

Fine sea salt and freshly ground black pepper

Extra-virgin olive oil, for drizzling

TOMATO SOUP WITH ZESTY CROUTONS

Serves 4 to 6 • Much as I used to love grilled cheese sandwiches, I don't usually miss eating them unless I'm having a bowlful of hot, creamy tomato soup. So I reimagined the classic combination by tossing cubes of grain-free bread with a bit of cheesy-tasting nutritional yeast before toasting them into croutons. Of course, if you tolerate dairy, go ahead and make a sandwich with some grass-fed raw cheese. To make the croutons crunchy, use stale bread. I cut it up and allow it to dry out on a baking sheet overnight.

CROUTONS

½ loaf Nut-Free Lunchbox Bread (page 48), cut into 1-inch cubes

2 tablespoons melted ghee or extra-virgin olive oil

2 teaspoons nutritional yeast

¼ teaspoon garlic powder

¼ teaspoon fine sea salt

3 pounds mixed tomatoes (such as heirloom and Roma), quartered

5 tablespoons extra-virgin olive oil

Fine sea salt and freshly ground black pepper

4 cloves garlic, chopped

1 shallot, coarsely chopped

3 cups Chicken Bone Broth (page 310)

¼ cup tomato paste

½ cup packed fresh basil leaves

1 teaspoon fresh thyme leaves

To make the croutons, preheat the oven to 300°F.

In a large bowl, combine the bread cubes, ghee, nutritional yeast, garlic powder, and salt. Spread the bread cubes in a single layer on a rimmed baking sheet and bake for 30 minutes, stirring occasionally, until golden brown. Remove from the oven and let cool on a wire rack.

Increase the oven temperature to 400°F.

Place the tomatoes on a separate rimmed baking sheet and drizzle with 3 tablespoons of the oil and sprinkle with a pinch of salt and pepper. Roast for 30 minutes, then remove from the oven and let cool for 10 minutes.

Meanwhile, heat the remaining 2 tablespoons oil in a stockpot or Dutch oven over medium-high heat. Add the garlic and shallot and sauté for 3 to 5 minutes, until the garlic is fragrant and the shallot is translucent. Add the bone broth and tomato paste and turn off the heat.

Place the cooled tomatoes in a blender along with the bone broth mixture. Add the basil, thyme, 2 teaspoons salt, and ¼ teaspoon pepper. Blend on high speed until very smooth and all of the seeds are pureed, about 20 seconds if using a high-speed blender or 45 seconds if using a conventional blender.

CONTINUED

Return the soup to the stockpot and cook over low heat until warmed through. Ladle the soup into bowls and top each with a few croutons. Serve with additional croutons on the side.

Store leftover croutons in an airtight container in the pantry for 5 days. Store leftover soup in an airtight container in the refrigerator for 5 days, or in the freezer for 6 months. Defrost overnight in the refrigerator. Reheat in a saucepan over medium heat, stirring frequently, for 10 minutes.

Variation: If you don't have time to make the croutons, top the soup with pesto gremolata to give it a little crunch and herby–tart flavor. To make it, in a bowl, combine ¼ cup chopped fresh basil, 2 tablespoons chopped pine nuts, 3 teaspoons extra-virgin olive oil, ¼ teaspoon finely grated lemon zest, ¼ teaspoon freshly squeezed lemon juice, and ¼ teaspoon fine sea salt. Place a spoonful of gremolata on top of the soup just before serving.

Tidbits: To comply with SCD and make this EF, omit the croutons.

HEALING CHICKEN SOUP

Serves 4 to 6 • I'm often asked what I eat when I'm not feeling well. The answer is lots and lots of chicken soup . . . even for breakfast! The homemade chicken bone broth that is the foundation of this soup is calming for the gut and replenishes minerals and nutrients. I like to make this in my electric pressure cooker so it comes together quickly—especially if I'm not feeling well enough to cook anything elaborate. But you could also make this in a slow cooker or on the stovetop. The best part about this simple recipe is that you can just throw frozen chicken into the pot if you are using a pressure cooker.

Put the chicken in an electric pressure cooker. Add the bone broth, onion, leeks, garlic, 3 teaspoons salt, and ¾ teaspoon pepper. Secure the lid, select the manual setting, and set it to high pressure for 10 minutes for fresh chicken, or 20 minutes for frozen chicken.

When the pressure cooker timer is done, quick release the pressure. Remove the chicken, cut it into bite-size chunks, and return it to the pressure cooker. Add the celery, carrots, parsley, oregano, thyme, dill, lemon zest, and 1 teaspoon lemon juice (reserve the remaining juice for another use) and season with salt and pepper to taste. Secure the lid again, select the manual setting, and set it to high pressure for 2 minutes. Quick release the pressure. Ladle the soup into bowls and serve hot.

To freeze in individual portions, place 2 cups of soup in a resealable plastic bag and press out any excess air, or use an airtight glass container. Freeze the bag, lying flat for faster defrosting, for 4 months. Defrost at room temperature for 1 hour, then transfer the partially thawed contents to a saucepan and warm over medium-low heat for 15 minutes, until heated through.

5 boneless, skinless chicken breasts, fresh or frozen

6 cups Chicken Bone Broth (page 310)

1 yellow onion, chopped

2 leeks, washed well and thinly sliced

3 cloves garlic, minced

Fine sea salt and freshly ground black pepper

6 celery stalks, sliced

6 carrots, sliced

3 tablespoons chopped fresh flat-leaf parsley

1½ tablespoons chopped fresh oregano

1½ teaspoons fresh thyme leaves

1½ teaspoons chopped fresh dill

Finely grated zest and juice of 1 lemon

CONTINUED

Variations: To make in a slow cooker, use fresh or thawed frozen chicken breasts. Add all of the ingredients to a slow cooker. Cover and cook for 4 hours on high or 8 hours on low. Remove the chicken, cut it into bite-size chunks, and return it to the slow cooker. Serve immediately.

To make on the stovetop, use fresh or thawed frozen chicken breasts. Place the chicken and broth in a stockpot over medium-high heat. Bring it to a boil, turn the heat to low, and cook, covered, for 30 minutes. Add the remaining ingredients and cook over medium-high heat for 20 to 25 minutes more, until the vegetables are tender. Remove the chicken, cut it into bite-size chunks, and return it to the pot. Serve immediately.

CHICKEN 'N' DUMPLINGS SOUP

Serves 4 to 6 • To make this soup extra flavorful and economical, I cut a whole chicken into pieces and brown the pieces in the pot in which I make the soup; the browned skin adds a rich flavor. Then I simmer the chicken in a homemade broth until it's tender, so the flavor and nutrients from the bones aren't lost. The resulting broth is thick and nutritious, and the herb-flecked dumplings add a lovely richness to the dish. If you're like me, and butchering a chicken isn't in your repertoire, just ask your butcher to cut a whole chicken into 8 pieces, making sure to save the backbone and wingtips for making the broth.

To make the soup, heat the ghee in a large pot or Dutch oven over medium-high heat. Season the chicken pieces with 1 teaspoon salt and 1 teaspoon pepper. Working in batches to avoid crowding, add the chicken and cook for 4 to 6 minutes per side, until well browned. Transfer the chicken to a plate and leave the drippings in the pot.

Add the shallots, carrot, celery, thyme, and garlic to the pot and sauté until the vegetables begin to soften, 5 to 7 minutes. Remove and discard the browned skin from the chicken pieces and return the chicken to the pot along with the bay leaves and bone broth. Bring to a boil, then turn the heat to medium and simmer, covered, until the chicken is cooked through and easily pulls away from the bone, about 1 hour.

To make the dumplings, meanwhile, in a bowl, whisk together the almond flour, coconut flour, ¼ cup arrowroot, baking powder, chives, dill, and salt. Whisk in the egg and almond milk.

Transfer the chicken pieces to a cutting board and discard the bay leaves. Shred the chicken, discarding the bones, and return the meat to the soup.

SOUP

1 tablespoon ghee or extra-virgin olive oil

1 (3-pound) whole chicken, cut into 8 pieces

Fine sea salt and freshly ground black pepper

2 shallots, minced

½ cup diced carrot

½ cup diced celery

2 tablespoons fresh thyme leaves

2 cloves garlic, minced

2 bay leaves

8 cups Chicken Bone Broth (page 310)

3 tablespoons arrowroot powder (see Tidbits)

Chopped fresh flat-leaf parsley, for serving

DUMPLINGS

1 cup blanched almond flour

¼ cup coconut flour

¼ cup arrowroot powder

CONTINUED

1 tablespoon Grain-Free Baking Powder (page 312; see Tidbits)

1 tablespoon finely chopped fresh chives

1 tablespoon chopped fresh dill

½ teaspoon fine sea salt

1 egg, beaten

½ cup Almond Milk (page 308)

In a small bowl, whisk together ¼ cup water and the 3 tablespoons arrowroot, then whisk it into the soup. Bring the soup back to a boil over medium-high heat and cook for 3 to 5 minutes, until the broth has thickened. Season with salt and pepper to taste.

Turn the heat to low and allow the boil to calm (the dumplings will break apart if the soup is boiling when you add them). Skim the fat from the surface using a wide spoon, then drop the dumpling mixture into the soup in eight large spoonfuls. Cover the pot and cook until the dumplings are firm, 10 to 12 minutes. Ladle the soup into bowls, being sure to get plenty of chicken and a dumpling or two in each serving. Sprinkle with parsley and serve immediately.

Store leftover soup and dumplings in an airtight container in the refrigerator for 5 days. Reheat in a covered saucepan over medium-low heat for 8 to 10 minutes, until heated through.

Variation: To make in an electric pressure cooker, working in batches, brown the chicken pieces in the ghee directly in the pressure cooker using the sauté setting. Add the bone broth and secure the lid. Select the manual setting and cook at high pressure for 25 minutes. Quick release the pressure and add the shallots, carrot, celery, thyme, garlic, and bay leaves. Cook again at high pressure for 1 minute, then quick release the pressure. Follow the instructions to make the dumplings, then remove the lid and return the pressure cooker to the sauté function so the soup simmers. Discard the bay leaves, then drop the dumplings into the pot and cook, with the cover propped atop the machine but not secured, for 10 to 12 minutes, until the dumplings are firm.

Tidbits: To comply with SCD, substitute ½ cup cashew butter for the water and arrowroot used to thicken the soup. For the dumplings, omit the arrowroot and increase the coconut flour to ⅓ cup, and use 1 teaspoon baking soda in place of the baking powder.

BETTY'S BEEF STEW

Serves 4 to 6 • Ryan always speaks so fondly of his Grandmother Betty's, aka Nanny's, beef stew and mashed potatoes that I wanted to create a version our family could enjoy. The original recipe calls for Worcestershire sauce, which often contains wheat and sugar. I use a mix of coconut aminos and fish sauce to mimic that briny taste. My kids love anything that is slow-cooked and fork-tender, and they seem to love this stew just as much as their dad does. Nanny always said the secret to good slow-cooked meat is to brown the meat really well first. Don't skip the browning, even if you do this in a slow cooker or electric pressure cooker.

Pat the beef dry with paper towels and season it generously with 1 tablespoon salt and 1 teaspoon pepper.

Melt 2 tablespoons of the tallow in a 3.5-quart (or larger) Dutch oven over medium-high heat. Working in two batches, brown the meat really well on all sides, about 10 minutes per batch. Using a slotted spoon, transfer the meat to a bowl. If the pan is dry, add the remaining 1 tablespoon tallow. Once it has melted, add the onion and garlic and sauté for 5 to 7 minutes, until the onion is soft. Add the bone broth and use a wooden spoon to scrape up the brown bits from the bottom of the pan. Carefully transfer the mixture to a conventional blender, or use an immersion blender, and puree until smooth. (If using a conventional blender, remove the cap in your blender top and place a kitchen towel over the top to allow steam from the hot liquid to release while you blend.)

Return the sauce to the pot and add the browned beef, lemon juice, coconut aminos, fish sauce, bay leaves, paprika, and allspice. Turn the heat to medium, cover the pot, and simmer for 1½ hours, until the sauce has reduced by half.

3 pounds beef chuck roast, cut into 2-inch cubes

Fine sea salt and freshly ground black pepper

2 or 3 tablespoons beef tallow or ghee

1 large yellow onion, coarsely chopped (about 1½ cups)

3 cloves garlic, chopped

3 cups Beef Bone Broth (page 310)

1 tablespoon freshly squeezed lemon juice

1 teaspoon coconut aminos

½ teaspoon fish sauce

2 bay leaves

½ teaspoon sweet paprika

¼ teaspoon ground allspice

3 large carrots, sliced

3 celery stalks, chopped

Roasted Garlic Mashed Cauliflower (see page 250), for serving

CONTINUED

Add the carrots and celery and simmer, uncovered, for 30 to 40 minutes more, until the beef is fork-tender and the vegetables are cooked through. Serve the stew over the garlic mashed cauliflower.

Variations: To make in a slow cooker, decrease the bone broth to 2½ cups. Brown the meat as directed, then place it in a 6- or 7-quart slow cooker. Add all of the ingredients except the carrots, celery, and caulifower. Cover and cook for 7 hours on low. Remove the meat from the pot and use an immersion blender to puree the sauce. Return the meat to the pot, add the carrots and celery, and cook for 1 hour on low.

To make in an electric pressure cooker, decrease the bone broth to 1 cup. Working in batches, brown the meat in the tallow directly in the pressure cooker using the sauté setting. Add all of the remaining ingredients except the carrots, celery, and cauliflower. Secure the lid, select the manual setting, and cook at high pressure for 50 minutes. Quick release the pressure, remove the meat from the pressure cooker, and use an immersion blender to puree the sauce. Return the meat to the pressure cooker and add the carrots and celery. Cook again at high pressure for 1 minute, then let the pressure release naturally.

Make It Ahead: Chop the onion and garlic and store them in an airtight container in the refrigerator for 5 days. The meat can be cooked from frozen in an electric pressure cooker, but increase the time to 40 minutes. Cool the browned meat, sauce, lemon juice, coconut aminos, fish sauce, bay leaves, paprika, and allspice to room temperature and freeze in a large resealable plastic bag, lying flat for faster defrosting, for 4 months. Defrost overnight in the refrigerator before completing the cooking process. Chop the carrots and celery and store them in a bowl of water, tightly covered, for 5 days.

Tidbits: If you prefer the sauce to be really thick like gravy, in a small bowl, whisk together 2 tablespoons water and 1 tablespoon arrowroot powder until smooth. Pour the arrowroot slurry into the pot when the vegetables are added, and the sauce will thicken quickly as it heats up.

To make this NSF, omit the paprika.

CHAPTER 6

QUICK AND EASY MEALS

Minimize your meal prep and save time on kitchen cleanup with the one-pot, sheet-pan, electric-pressure-cooker, and slow-cooker recipes in this chapter. No-fuss, simplified cooking techniques can be lifesavers during busy weeks, and these recipes typically double and freeze easily, require minimal ingredients, and use familiar methods. Even better—most have a cook time of 30 minutes or less.

In other words, these are the dishes you'll come back to again and again for weeknight meals, and any other time you want to get dinner on the table quickly without sacrificing flavor. These are also really forgiving recipes: you can easily modify the ingredients or substitute with what you have on hand if you're facing hungry mouths and don't have exactly what you need in the pantry.

If some of these dishes sound like food you usually order in, that's deliberate! It's difficult to compete with the allure of takeout, which is why I've designed these recipes to come together in the amount of time it would take you to read a menu, make a call, and wait for delivery. And this way, you know exactly what's going into your dinner, and your body.

If you're really feeling ambitious, set aside one day at the beginning of the month to prep the ingredients for multiple meals. Double or triple a recipe and store the uncooked ingredients for each individual meal in a resealable plastic bag. If a recipe calls for browning the meat first, go ahead and brown it, then let it cool to room temperature before putting it and its juices in the bag. Store the bags in the freezer for up to four months. Remove the bag from the freezer the day before you want to cook it and let the contents defrost in the fridge, then let the slow cooker or electric pressure cooker do the work for you. I love to prep meals like this for Ryan and the kids when I'm traveling, or when I know we have a hectic week coming up and I won't have time to plan dinner. It's so convenient, and it beats going out to eat.

BEEF AND BROCCOLI

Serves 4 to 6 • I have fond memories of going out for Chinese food with my dad when I was growing up. He always ordered the beef and broccoli, so of course it became a favorite of mine too. Since most restaurants use cornstarch and even MSG in their sauces, I haven't been able to eat this in a restaurant for a long time. So I developed this recipe, which I frequently make at home, and it has become an often-requested dish with my family. Serve it over cauliflower rice or with some zucchini noodles.

2 pounds flank steak (see Tidbits)

⅔ cup coconut aminos

2 tablespoons arrowroot powder

3½ teaspoons toasted sesame oil

1¼ teaspoons unseasoned rice vinegar

4 tablespoons beef tallow, avocado oil, or ghee

4 cloves garlic, minced

1 teaspoon peeled and minced fresh ginger

5 cups broccoli florets (about 2 pounds)

⅓ cup Beef Bone Broth (page 310)

Fine sea salt

¼ teaspoon ground white pepper

Basic Cauli Rice (page 309), for serving

Place the steak in the freezer for 20 minutes to make it easier to slice. Cut it on the diagonal into ⅛-inch slices, then cut each slice into 2-inch pieces. Place the steak pieces in a shallow bowl. In a separate bowl, whisk together the coconut aminos, arrowroot, 3 teaspoons of the sesame oil, and the vinegar and pour the mixture over the steak, stirring to coat each piece well. Marinate for 30 minutes.

Heat 2 tablespoons of the tallow in a wok or large skillet over medium-high heat. Stir in the garlic and ginger, and let them sizzle in the hot oil for about 30 seconds. Stir in the broccoli and toss the florets in the hot oil until they turn bright green and almost tender, 5 to 7 minutes. Remove the broccoli from the wok and set aside.

Add the remaining 2 tablespoons tallow to the wok. Let the pan get very hot again. With tongs, add the marinated meat to the wok in a single layer, reserving the marinating liquid and working in batches to avoid crowding the meat. Do not stir the meat until it has browned, about 1 minute. Flip the meat and cook the other side for 30 seconds more, then transfer the meat to a clean plate to rest.

Pour the reserved marinating liquid into the wok along with the bone broth, 1¼ teaspoons salt, and white pepper. Cook over medium-high heat until the sauce starts to thicken, about 45 seconds. Add the beef and broccoli back to the wok and toss to coat. Season with salt to taste and finish with the remaining ½ teaspoon sesame oil. Serve warm over the cauliflower rice.

Tidbits: You can also use boneless, skinless chicken thighs or even uncooked large shrimp.

CHICKEN PICCATA WITH ARTICHOKES AND SPINACH

Serves 4 to 6 • My mom loves a traditional chicken piccata, with its thin chicken breasts cooked in a silky, tart lemon sauce. To make this recipe more of a one-pot meal, I cook down spinach and artichoke hearts along with the sauce. It makes this a heartier dish, and the kids don't notice the extra vegetables—that's a win.

Slice the chicken breast halves horizontally to make thin cutlets. If the pieces are still thick, place the chicken between two pieces of plastic wrap and, using a kitchen mallet or heavy skillet, pound to ¼-inch thickness. Season with the salt and pepper.

Warm a large stainless-steel or cast-iron skillet over medium-high heat. Add the oil and swirl to coat the pan. Working in batches, add a few chicken pieces to the pan and cook for 2 minutes per side, until cooked through. Transfer the chicken to a plate while you cook the rest of the chicken.

Wipe the pan clean with paper towels and return it to medium heat. Add 1½ teaspoons of the ghee and swirl the pan until the ghee melts. Add the garlic and thyme and cook for 1 minute. Add the bone broth and lemon juice, scraping the pan to loosen any browned bits. Bring the mixture to a boil, then cook for 3 minutes, until the liquid is reduced to about ¾ cup.

Whisk the arrowroot and 1 tablespoon water in a small bowl, until there are no lumps. Pour the mixture into the pan. Bring to a boil, then lower the heat and simmer for 3 to 4 minutes, until the sauce is thickened and reduced to about ½ cup. Remove the pan from the heat and discard the thyme. Stir in the remaining 1½ tablespoons ghee, the artichoke hearts, spinach, and capers and cook, stirring often, until the spinach wilts, about 2 minutes. Return the chicken and any juices to the pan and coat with the sauce. Sprinkle the parsley over the top and serve immediately.

Tidbit: Have all of your ingredients prepped and ready to go before you start cooking, as this dish comes together quickly. You want everything at your fingertips so the chicken doesn't dry out.

2 pounds boneless, skinless chicken breasts

¾ teaspoon fine sea salt

½ teaspoon freshly ground black pepper

2 teaspoons extra-virgin olive oil

2 tablespoons ghee

2 cloves garlic, minced

1 sprig fresh thyme

¾ cup Chicken Bone Broth (page 310)

⅓ cup freshly squeezed lemon juice

2 teaspoons arrowroot powder

1 (6.5-ounce) jar artichoke hearts, drained, rinsed, and quartered

3 cups baby spinach

2 tablespoons capers, drained and rinsed

2 tablespoons chopped fresh flat-leaf parsley

BUFFALO-STUFFED SWEET POTATOES

Serves 4 to 6 • I didn't eat sweet potatoes for years, when I was following more of an SCD-style diet, so I was extremely happy when I reintroduced them a few years ago and found that, as long as I limit my consumption to about once a week, I tolerate them pretty well. Ryan loves anything topped with buffalo sauce, so I decided to toss leftover chicken with my homemade buffalo sauce and use it as a filling for sweet potatoes.

6 Garnet sweet potatoes, scrubbed

1 tablespoon melted ghee or bacon fat

2½ teaspoons coarse sea salt

1½ pounds boneless, skinless chicken breasts or thighs

½ cup hot pepper sauce (such as Frank's)

⅓ cup ghee or expeller-pressed coconut oil

2 teaspoons white wine vinegar

½ teaspoon cayenne pepper

¼ cup diced celery

¼ cup diced carrot

½ cup Herb Ranch Dressing (page 92), for serving

Chopped fresh cilantro, for garnish

Preheat the oven to 425°F. Line a rimmed baking sheet with parchment paper.

Rub the skins of the sweet potatoes all over with the 1 tablespoon melted ghee and pat with 1½ teaspoons of the salt. Prick the potatoes with a fork a few times and place on the prepared baking sheet. Bake until tender, about 30 minutes.

Meanwhile, in a large pot, combine the chicken breasts, hot sauce, the ⅓ cup ghee, the remaining 1 teaspoon salt, the vinegar, and cayenne and simmer over low heat for 20 minutes, until the chicken is fully cooked.

Remove the chicken from the pot and use two forks to shred the meat. Return the shredded chicken to the pot, add the celery and carrot, and cook over medium heat for 10 minutes.

Cut slits in the tops of the roasted sweet potatoes and open them up a bit with a fork. Spoon the filling into the potatoes, drizzle with the ranch dressing, sprinkle with cilantro, and serve warm.

Make It Ahead: Cook the sweet potatoes and store them in an airtight container in the refrigerator for 5 days. Warm them in a 425°F oven for 15 minutes before serving. Alternately, cook the sweet potatoes in an electric pressure cooker (see page 316). Store the chicken in an airtight container in the refrigerator for 5 days. Reheat in a dry skillet over medium-high heat for 5 minutes, stirring frequently.

FRIED CHICKEN

Serves 4 to 6 • I have been trying to develop a good fried-chicken recipe for ages. It wasn't until I coated the chicken first with a dry mix of arrowroot and coconut flour that I got it right. Serve this with slaw (see page 206) or with my Crispy Nut-Free Waffles (page 237) for a classic chicken-and-waffles breakfast. Purchase the chicken whole, with bones and skin, and ask the butcher to cut it into 10 pieces (2 drumsticks, 2 thighs, 2 wings, and 2 breasts, each breast cut in half). Save the backbone and wingtips for making homemade bone broth (see page 310).

8 cups lukewarm water

2 tablespoons brine from a jar of pickles

2 tablespoons apple cider vinegar

½ cup fine sea salt

1 (4-pound) whole chicken, cut into 10 pieces

4 cups duck fat, palm shortening, or pastured lard, for frying

BREADING

¼ cup plus ⅔ cup arrowroot powder

1 tablespoon coconut flour

2 egg whites (see Tidbits)

¼ cup full-fat coconut milk

1 teaspoon hot pepper sauce (such as Frank's)

2 cups blanched almond flour

3 teaspoons garlic powder

1½ teaspoons onion powder

1 teaspoon fine sea salt

1 teaspoon sweet paprika

½ teaspoon cayenne pepper

½ teaspoon freshly ground black pepper

Whisk together the water, pickle brine, vinegar, and salt in a large stockpot until the salt has dissolved. Add the chicken, cover, and refrigerate overnight or for up to 24 hours. Remove the chicken from the brine, rinse well, and pat dry with paper towels.

To make the breading, in a shallow bowl, combine the ¼ cup arrowroot and the coconut flour. In a separate shallow bowl, beat the egg whites until frothy, then stir in the coconut milk and hot sauce. In a third shallow bowl, combine the almond flour, the remaining ⅔ cup arrowroot, the garlic powder, onion powder, salt, paprika, cayenne, and black pepper.

Line a baking sheet with paper towels and set a wire rack on top. Scoop the duck fat into a deep cast-iron skillet and heat to 350°F over medium-high. Once melted, the fat should be about 2 inches deep in the skillet.

Working with one piece at a time, dip the brined chicken pieces in the arrowroot–coconut flour mixture, turning to coat the pieces well and shaking off any excess flour. Next, dip the pieces in the egg white mixture, gently shaking to remove any excess egg white. Finally, coat each piece well in the almond flour mixture.

Working in batches of 2 or 3 pieces at a time, fry the chicken in the duck fat for 8 to 10 minutes (for white meat) or 12 to 14 minutes (for dark meat), until brown and crisp, turning each piece over a few times if the piece is not fully submerged. Use tongs to transfer the fried chicken to the prepared rack to cool for 10 minutes. Serve immediately.

The chicken is best eaten right away, when it is most crispy, but leftovers can be stored in an airtight container in the refrigerator for 3 days. Enjoy cold, or reheat on a wire rack set on a baking sheet in a 400°F oven for 10 to 12 minutes, until heated through.

Tidbits: Your fat will drop in temperature when you add the chicken. Keep a thermometer in the pan and adjust the heat of the stove as needed to maintain a constant temperature.

To reuse your frying oil, see Tidbits on page 127.

To make this EF, use 1 cup full-fat coconut milk in place of the egg whites.

SLOPPY JOES

Serves 4 to 6 • My sister's husband, Tyson, has been requesting a sloppy joes recipe for years. I make a quick, from-scratch tomato sauce here so you don't have to make ketchup or find a BBQ sauce that is free of refined sugar. My favorite way to eat this is over a sweet potato mash, but you could also serve this on individual Sandwich Rolls (page 317) or on the biscuits from Biscuits and Sausage Gravy (page 26).

SAUCE

2 cups tomato puree

3 tablespoons coconut aminos

2 tablespoons tomato paste

2 tablespoons coconut sugar

2 tablespoons white wine vinegar

1 tablespoon Dijon mustard

1 tablespoon light-colored raw honey

1¾ teaspoons fine sea salt

1 teaspoon fish sauce

1 teaspoon chili powder

½ teaspoon sweet paprika

⅛ teaspoon ground cloves

2 tablespoons beef tallow or avocado oil

1½ pounds ground beef

¾ cup diced yellow onion

½ cup diced carrot

½ cup diced celery

1 red bell pepper, seeded and diced

3 cloves garlic, minced

Savory Sweet Potato Mash (page 130), for serving

To make the sauce, combine all of the ingredients in a bowl and stir to mix well. Set aside.

Heat the tallow in a Dutch oven or deep skillet over medium-high heat. Add the ground beef and cook, stirring only occasionally, until the beef is well browned, 6 to 8 minutes. Drain off all but 1 tablespoon of the fat from the pan and return the pan to the heat. Add the onion, carrot, celery, bell pepper, and garlic and sauté for 3 to 5 minutes, until the vegetables have softened and the onion is translucent.

Pour in the sauce and stir well to combine. Simmer for 15 minutes. Spoon the beef mixture over the sweet potato mash and serve warm.

Make It Ahead: Brown the meat and vegetables, then combine them with the sauce. Place the mixture in a resealable plastic bag, lying flat for faster defrosting, and freeze for 4 months. Defrost at room temperature for 1 hour. Reheat in a covered saucepan over medium heat until heated through, about 20 minutes.

SHRIMP FRIED RICE

Serves 4 to 6 • I'm always looking for ways to incorporate more vegetables into my family's meals, and using riced cauliflower in this fried rice recipe inspired by Chinese takeout is a great way to do it. The salty sauce can make any vegetable taste appealing, and this dish is pretty much all veggies! While it's super-simple to make cauliflower rice at home, many supermarkets sell fresh or frozen riced cauliflower, so that's what I use more often than not. Go ahead and use it straight from the freezer; there's no need to thaw it first.

Combine the shrimp, 1 tablespoon of the coconut aminos, and 1 tablespoon of the sesame oil in a bowl.

Place the cauliflower in a food processor fitted with the grating attachment, or use the large holes on a box grater, and process the florets into rice-size pieces. Pick out any large fragments that didn't shred and chop them up by hand with a knife or save for another use. You should have around 3 cups riced cauliflower.

Heat 2 tablespoons of the avocado oil in a wok over medium-high heat. Add the onion, garlic, and ginger and cook, stirring continuously with a wooden spoon, for 2 minutes, until fragrant. Add the carrot and cook, stirring continuously, for 2 minutes. Add the remaining 3 tablespoons avocado oil and the cauliflower and cook, stirring occasionally, for 4 minutes more. Transfer the cauliflower mixture to a plate and return the wok to the heat.

Add the shrimp mixture to the wok and sear for 1 minute per side, until pink all over and just cooked through. Transfer the shrimp to the plate with the cauliflower and return the wok to the heat.

Pour the eggs into the wok and stir to scramble them for 10 seconds, until mostly cooked through. Pour the cauliflower mixture and shrimp back into the wok and add the remaining 5 tablespoons coconut aminos, the remaining 1 tablespoon sesame oil, and the salt. Stir in the peas and cook for 1 minute longer. Top with the green onions and serve immediately.

1½ pounds jumbo raw shrimp, peeled and deveined, with tails removed

6 tablespoons coconut aminos

2 tablespoons toasted sesame oil

1 head cauliflower, cut into florets

5 tablespoons avocado oil

½ small yellow onion, minced

3 cloves garlic, minced

2 teaspoons peeled and minced fresh ginger

1 carrot, diced

2 eggs, beaten

1¼ teaspoons fine sea salt

¼ cup frozen peas

2 green onions, tender green tops only, chopped

THAI YELLOW CURRY

Serves 4 to 6 • The sweet and ever-so-slightly-spicy flavor of Thai yellow curry has always been my favorite of the curry varieties. I make a big batch of homemade curry paste and store it in the freezer to use for quick meals throughout the month. Many people believe that a curry dish is simply a few tablespoons of curry powder mixed with a can of coconut milk. But for a truly authentic Thai curry, you need the paste, which is full of shallots, garlic, lemongrass, and spices. Traditional Thai curry features onions, potatoes, and sometimes bell peppers, but feel free to add any of your favorite vegetables to this version.

½ cup Yellow Curry Paste (see page 196)

2 (13.5-ounce) cans full-fat coconut milk

3 teaspoons fish sauce

2½ teaspoons fine sea salt

3 pounds bone-in chicken legs and breasts, skin removed

4 Thai lime leaves, fresh or dried (see Tidbits)

1 white-fleshed sweet potato (such as Hannah), peeled and cut into 2-inch cubes

1 red bell pepper, seeded and thinly sliced

1 yellow onion, halved and thinly sliced into half-moons

Basic Cauli Rice (page 309), for serving

In an electric pressure cooker, combine the curry paste, coconut milk, fish sauce, and salt. Add the chicken and lime leaves and stir to coat. Secure the lid and select the meat/stew setting, or select the manual setting and cook it at high pressure for 10 minutes. Quick release the pressure, remove the chicken, and skim off any fat from the top of the sauce. Strip the chicken from the bones and chop it coarsely. Discard the bones and return the chicken to the pot. Add the sweet potato, bell pepper, and onion and secure the lid again. Select the manual setting and cook at high pressure for 1 minute. Quick release the pressure and remove the lid. Serve warm over the cauliflower rice.

Variation: To make this in a slow cooker, combine the curry paste, coconut milk, fish sauce, salt, chicken, and lime leaves in the slow cooker. Cover and cook for 6 hours on low or 4 hours on high. Once the chicken is cooked, debone and shred it and return it to the slow cooker. Add the vegetables and continue cooking for 2 hours on low or 1 hour on high, until the vegetables are cooked.

Make It Ahead: Combine the yellow curry paste, coconut milk, fish sauce, salt, chicken, and lime leaves in a resealable plastic bag or airtight container. Combine the vegetables in a separate container. Store them, uncooked, in the freezer for up to 4 months. Remove the containers from the freezer at least 2 hours or up to 1 day before you

CONTINUED

want to prepare the dish. Place the semithawed contents directly into the electric pressure cooker and follow the main method, but increase the cook time for the chicken mixture to 20 minutes. Thaw the contents completely in the fridge if you plan to use a slow cooker.

Tidbits: I find fresh Thai lime leaves in the produce aisle near the fresh herbs, or dried in a jar in the international foods aisle. Thai lime yields the most authentic flavor, but you can also substitute 2 teaspoons finely grated lime zest plus 3 small bay leaves.

To comply with SCD, omit the coconut sugar from the curry paste.

YELLOW CURRY PASTE

Makes 1½ cups

4 heads garlic

5 small shallots, unpeeled

6-inch piece fresh ginger, peeled and sliced

2 tablespoons melted virgin coconut oil

5 to 15 dried Thai or bird's-eye chiles

3 stalks lemongrass, tops trimmed, outer layers removed, and stalks cut into half-moons

2 tablespoons mild curry powder

3 teaspoons ground turmeric

2 teaspoons ground coriander

1 teaspoon ground cumin

¼ cup packed fresh cilantro leaves

2 tablespoons coconut sugar (see Tidbits)

1½ tablespoons fine sea salt

Preheat the oven to 400°F.

Cut the tops off the heads of garlic so the cloves are partially exposed. Place the garlic heads, shallots, and ginger in an oven-safe skillet. Drizzle with the coconut oil and cover the skillet tightly with aluminum foil. Bake for 10 minutes; remove the ginger and reserve it in a small bowl. Return the covered pan to the oven and roast the garlic and shallots for 30 minutes more, until they are golden brown and very fragrant. Remove the pan from the oven and let cool until the garlic and shallots are cool enough to handle.

Meanwhile, place the chiles in a small bowl and add enough boiling water to cover. Soak for 15 minutes to rehydrate the chiles, then drain the water and remove the stems. Place the chiles in the bowl of a food processor.

Squeeze the garlic cloves out of their papery skins. Peel the shallots and coarsely chop the bulbs. Add the garlic cloves, shallots, ginger, lemongrass, curry powder, turmeric, coriander, cumin, cilantro, coconut sugar, and salt to the food processor. Process for 30 seconds, until the paste is very smooth. Transfer the paste to a jar and refrigerate for up to 2 weeks, or freeze for up to 6 months.

NO-MATO BOLOGNESE WITH SPAGHETTI SQUASH

Serves 4 to 6 • I published this Bolognese sauce recipe years ago on my blog. Judging from the comments on the original post, it sounds like this sauce has become an essential part of the pantry for those of you with nightshade or tomato allergies. Tomatoes, and other vegetables in the nightshade family, can cause inflammation for many people. But all cooks need a good Italian meat sauce, and this one is a fabulous stand-in. Served over spaghetti squash, or even zucchini noodles (to make zucchini noodles, see Spaghetti and Meatballs, page 204), it makes a hearty but healthful meal.

In a large saucepan over medium-high heat, melt together the ghee and 2 tablespoons of the oil. Add the onion and garlic and sauté for 3 to 4 minutes, until the onion begins to soften. Add the bacon and cook for 2 to 3 minutes more, until the onion is translucent. Add the carrots, beets, celery, 2½ teaspoons salt, and ¼ teaspoon pepper and cook until the vegetables have softened slightly, 5 to 6 minutes.

Pour in the wine and bone broth and bring the mixture to a boil. Turn the heat to medium-low and simmer for 10 minutes. Carefully pour the sauce into a blender. (Remove the cap in the blender top and place a kitchen towel over the top to allow steam from the hot liquid to release while you blend.) Blend on low speed for 15 seconds, then increase the speed to high and blend until you have a smooth sauce, about 15 seconds more.

Return the sauce to the pan and cook over medium heat. Add the bay leaves, 1 tablespoon of the basil, the oregano, thyme, and vinegar. Once the sauce is simmering, crumble the ground beef into the sauce and cook for 40 minutes, until the meat is cooked through. If the sauce is too thick, add a little more broth toward the end of the cooking process to reach your desired consistency.

CONTINUED

2 tablespoons ghee or bacon fat

4 tablespoons extra-virgin olive oil

1 cup diced yellow onion

5 cloves garlic, minced

3 slices bacon, chopped

2 cups diced carrots

2 cups peeled and diced beets

1 celery stalk, chopped

Fine sea salt and freshly ground black pepper

¾ cup dry red wine

1½ cups Chicken Bone Broth (page 310), plus more as needed

2 bay leaves

3 tablespoons chopped fresh basil

1½ teaspoons dried oregano

½ teaspoon dried thyme

1 tablespoon apple cider vinegar

1 pound ground beef or turkey

Meanwhile, preheat the oven to 425°F and line a rimmed baking sheet with parchment paper.

Cut each spaghetti squash in half lengthwise. Scoop out the seeds and membranes and drizzle the cut sides with the remaining 2 tablespoons oil. Season the squash generously with salt and pepper. Place the squash, cut side down, on the prepared baking sheet and bake for 20 minutes, until the skin gives a little when pressed with a spoon or finger. Remove the squash from the oven and use a fork to pull the spaghetti-like strands away from the skin. Place the strands in a serving bowl and season with salt and pepper to taste.

Spoon the Bolognese sauce over the spaghetti squash noodles and sprinkle with the remaining 2 tablespoons basil and the Parmesan cheese. Serve immediately.

Store leftover sauce in an airtight container in the fridge for 1 week. Reheat in a saucepan over medium-high heat for 5 to 10 minutes. Store leftover spaghetti squash in an airtight container in the fridge for 5 days. To reheat, sauté the squash in a skillet with 1 tablespoon extra-virgin olive oil over medium-high heat for 3 to 5 minutes.

Make It Ahead: **Prepare the sauce, then divide it between two resealable plastic bags and press out any excess air. Freeze the bags, lying flat for faster defrosting, for 4 months. Defrost at room temperature for 1 hour. Reheat in a saucepan over medium-low heat until heated through, about 20 minutes.**

3 spaghetti squash (about 2 pounds each)

2 tablespoons Parmesan Cheese (page 315; optional)

CRAB CAKES WITH REMOULADE SAUCE

Serves 4 to 6 • Because crab cakes typically contain ground-up crackers or bread crumbs to bind them together, I needed an alternative. The winner was ground-up plantain chips. Fresh crab is always best if you can find it. I use a pound each of lump and claw meat.

REMOULADE SAUCE

¼ cup Mayonnaise (page 314)

2 tablespoons freshly squeezed lemon juice

2 teaspoons Dijon mustard

2 cloves garlic, crushed

2 teaspoons anchovy paste

2 teaspoons chopped capers

½ teaspoon grated horseradish

½ teaspoon apple cider vinegar

¼ teaspoon cayenne pepper

CRAB CAKES

4 cups crabmeat (about 2 pounds), picked through for shells

5 ounces Plantain Chips (page 98)

1 cup Mayonnaise (page 314)

2 eggs

2 tablespoons Dijon mustard

1 tablespoon plus 1 teaspoon coconut aminos

2 teaspoons fish sauce

1 teaspoon hot pepper sauce (such as Frank's)

½ teaspoon fine sea salt

¼ teaspoon freshly ground black pepper

½ cup melted ghee

6 cups mixed salad greens, for serving

To make the remoulade, in a small bowl, stir together the mayonnaise, lemon juice, mustard, garlic, anchovy paste, capers, horseradish, vinegar, and cayenne. Cover and refrigerate.

To make the crab cakes, place the crabmeat in a large mixing bowl. Process the plantain chips in a food processor until they have the texture of sand; you should have about 1 cup. Gently mix the crushed chips into the crabmeat.

In a separate bowl, mix together the mayonnaise, eggs, mustard, coconut aminos, fish sauce, hot sauce, salt, and pepper and pour it into the crab mixture. Using your hands, gently mix together until just incorporated. Do not overmix. Place the crab mixture in the fridge to chill for 15 minutes or up to 1 hour.

Heat the ghee in a large skillet over medium heat. With damp hands, loosely form eight cakes from the crab mixture, each about 3 inches in diameter. Working in batches, place the cakes in the skillet and cook for 3 to 5 minutes per side, until they are browned and easily release from the pan. Transfer the crab cakes to a plate and serve with mixed greens and a drizzle of the remoulade over all.

Make It Ahead: Store the sauce in an airtight container in the refrigerator for 3 days.

Tidbits: To make this NSF, omit the cayenne pepper in the remoulade and the hot pepper sauce in the crab cakes.

INDIAN BUTTER CHICKEN

Serves 4 to 6 • Butter chicken is definitely a comforting dish, with its warm, velvety sauce of curry spices coating tender chicken. I use a creamy cashew puree to mellow out the spices and thicken the luscious sauce.

Bring a kettle of water to a boil. Place the cashews in a bowl and add enough boiling water to cover. Soak for 30 minutes.

Heat 2 tablespoons of the ghee in an electric pressure cooker using the sauté setting. Add the chicken, shallots, and onion and sauté for 8 minutes, until the chicken is browned and the onion is translucent. Add the remaining 4 tablespoons ghee, the tomato puree, tomato paste, lemon juice, garlic, cardamom, cinnamon stick, bay leaves, ginger, garam masala, cumin, salt, turmeric, and fenugreek and stir to combine. Secure the lid and select the meat/stew setting, or select the manual setting and cook at high pressure for 10 minutes.

Meanwhile, drain the cashews, rinse, and drain again. Combine the cashews and ¾ cup water in a blender. Blend on high speed until very smooth and creamy, about 30 seconds in a high-speed blender, or 1 minute in a conventional blender.

When the pressure cooker timer is done, quick release the pressure and stir in the cashew cream. Spoon the butter chicken into serving bowls. Sprinkle with almonds and cilantro and serve with naan on the side.

Variation: To make on the stovetop, heat 2 tablespoons ghee in a large skillet over medium-high heat. Add the chicken, shallots, and onion and sauté for 8 minutes, until the chicken is browned and the onion is translucent. Add the remaining 4 tablespoons ghee, the tomato puree, tomato paste, lemon juice, garlic, cardamom, cinnamon stick, bay leaves, ginger, garam masala, cumin, salt, turmeric, and fenugreek and stir to combine. Cover and simmer over medium-low heat for 20 minutes. Stir in the cashew cream and serve immediately.

Tidbits: Repurpose any leftover sauce by adding it to some sautéed vegetables and rotisserie chicken or cooked shrimp for a quick dinner the next day.

½ cup (about 75g) whole raw cashews (see Tidbits, page 310)

6 tablespoons ghee or unsalted grass-fed butter

3 pounds boneless, skinless chicken thighs, trimmed of fat and cut into 2-inch cubes

2 shallots, chopped (about ½ cup)

½ yellow onion, chopped

1 cup tomato puree

¾ cup tomato paste

3 tablespoons freshly squeezed lemon juice

4 cloves garlic, minced

6 green cardamom pods, bruised with the butt of a knife

1 cinnamon stick

2 bay leaves

3 tablespoons peeled and minced ginger

2½ tablespoons garam masala

1 tablespoon ground cumin

1 tablespoon fine sea salt

2 teaspoons ground turmeric

1 teaspoon fenugreek seeds

Toasted slivered almonds, for garnish

Chopped fresh cilantro, for garnish

Garlic Naan (page 268), for serving

SPAGHETTI AND MEATBALLS

Serves 4 to 6 • Although this meal isn't quick if you make it from scratch, it's one of my favorite last-minute meals when the meatballs are already prepped and in the freezer. I default to store-bought marinara sauce quite often for convenience, doctoring it up so the flavors are bolder. Look for sauces that are free from soybean oil, sugars, canola oil, or citric acid, which is often derived from corn or white potatoes. If you already have some Pesto Power Meatballs (page 244) in the freezer, you could substitute them here. You could also use spaghetti squash noodles (see No-Mato Bolognese with Spaghetti Squash, page 197).

6 zucchini

¼ teaspoon fine sea salt

MEATBALLS

3 eggs

3 pounds ground beef

¾ cup coarse almond meal or 3 tablespoons coconut flour

2 tablespoons nutritional yeast

3 cloves garlic, minced

2 teaspoons Italian seasoning

2½ teaspoons coconut aminos

1½ teaspoons dried oregano

1½ teaspoons fine sea salt

1½ teaspoons fish sauce

2 tablespoons olive oil or ghee

SAUCE

5 cups marinara sauce

3 teaspoons Italian seasoning

1 tablespoon dried parsley

2 teaspoons onion powder

Fine sea salt and freshly ground black pepper

½ teaspoon red pepper flakes

Chopped fresh flat-leaf parsley, for garnish

Preheat the oven to 200°F. Line a baking sheet with paper towels.

Peel the zucchini and slice off the ends. Using a spiral slicer or julienne peeler, turn the zucchini into long noodles, discarding the seedy core. Place the noodles on the prepared baking sheet. Sprinkle with the salt. Place the zucchini in the oven to sweat out some of its water while you make the meatballs and cook the sauce, about 30 minutes.

To make the meatballs, whisk the eggs in a large bowl. Add the ground beef, almond meal, nutritional yeast, garlic, Italian seasoning, coconut aminos, oregano, salt, and fish sauce. Using your hands, gently knead the mixture until the ingredients are just incorporated; do not overmix. Form the mixture into golf ball–size meatballs.

Warm the oil in a large Dutch oven or other heavy pot over medium heat. Panfry the meatballs in batches until browned all over, 10 to 12 minutes. (They do not need to cook all the way through since they will simmer in the sauce.) Transfer the meatballs to a plate, drain the fat from the pot, and return the pot to the stove over medium-low heat.

To make the sauce, add the marinara sauce, Italian seasoning, parsley, onion powder, 1½ teaspoons salt, ½ teaspoon black pepper, and the red pepper flakes to the pot and stir to combine.

Add the meatballs to the sauce and simmer for 20 minutes, stirring occasionally, until the meatballs are cooked through and the sauce is thickened.

Remove the zucchini noodles from the oven. Gather the ends of the paper towel and give the noodles a squeeze to wring out some of the liquid. Spoon the meatballs and sauce over the noodles, garnish with parsley, and serve immediately.

Make It Ahead: Prepare the meatballs and the sauce (I like to double both recipes). Freeze the cooled meatballs in a single layer on a baking sheet, covered with plastic wrap, for 4 hours. Store the frozen meatballs in an airtight container for 4 months. Divide the sauce between two resealable plastic bags and press out any excess air. Freeze the bags, lying flat for faster defrosting, for 4 months. To reheat, defrost the sauce at room temperature for 1 hour. Reheat in a saucepan over medium-low heat until fully defrosted, then add the frozen meatballs. Cook until the meatballs are heated through, about 20 minutes.

Tidbits: To make this NF, use coconut flour instead of almond meal for the meatballs.

PULLED PORK WITH SLAW

Serves 6 to 8 • Nothing beats juicy and tender pulled pork smothered in barbecue sauce and topped with a fresh and tangy coleslaw. Normally, this kind of slow-cooked dish takes hours, but with an electric pressure cooker, all you need is 40 minutes. (If you don't have a pressure cooker, I've also given instructions for making this in a slow cooker.) I use my super-easy sugar-free BBQ sauce here, but you could always use your favorite paleo-friendly store-bought sauce as well. I serve this simply over a bed of greens or stuffed into a baked sweet potato with the slaw on top.

SLAW

1 small head green cabbage, shredded

2 carrots, grated

1 red onion, thinly sliced

2 green onions, tender green and white parts only, chopped

1 jalapeño chile, halved, seeded, and thinly sliced

1 cup Mayonnaise (page 314; see Tidbits)

3 tablespoons Dijon mustard

2 teaspoons apple cider vinegar

1 teaspoon freshly squeezed lemon juice

½ teaspoon celery seeds

Hot pepper sauce (such as Frank's)

Fine sea salt and freshly ground black pepper

Chopped fresh cilantro, for garnish (optional)

PULLED PORK

1 (4-pound) boneless pork roast, shoulder, or Boston butt

2 tablespoons sweet paprika

To make the slaw, combine the cabbage, carrots, red and green onions, and jalapeño in a large bowl. In a separate bowl, stir together the mayonnaise, mustard, vinegar, and lemon juice. Pour the dressing over the cabbage mixture and toss gently to mix. Season the slaw with the celery seeds, several dashes of hot sauce, and salt and pepper to taste. Toss to combine. Cover and chill for 2 hours in the refrigerator before serving, garnished with the cilantro.

To make the pulled pork, cut the pork into four pieces, trim the fat, and place the pork in a large bowl. Add the paprika, chili powder, garlic powder, dry mustard, and 2 tablespoons salt and toss to coat well.

Pour the bone broth into an electric pressure cooker and add the pork. Secure the lid, select the manual setting, and cook at high pressure for 40 minutes.

When the pressure cooker timer is done, quick release the pressure. Remove the pork and use two forks to shred the meat. Skim the fat from the liquid left in the cooker and discard all but 1 cup of the liquid. Return the shredded pork and the reserved liquid to the pressure cooker and stir in the BBQ sauce and vinegar. Season with salt and pepper to taste before serving.

Variation: To make in a slow cooker, follow the given method, but increase the bone broth to 1½ cups. Cover and cook for 8 hours on low, then finish the dish as directed.

Make It Ahead: Prepare the pork and BBQ sauce up to 3 days in advance. Store in an airtight container in the refrigerator. Reheat in a saucepan over medium heat, stirring occasionally, for 15 minutes.

Tidbits: To make this EF, use an egg-free mayonnaise in the slaw.

1 tablespoon chili powder

1 tablespoon garlic powder

1 tablespoon dry mustard powder

Fine sea salt

1 cup Chicken Bone Broth (page 310)

3 cups BBQ Sauce (page 309), or any paleo-friendly barbecue sauce

2 tablespoons apple cider vinegar

Freshly ground black pepper

SHRIMP AND SAUSAGE JAMBALAYA

Serves 4 to 6 • This may not be a surprise if you already know how much I love Disneyland, but the only time I have ever eaten jambalaya was at Disneyland's Blue Bayou restaurant. Traveling to Louisiana to taste the real thing is on my to-do list, but until then, I've relied on some of my fans from the South to reassure me that this rendition tastes authentic.

Using a food processor fitted the shredding disk, or the large holes of a box grater, shred the sweet potato. Remove the shredding disk, insert the standard blade, and pulse the shredded potato a few times, until the shreds resemble grains of rice.

Heat the oil in a Dutch oven over medium-high heat. Add the sausage and cook, turning once, until golden brown, about 2 minutes per side. Transfer the sausage to a plate using a slotted spoon.

Add the yellow onion, 1 cup of the green onions, the celery, bell pepper, and garlic to the pan and sauté for 5 to 7 minutes, until the onion is translucent. Add the tomatoes and juice, parsley, oregano, thyme, black pepper, cayenne, salt, and bay leaves and bring to a boil. Stir in the minced sweet potato and the bone broth, turn the heat to medium-low, and simmer for 10 minutes, stirring occasionally, until the sweet potato is tender.

Add the shrimp and sausage and cook for 5 to 7 minutes more, until the stew has thickened but is still slightly soupy. Serve warm in bowls with the remaining ½ cup green onions on the side for garnish.

Tidbits: To comply with SCD, substitute 6 cups riced cauliflower for the sweet potato.

I typically buy tomatoes in jars or boxes that are BPA-free and don't contain citric acid.

12 ounces white-fleshed sweet potato (such as Hannah; see Tidbits), peeled

2 tablespoons avocado oil or ghee

12 ounces andouille sausage or kielbasa, thinly sliced on the diagonal

1 yellow onion, chopped

1½ cups finely chopped green onions, tender green and white parts only

4 celery stalks, chopped

1 green bell pepper, seeded and chopped

4 cloves garlic, minced

3 cups canned chopped tomatoes, with juice (see Tidbits)

2 teaspoons dried parsley

1 teaspoon dried oregano

½ teaspoon dried thyme

½ teaspoon freshly ground black pepper

¼ teaspoon cayenne pepper

1 teaspoon fine sea salt

2 bay leaves

½ cup Chicken Bone Broth (page 310)

1 pound large raw shrimp, peeled and deveined, with tails on

MOROCCAN CHICKEN SHEET-PAN SUPPER

Serves 4 to 6 • I'm a huge fan of sheet-pan suppers, but sometimes the meals lack flavor, or worse yet, all of the flavors blend together on the baking sheet and everything tastes the same. Don't worry, this is not one of those dishes! I love Moroccan flavors, and they are easy to replicate with just a handful of dried spices you likely already have in your pantry. The dried fruits and vegetables really stand out on their own, making this a winning dinner.

1½ cups mixed dried fruit (such as dates, apricots, figs, and cherries)

2 tablespoons dried parsley

Fine sea salt

½ teaspoon ground cumin

½ teaspoon ground cinnamon

½ teaspoon sweet paprika

¼ teaspoon cayenne pepper

¼ teaspoon ground turmeric

¼ teaspoon ground ginger

4 tablespoons extra-virgin olive oil

1 tablespoon freshly squeezed lemon juice

4 cloves garlic, crushed

6 chicken leg quarters (drumstick and thigh)

1 large yellow onion

1 medium butternut squash, peeled, halved, seeded, and cut into 2-inch cubes

Freshly ground black pepper

¼ cup fresh mint leaves, for garnish

2 tablespoons pomegranate seeds, for garnish

Place the dried fruit in a bowl and add enough hot water to cover. Soak for 10 minutes to rehydrate the fruit. Drain the water and cut the fruits in half if they are large.

Preheat the oven to 400°F.

In a small bowl, combine the parsley, 1 tablespoon salt, cumin, cinnamon, paprika, cayenne, turmeric, and ginger. In a large bowl, combine 2 tablespoons of the oil, the lemon juice, 2 cloves garlic, and 3 tablespoons of the spice mixture. Add the chicken pieces and toss, rubbing the chicken to coat each piece well. Arrange the chicken pieces, skin side up, on one side of a large rimmed baking sheet.

Cut the onion into ½- to ¾-inch wedges, leaving some of the core attached so the slices stay intact. In the same bowl that held the chicken, toss together the butternut squash, onion, the remaining 2 cloves garlic, the remaining 2 tablespoons oil, and the remaining spice blend. Season with salt and black pepper and toss again. Arrange the vegetable mixture in a single layer on the other side of the baking sheet.

Roast the chicken and vegetables for 20 minutes, then carefully sprinkle the rehydrated fruits around the baking sheet. Continue to roast until a thermometer inserted into the thickest part of the chicken leg registers 165°F and the butternut squash is tender, about 25 minutes more.

Serve the chicken with the roasted vegetables and fruits. Sprinkle the mint leaves and pomegranate seeds over the top.

HONEY-MUSTARD SHEET-PAN SALMON

Serves 4 to 6 • Sometimes to speed up dinner, I like to prep while I cook, especially if there are preliminary steps like preheating the oven or marinating. For this recipe, I marinate the salmon as the oven warms up, and at the same time, cut up vegetables and toss them with spices.

Whisk together the honey, mustard, vinegar, oregano, ½ teaspoon salt, and ¼ teaspoon pepper in a small bowl. Place the salmon fillet in a baking dish and pour the marinade over the fish. Marinate for 15 minutes.

Preheat the oven to 400°F.

Meanwhile, in a large bowl, toss together the butternut squash, brussels sprouts, tomatoes, oil, lemon juice, garlic powder, onion powder, oregano, turmeric, ¼ teaspoon salt, and ⅛ teaspoon pepper. Scatter the vegetables around the outer edges of a large rimmed baking sheet.

Remove the salmon from the marinade, allowing any excess to drip back into the baking dish. Reserve the marinade. Place the salmon in the center of the baking sheet and arrange the lemon slices on top of the fish.

Roast for 16 to 18 minutes, brushing the fish with the reserved marinade every 5 minutes, until the fish flakes in the center and the vegetables are crisp-tender. Serve immediately with the roasted vegetables.

Make It Ahead: Store the prepped vegetables in an airtight container in the fridge for 3 days. Store the spices in an airtight glass container in the pantry for 6 months.

Tidbits: To make this NSF, omit the tomatoes.

1 tablespoon light-colored raw honey

1 tablespoon coarse-grain mustard

½ teaspoon white wine vinegar

½ teaspoon dried oregano

Fine sea salt and freshly ground black pepper

1 (2-pound) salmon fillet, pinbones removed

2½ cups peeled, seeded, and cubed butternut squash

12 ounces brussels sprouts, trimmed and halved

2 cups cherry tomatoes (see Tidbits)

2 tablespoons avocado oil or melted ghee

½ teaspoon freshly squeezed lemon juice

¼ teaspoon garlic powder

¼ teaspoon onion powder

¼ teaspoon dried oregano

⅛ teaspoon ground turmeric

1 lemon, thinly sliced crosswise

CHICKEN PARMESAN WITH ROASTED SPAGHETTI SQUASH

Serves 4 to 6 • I have always loved chicken parmesan. In fact, it was the first recipe I attempted back in my college days (for Ryan and a bunch of his roommates). It was a disaster, but the failure spurred me to learn more about cooking, so it has a special place in my memory. I still enjoy this dish even without the dairy cheese and grain-based noodles. To keep things simple, I use store-bought marinara sauce most of the time (look for one that is free from soybean oil, sugars, canola oil, or citric acid, which is often derived from corn or white potatoes). To make this a one-pan meal, I skip panfrying the chicken and cook it along with the spaghetti squash on the same baking sheet.

1 (3-pound) spaghetti squash

Fine sea salt

Extra-virgin olive oil, for brushing and drizzling

6 boneless, skinless chicken breasts (about 2 pounds)

2 eggs (see Tidbits)

1½ cups blanched almond flour

1 cup Parmesan Cheese (page 315)

2 teaspoons dried oregano

1 teaspoon dried basil

½ teaspoon dried thyme

2½ teaspoons garlic powder

1½ cups marinara sauce

2 tablespoons melted ghee

Chopped fresh basil, for garnish

Preheat the oven to 350°F.

Lightly grease a rimmed baking sheet with extra-virgin olive oil. Slice the ends off the squash, then cut it crosswise into 2-inch rings. Run a knife around the interior of each ring to remove the seeds, or use a spoon to scrape them out.

Set a wire rack on the counter, line with a few paper towels, and set the squash rounds on top. Sprinkle both sides of the squash liberally with salt and let the rounds sit for 15 minutes to release some of their moisture. Wipe away the excess salt and moisture, brush both sides of the squash with oil, and arrange the rounds around the outer edges of the baking sheet, leaving an open space in the center.

Meanwhile, place each chicken breast between two pieces of parchment paper or plastic wrap. Using a kitchen mallet or heavy skillet, pound the chicken breasts until they're about ½ inch thick.

CONTINUED

In a shallow bowl, lightly beat the eggs. In a separate shallow bowl, combine the almond flour, ⅓ cup of the Parmesan, 1 teaspoon salt, the oregano, basil, thyme, and ½ teaspoon of the garlic powder. One at a time, dip the chicken breasts into the egg, allowing any excess to drip back into the bowl, then dip into the almond flour mixture, turning to coat each piece and shaking off any excess. Place the chicken pieces on the baking sheet and lightly drizzle with oil.

Bake the chicken and squash for 30 minutes, until the breading is golden brown. Pour about ¼ cup of the marinara sauce over each chicken breast and top with ⅓ cup Parmesan. Return the pan to the oven and bake for about 10 minutes more, until a thermometer inserted into the thickest part of each breast reads 165°F and the sauce is heated through.

Use a fork to pull the spaghetti-like strands away from the insides of the spaghetti squash rounds. Place into a bowl and toss with the ghee, the remaining 2 teaspoons garlic powder, and ½ teaspoon salt.

Divide the "noodles" among plates and top each with a piece of chicken. Spoon any additional sauce from the baking sheet over the top and sprinkle with the remaining ⅓ cup Parmesan and the basil.

Tidbits: To make this EF, substitute ¼ cup extra-virgin olive oil for the eggs.

FRENCH DIP SANDWICHES

Serves 4 to 6 • I loved French dip sandwiches growing up, and this was probably one of the first few dishes I learned how to make myself. Back then, we bought sliced roast beef and a packet of dried au jus, both of which were likely filled with sodium, MSG, and other additives. This super-easy slow cooker version makes the most delicious, savory dipping broth, and the meat becomes really tender from cooking all day. In my family, we always served these with seasoned fries (see my version on page 125) and a side salad.

Trim any visible fat from the chuck roast. In a cast-iron or other heavy pot, or using a cast-iron slow-cooker insert, heat the oil and ghee over medium-high heat. Add the chuck roast and brown the meat well on all sides, about 10 minutes total.

Carefully transfer the chuck roast and any juices to your slow cooker insert and add the bone broth, coconut aminos, fish sauce, vinegar, lime juice, thyme, onion powder, garlic powder, cloves, bay leaf, salt, and peppercorns. Cover and cook for 7 hours on low or 4 hours on high.

Remove the meat from the slow cooker and slice it very thinly on the diagonal, against the grain. Using a wide, shallow spoon, skim off and discard any fat from the juices, and strain out the bay leaf and peppercorns. Return the meat slices to the slow cooker. Cover and cook for 30 minutes more on high, allowing the meat to absorb some of the flavorful jus.

Toast the sandwich rolls and spread each with about 1 tablespoon mayonnaise. Use tongs to remove the meat from the jus and fill the rolls with six to eight slices each. Serve warm with a side of jus for dipping.

1 (3-pound) beef chuck roast

1 tablespoon extra-virgin olive oil

1 tablespoon ghee

1½ cups Beef Bone Broth (page 310)

¼ cup coconut aminos

2 teaspoons fish sauce

2 teaspoons apple cider vinegar

½ teaspoon freshly squeezed lime juice

1 teaspoon dried thyme

1 teaspoon onion powder

1 teaspoon garlic powder

¼ teaspoon ground cloves

1 bay leaf

1 tablespoon fine sea salt

½ teaspoon whole black peppercorns

4 to 6 Sandwich Rolls (page 317), 8 to 12 pieces Nut-Free Lunchbox Bread (page 48), or any grain-free rolls, split in half

4 to 6 tablespoons Mayonnaise (page 314)

CONTINUED

Variation: To make in an electric pressure cooker, decrease the bone broth to 1 cup. Brown the chuck roast in the oil and directly in the pressure cooker using the sauté setting. Add all of the remaining ingredients, except the rolls and mayo, and secure the lid. Select the meat/stew setting or select the manual setting and cook at high pressure for 25 minutes. Let the pressure release naturally before slicing the meat. Using a wide, shallow spoon, skim off and discard any fat from the juices, and strain out the bay leaf and peppercorns. Return the meat slices to the jus and cook, uncovered, on the sauté function for 10 minutes.

Tidbits: When I was little, I ate these with melted cheese, so if you tolerate dairy, a nice Gruyère or grass-fed Cheddar would taste delicious melted on the bread before adding the meat. To turn this into a cheesesteak-style sandwich, add some sautéed onions and bell peppers.

SAUSAGE-SPINACH SKILLET LASAGNA

Serves 4 to 6 • Between the number of pots and pans usually required to make it and the multiple layers involved, lasagna can be an overwhelming task for a weeknight. That's why I designed this skillet lasagna to be made in a single pan; the prep and cleanup are much easier. I sneak a little spinach into this recipe to give all of us some added greens. Instead of standard lasagna noodles, my grain-free wraps stand in here. Serve this with a simple salad, and dinner is done.

2 tablespoons extra-virgin olive oil or ghee

8 ounces uncooked mild Italian chicken sausage

8 ounces ground turkey

3 cups marinara sauce (see Tidbits)

1¼ cups Ricotta Cheese (page 316), or any store-bought dairy-free ricotta

1 egg

1 tablespoon chopped fresh flat-leaf parsley

1 tablespoon chopped fresh basil, plus more for garnish

½ teaspoon fine sea salt

¼ teaspoon freshly ground black pepper

5 Grain-Free Wraps (page 313)

2 cups baby spinach

Preheat the oven to 375°F.

Warm the oil in a deep ovenproof 9-inch skillet over medium-high heat. Remove the casings from the sausage and crumble it into the skillet with the ground turkey. Cook, breaking up the meat with a wooden spoon, for 5 to 6 minutes, until the meat is browned and cooked through. Drain the meat of excess fat and transfer it to a bowl. Add the marinara sauce to the bowl and mix well.

In a small bowl, mix together the ricotta, egg, parsley, basil, salt, and pepper.

Spoon 2 tablespoons of the meat sauce evenly into the bottom of the skillet. Gently spread ¼ cup of the cheese mixture onto one of the wraps. Place the cheese-covered wrap on top of the sauce and top with ½ cup spinach. Spread a little more meat sauce on top of the spinach. Repeat these layers four more times, until you reach the top of the skillet. Finish with the last of the meat sauce and dollops of the remaining cheese mixture.

Bake the lasagna, uncovered, for 20 to 30 minutes, until the edges are bubbling. Let the lasagna stand for 10 to 15 minutes before cutting. Sprinkle with fresh basil and serve warm.

Tidbits: Look for a marinara that is free from soybean oil, sugars, canola oil, or citric acid, which is often derived from corn or white potatoes.

To make this NSF, substitute No-Mato Bolognese sauce (see page 197) for the marinara and omit the sausage, which typically includes red pepper flakes.

SHEET-PAN STEAK FAJITAS

Serves 4 to 6 • Fajitas is the dish I turned to when eating at Mexican restaurants after going grain-free. It is easy to avoid the tortillas, and the sizzling Tex-Mex protein and vegetables really fill me up. This homemade version substitutes my grain-free wraps for the tortillas. I love to serve this with Refried "Beans" (page 122) or Mexican Cauli Rice (see Variation, page 309).

Preheat the broiler with a rack placed about 4 inches from the heating element. Place a large rimmed baking sheet on the rack to preheat along with the broiler.

In a large bowl, combine the steak, 3 tablespoons of the oil, 1 tablespoon of the lime juice, the orange juice, garlic, chili powder, cumin, 1 teaspoon salt, and ½ teaspoon black pepper. Toss the steak to coat, then marinate for 15 minutes, or cover and store in the fridge for up to 2 days.

Place the bell peppers and onion in a second bowl and toss with the remaining 2 tablespoons oil and the remaining 1 tablespoon lime juice. Season generously with salt and black pepper.

Carefully remove the hot baking sheet from the oven and arrange the bell pepper and onion mixture in a single layer on it. Broil for 10 minutes, until the vegetables are crisp-tender. Remove the baking sheet from the oven and push the peppers and onion to the outer edges of the pan. Arrange the steak strips in the center of the baking sheet in a single layer. Broil for 3 minutes, until the steak is medium-rare and the vegetables are tender.

Serve the fajita filling with the wraps, guacamole, cilantro, and lime wedges on the side.

Tidbits: To make the steak easier to slice thinly, freeze it for 20 minutes before slicing.

To make this EF and NF, use the lettuce cups for serving.

1½ pounds flank steak, sliced against the grain into ¼-inch strips

5 tablespoons avocado oil

2 tablespoons freshly squeezed lime juice

2 tablespoons freshly squeezed orange juice

2 cloves garlic, minced

2 teaspoons chili powder

2 teaspoons ground cumin

Fine sea salt and freshly ground black pepper

1 red bell pepper, seeded and thinly sliced

1 yellow bell pepper, seeded and thinly sliced

1 orange bell pepper, seeded and thinly sliced

1 small yellow onion, halved and thinly sliced into half-moons

8 to 12 Grain-Free Wraps (page 313) or lettuce cups, for serving (see Tidbits)

Guacamole (page 95), for serving

¼ cup fresh cilantro leaves, for serving

1 lime, cut into wedges, for serving

SHEET-PAN TERIYAKI SALMON WITH BROCCOLI AND ASPARAGUS

Serves 4 to 6 • A sheet-pan meal made with salmon is one of my fallback recipes when I don't have anything planned for dinner. I always keep a few fillets of wild-caught salmon in the freezer so I can defrost them quickly and throw them on a pan with some vegetables for an easy meal. My kids don't particularly love fish, but they *will* eat salmon, so I'm always on the lookout for new ways to prepare it. This teriyaki version with broccoli and asparagus is one of our favorites.

4 tablespoons coconut aminos

2 teaspoons fish sauce

½ teaspoon ground ginger

½ teaspoon garlic powder

1 teaspoon fine sea salt

⅛ teaspoon freshly ground black pepper

1 (2-pound) salmon fillet, pinbones removed

8 ounces broccoli florets

1 bunch asparagus, trimmed and cut into 2-inch pieces

2 tablespoons avocado oil

½ teaspoon apple cider vinegar

¼ to ¾ teaspoon red pepper flakes, to taste (see Tidbits)

2 teaspoons toasted sesame oil

2 green onions, tender green and white parts only, chopped, for garnish

Preheat the oven to 400°F.

In a small bowl, whisk together 3 tablespoons of the coconut aminos, the fish sauce, ¼ teaspoon of the ginger, ¼ teaspoon of the garlic powder, ½ teaspoon of the salt, and the black pepper. Place the salmon fillet in a baking dish and pour the marinade over the fish. Marinate for 15 minutes.

Meanwhile, in a separate bowl, toss together the broccoli, asparagus, avocado oil, the remaining 1 tablespoon coconut aminos, the remaining ¼ teaspoon ginger, the remaining ¼ teaspoon garlic powder, the remaining ½ teaspoon salt, the vinegar, and red pepper flakes. Scatter the vegetables around the outer edges of a large rimmed baking sheet.

Remove the salmon from the marinade, allowing any excess to drip back into the baking dish. Reserve the marinade. Place the salmon in the center of the baking sheet.

Roast for 16 to 18 minutes, brushing the fish with the reserved marinade every 5 minutes, until the fish flakes in the center and the vegetables are crisp-tender. Drizzle the vegetables and salmon with the sesame oil, top with the green onions, and serve immediately.

Tidbits: To make this NSF, omit the red pepper flakes.

ONE-PAN DECONSTRUCTED TURKEY DINNER

Serves 4 to 6 • Anytime I'm cooking celery, onions, and garlic with fresh herbs, my mind goes to Thanksgiving. I think of family time spent around the table and the months when there is finally a chill in the air and excitement about Christmas starts to build. This sheet-pan supper incorporates the best parts of a traditional Thanksgiving meal but without the hassle and time laboring in the kitchen. I like to thinly slice any leftover turkey for sandwiches or wraps and enjoy it for lunch the next day.

1 (3- to 4-pound) bone-in turkey breast

½ loaf Nut-Free Lunchbox Bread (page 48), cut into 1-inch pieces (around 6 cups; see Tidbits)

1 apple, such as Fuji or Pink Lady, cored and cut into 1-inch cubes

2 celery stalks, sliced crosswise

1 small yellow onion, diced

¼ cup dried cranberries (see Tidbits)

4 tablespoons melted ghee

2 cloves garlic, minced

2 tablespoons chopped fresh sage, plus 3 whole leaves for seasoning

5 sprigs thyme

2 tablespoons extra-virgin olive oil

Fine sea salt and freshly ground black pepper

1½ cups Chicken Bone Broth (page 310)

Preheat the oven to 450°F with a rack placed in the upper third of the oven. Let the turkey sit at room temperature on the counter while the oven preheats.

On a large rimmed baking sheet, toss together the bread, apple, celery, onion, cranberries, 2 tablespoons of the ghee, the garlic, and chopped sage. Strip the leaves from 2 sprigs of the thyme and add to the baking sheet. Spread the mixture into an even layer and bake for 10 minutes.

Meanwhile, in a small bowl, combine the remaining 2 tablespoons ghee and the oil. Rub the turkey with the oil mixture and season generously with salt and pepper. Gently loosen the turkey skin and rub some of the oil, salt, and pepper under the skin. Place the remaining thyme sprigs and the sage leaves under the skin, then pull the skin back to cover the meat as much as possible.

Remove the bread mixture from the oven, pour the bone broth over the top, and stir until the liquid is absorbed. Arrange the moistened bread mixture around the outer edges of the baking sheet, leaving an open space in the center. Place the turkey in the center of the sheet, skin side up. Season the bread mixture with salt and pepper.

Decrease the oven temperature to 350°F. Roast the turkey and stuffing for 50 minutes, then begin checking the temperature every 10 minutes until a thermometer inserted into the thickest part of the breast reads 165°F. Stir the stuffing if the bread looks like it's browning too much.

Remove the baking sheet from the oven, tent it loosely with aluminum foil, and let the turkey rest for 15 minutes. Remove the herb sprigs, then place the turkey on a cutting board. Slice it against the grain at a slight angle into pieces about ¼ inch thick. Serve the stuffing alongside the turkey.

Variation: Substitute one 3- to 4-pound whole chicken, cut into 10 pieces, for the turkey breast. Bake at 450°F for 20 to 25 minutes, until a thermometer inserted into the thickest part of the breast reads 165°F.

Tidbits: To comply with SCD, use an SCD-legal grain-free bread in place of the Lunchbox Bread.

Eden Organics dried cranberries are sweetened only with apple juice and do not contain added oils.

CHAPTER 7

MAKE IT AHEAD

Batch cooking is a home cook's best friend. All the prep work may seem a little intimidating up front, but you will be so relieved to come home after a long, exhausting day and have something in the freezer to heat up for dinner. A lot of these recipes will also come in handy for packing work or school lunches.

Although you might think make-ahead dishes are limited to casseroles, I keep my freezer stocked with a variety of meals. Sure, you'll find some casseroles in there, but I also freeze soups, stews, pizza crusts, chicken nuggets, and breakfast foods such as muffins and waffles. Of course, my freezer is also stocked with meat, vegetables and fruit, and bone broth (see page 310). There are many dishes throughout this book that freeze and reheat well—not just the ones in this chapter. Watch for freezing tips at the end of recipes, and review the following list if you are (or want to be) an avid make-it-ahead cook.

Freezing and reheating isn't hard, but I've learned a few secrets along the way.

MY FREEZING TIPS

- To prevent foods from sticking together, freeze them in a single layer on a rimmed baking sheet, tightly covered with plastic wrap, for 4 hours. Place the frozen food in a resealable plastic freezer bag or airtight container.

- Glass containers are great for make-ahead meals because you can freeze and reheat them in the same container. If you're using plastic containers, wait until the food has cooled to room temperature before putting it into the container to avoid harmful chemicals leaching out of the plastic and into the food. While I use glass containers with airtight lids to store foods in my refrigerator, I prefer resealable plastic freezer bags for the freezer because they take up less space. And if you freeze the bag lying flat, the contents can be defrosted more quickly.

- Use fresh, not previously frozen, meat if you are freezing the dish before cooking it. Raw meat should never be thawed and then refrozen.

- Cool a cooked dish to room temperature, or at least until it stops steaming, then chill it thoroughly in the refrigerator before freezing. This helps avoid freezer burn and having excess moisture in the dish when it is reheated.

- Get all of the air out of any resealable plastic bags or storage containers. Air is the enemy when it comes to freezer burn and shelf life. Ryan thinks I'm crazy, but since I don't own a vacuum sealer, I close a resealable plastic bag 90 percent of the way, suck out any air from the small opening with my mouth, then zip it up quickly before any air reenters.

- Double or triple a recipe, then freeze the batches separately. You only have to dirty the dishes once to make it, and will have multiple meals ready to go. I find it's easier to make more food if you have an assembly-line process for preparing each dish.

- Label everything you freeze with the name of the dish, the date it was prepared, and thawing and reheating instructions so someone else can prepare dinner. Use a permanent marker to label plastic bags, or write on a piece of painter's tape and stick it to the container.

- Clean as you go—that massive sink full of dishes at the end of the day can be overwhelming. If something is cooking on the stove, I clean up as much as possible while I wait for the next active step. I hand wash tools that I may use again and again, like measuring cups and spoons, so they're always ready to go.

- Skip the microwave! Microwaving frozen foods and leftovers causes them to reheat inconsistently, which can make foods mushy. The best way to reheat frozen foods is to thaw them in the refrigerator and then warm them up in a low oven or over medium-low heat on the stove. I use a countertop toaster oven much of the time so I don't have to turn on my big oven.

BREAKFAST "HAMBURGERS"

Makes 24 • These sausages have become my breakfast lifeline on busy weekday mornings. All my kids love these, and I like that they are baked rather than fried (which makes them healthier and easier to clean up), packed with iron and vitamin B–rich liver, and readily accessible in the freezer. Just remove what you need and pop them in a toaster oven to defrost and warm quickly. Even though these are really little sausage patties, I called them "hamburgers" when I first started making them because it convinced my oldest son to eat them. He knows the difference now and still happily eats these, but the name stuck.

Preheat the oven to 375°F. Line a plate with paper towels.

Rinse the livers and use kitchen shears to trim them of any fat or connective tissues. Pat them dry with a paper towel. Melt the ghee in a skillet over medium-high heat. Add the livers and cook for 4 to 5 minutes per side, until firm and grayish brown.

Place the cooked livers in a food processor and pulse a few times to coarsely grind. Remove the blade and add the pork, maple syrup, salt, pepper, sage, garlic powder, onion powder, cinnamon, and nutmeg. Mix by hand until just combined.

Form the sausage mixture into 3-inch patties that are about 1 inch thick; you should have two dozen patties. Place the patties—without touching—on two large rimmed baking sheets. Bake the sausages for 7 minutes, then flip them over and bake for 7 minutes more, until a thermometer inserted into the center of a patty reads 165°F.

Turn off the oven, set the broiler, and place a rack about 3 inches from the heating element. Brown the sausages for 1 minute on each side, then transfer them to the prepared plate to drain. Serve warm.

Freeze the cooled hamburgers in a single layer on a rimmed baking sheet, tightly covered with plastic wrap, for 4 hours. Place the frozen hamburgers in an airtight container and freeze for 4 months. Reheat on a baking sheet in a 400°F oven until heated through, 12 to 15 minutes.

8 ounces chicken livers

2 tablespoons ghee

3 pounds ground pork

2 tablespoons pure maple syrup

2½ teaspoons sea salt

¼ teaspoon freshly ground black pepper

1 teaspoon ground sage

½ teaspoon garlic powder

½ teaspoon onion powder

½ teaspoon ground cinnamon

½ teaspoon ground nutmeg

CHOCOLATE-ZUCCHINI MUFFINS

Makes 24 • These muffins are moist and fluffy, plus they're nut-free. I keep them in the freezer for a quick breakfast when we're frazzled and trying to get out the door for school, or to send as a snack in Asher's lunchbox. If zucchini isn't in season, you could use shredded carrots. For a little extra protein, I often add collagen peptides powder (see Tidbits on page 43), which is also beneficial for immunity, digestion, and healthy hair and skin.

1½ cups shredded zucchini

8 eggs

1 cup unsweetened applesauce

1 cup pure maple syrup

⅔ cup coconut flour

½ cup unflavored collagen peptides powder or protein powder of your choice (optional)

½ cup raw cacao powder

6 tablespoons arrowroot powder

1 tablespoon baking soda

1 teaspoon ground cinnamon

¼ teaspoon ground nutmeg

½ teaspoon fine sea salt

½ cup dairy-free chocolate chips (optional)

Preheat the oven to 350°F and line two 12-cup muffin tins with baking cups, or grease the tins with coconut oil. Line a plate with paper towels.

Place the zucchini on the prepared plate and allow it to drain some of its moisture while you make the batter.

Place the eggs, applesauce, and maple syrup in a stand mixer fitted with the beater attachment, or use an electric handheld mixer. Mix on medium speed until combined. Add the coconut flour, collagen peptides powder, cacao powder, arrowroot, baking soda, cinnamon, nutmeg, and salt and mix on medium speed until combined.

Wrap the paper towels around the zucchini and give it a light squeeze to remove any remaining moisture. Add the zucchini to the batter along with ¼ cup of the chocolate chips and mix on low speed until incorporated. Divide the batter evenly among the muffin cups, filling each two-thirds full. Sprinkle the remaining chocolate chips over the top.

Bake for 22 to 25 minutes, until a toothpick inserted into the center of a muffin comes out clean. Remove the muffins from the pan and allow them to cool completely on a wire rack before serving or storing.

Freeze in a single layer on a rimmed baking sheet, tightly covered with plastic wrap, for 4 hours. Place the frozen muffins in an airtight container and freeze for 4 months. To eat the muffins directly from the freezer, heat them in a 350°F oven for 10 minutes, until warmed through. Or, defrost in an airtight container in the fridge overnight, or for up to 1 week. If you prefer, warm on a baking sheet in a 400°F oven for 2 to 3 minutes.

CRISPY NUT-FREE WAFFLES

Makes 12 • My original waffle recipe, published on my blog, uses cashews and has become a favorite over the years. However, I constantly get requests for a nut-free version. These waffles are crisper and lighter than the cashew-based ones, so even if you *do* tolerate nuts, you will love this new recipe. I also tested an egg-free version, so be sure to note the modifications below. You could also make Fried Chicken (page 188) for an awesome chicken-and-waffles breakfast.

Preheat a waffle iron to medium-high. In the bowl of a stand mixer fitted with the whisk attachment, or using an electric handheld mixer, beat the egg whites with the cream of tartar on medium-high speed until stiff peaks form, 2 to 3 minutes. Use a rubber spatula to transfer the whipped whites to a bowl.

Return the bowl to the stand mixer. Combine the egg yolks, ghee, coconut milk, honey, vinegar, arrowroot, coconut flour, baking soda, and salt. Mix on medium speed until well combined, scraping down the sides if needed.

Add 2 tablespoons of the whipped whites to the batter and mix on medium-low speed until well combined. Scrape down the sides and release any batter that is stuck on the bottom of the bowl. Using a rubber spatula, gently fold in the remaining egg whites, being careful to not deflate them.

Depending on the size of your waffle iron, spoon ¼ cup to ½ cup of batter into each quadrant. Close the iron and cook until the indicator light turns on, or the steam has stopped releasing from the machine. Open the iron and use a fork to release the waffles. Transfer the waffles to a baking sheet and place in an oven turned to its lowest setting to keep warm while you cook the remaining batter. Serve the waffles hot with a drizzle of maple syrup and your favorite fruit on top.

Freeze the cooked waffles in an airtight container for 4 months. Reheat from frozen in a toaster until warm, about 5 minutes.

8 eggs, separated (see Tidbits)

½ teaspoon cream of tartar

½ cup melted ghee or expeller-pressed coconut oil

½ cup full-fat coconut milk

2 tablespoons light-colored raw honey

2 teaspoons apple cider vinegar

1⅓ cups arrowroot powder

¼ cup plus 1 tablespoon coconut flour

2 teaspoons baking soda

½ teaspoon fine sea salt

Pure maple syrup and sliced fresh fruit, for serving

Tidbits: To make this EF, substitute 2 tablespoons finely ground golden flax seeds whisked together with 6 tablespoons hot water for the eggs. Let the mixture rest for 2 minutes, then whisk again. Place all of the waffle ingredients in a blender and blend on high speed until smooth, about 30 seconds. Cook the waffles as directed.

MORNING GLORY MUFFINS

Makes 24 • I'm not a morning person, nor am I a night owl—I just like to sleep! Prior to having a houseful of kids, I enjoyed about 30 minutes of silence in the morning before even speaking a word to anyone. Now that I am up with the sun and my energetic children, I need something first thing to kick-start my energy. I keep some of these carrot and apple muffins in the freezer to give my morning a bit of glory instead of chaos. Well, there's still chaos, but at least we're all nourished and happy.

8 eggs, at room temperature

½ cup coconut sugar

6 tablespoons warm water

6 tablespoons melted virgin coconut oil

6 tablespoons light-colored raw honey

1½ teaspoons pure vanilla extract

1 cup coconut flour

½ cup arrowroot powder (see Tidbits)

2 tablespoons ground cinnamon

2 teaspoons baking soda

1 teaspoon ground nutmeg

1 teaspoon fine sea salt

2 carrots, grated (about ½ cup)

2 small apples (such as Fuji or Pink Lady), cored and grated

½ cup golden raisins

½ cup chopped pineapple, canned or fresh

1½ teaspoons apple cider vinegar

¼ cup raw sunflower seeds

Preheat the oven to 350°F and line two 12-cup muffin tins with baking cups.

Place the eggs in a blender and blend on high speed for 30 seconds, until frothy. Add the coconut sugar, warm water, coconut oil, honey, vanilla, coconut flour, arrowroot, cinnamon, baking soda, nutmeg, and salt. Blend on low speed for 15 seconds, then on high speed for 30 seconds, until the batter is smooth.

Fold the carrots, apples, raisins, pineapple, and vinegar into the batter in the blender. Divide the batter evenly among the muffin cups, filling each two-thirds full. Sprinkle the tops with the sunflower seeds.

Bake for 20 to 22 minutes, until a toothpick inserted into the center of a muffin comes out clean. Remove the muffins from the pan and allow them to cool completely on a wire rack before serving or storing.

Freeze in a single layer on a rimmed baking sheet, tightly covered with plastic wrap, for 4 hours. Place the frozen muffins in an airtight container and freeze for 4 months. To eat the muffins directly from the freezer, heat them in a 350°F oven for 10 minutes, until warmed through. Or, defrost in an airtight container in the fridge overnight, or for up to 1 week. If you prefer, warm on a baking sheet in a 400°F oven for 2 to 3 minutes.

Tidbits: To comply with SCD, omit the warm water and arrowroot powder. Increase the honey to 1 cup and omit the coconut sugar.

SMOOTHIE PACKETS

Each serves 2 • I used to think smoothie packets were silly. How hard is it to throw some fruit and veggies into a blender each morning? But one day, I was leaving for a business trip and wanted to make breakfast easy on Ryan and the kids. So I prepped a week's worth of smoothie ingredients in individual bags that Ryan could just dump into the blender. It worked out so well that I started prepping my smoothies even during weeks I was home. Here are four of my favorite blends; switch up the flavors as you like.

EF • NSF • SCD

CREAMY BLUEBERRY PEACH

In a resealable plastic freezer bag, combine 1 cup blueberries, 1 cup peeled and sliced peaches, 1 sliced banana, ¼ cup (about 35g) whole raw cashews (see Tidbits, page 310), and 2 teaspoons bee pollen (optional). Freeze until ready to use. Combine the smoothie packet with 1¼ cups unfiltered unsweetened apple juice, water, or unsweetened almond milk and 1 teaspoon freshly squeezed lemon juice, and blend on high speed for 30 seconds, until smooth.

EF • NSF

CHOCOLATE MINT

In a resealable plastic freezer bag, combine 1 sliced banana, 3 to 5 small pitted dates, 2 tablespoons unsweetened almond butter, ½ diced avocado, 2 tablespoons raw cacao powder, 2 tablespoons unflavored collagen peptides powder (optional), 1 cup packed baby spinach leaves, 1 teaspoon golden flaxseeds, and 6 fresh mint leaves. Freeze until ready to use. Combine the smoothie packet with 1½ cups unsweetened almond milk, cashew milk, or full-fat coconut milk and blend on high speed for 30 seconds, until smooth.

GREEN PIÑA COLADA

EF · NF · NSF · SCD

In a resealable plastic freezer bag, combine 2 cups diced pineapple, 2 sliced bananas, and 2 cups packed chard leaves. Freeze until ready to use. Combine the smoothie packet with 1 (13.5-ounce) can full-fat coconut milk and ½ cup unsweetened pineapple juice or water and blend on high speed for 30 seconds, until smooth.

BERRY SORBET

EF · NSF

In a resealable plastic freezer bag, combine 1 cup mango chunks, 1 cup strawberries, ½ cup raspberries, 4 tablespoons Dairy-Free Yogurt (page 312), and 2 teaspoons chia seeds. Freeze until ready to use. Combine the smoothie packet with 1½ cups unfiltered unsweetened apple juice, water, orange juice, or a mix, and blend on high speed for 30 seconds, until smooth.

Tidbits: If your favorite fruits are out of season, it may be more cost-effective to buy organic frozen fruit.

HONEY-MUSTARD CHICKEN

Serves 8 • This is my go-to chicken recipe during the summer. Whenever I see boneless, skinless chicken breasts on sale, I grab a bunch and marinate them in this flavorful honey-mustard mix. I like to throw two breasts and the marinade into plastic bags and freeze them so I can defrost a single packet anytime we fire up the grill for dinner. That way, we have delicious chicken to use on salads and in wraps for easy lunches all week.

8 boneless, skinless chicken breast halves (about 3 pounds)

½ cup Dijon mustard

½ cup light-colored raw honey

¼ cup avocado oil

2 teaspoons fine sea salt

1 teaspoon freshly ground black pepper

Place 2 breasts each into four resealable plastic freezer bags or glass containers with airtight lids. Whisk together the mustard, honey, oil, salt, and pepper in a bowl. Divide the marinade among the bags, seal, and toss to coat the chicken. Marinate in the refrigerator for 12 hours or up to 2 days, or freeze each packet for up to 4 months. Defrost the individual packets overnight in the refrigerator before grilling.

Preheat the grill to medium heat and oil the grates, or heat a grill pan on the stovetop over medium heat. While the grill heats, let the chicken sit at room temperature in its marinade.

Remove the chicken from the bags and shake off the excess marinade. Cook until a crust forms on both sides and the chicken is cooked through, 8 to 10 minutes per side. Let the chicken rest on a serving platter for 10 minutes before serving. Serve warm.

PESTO POWER MEATBALLS

Makes 36 • A paleo diet focuses on nutrient-dense foods, but including lots of organ meats in your diet can be difficult for some people to stomach. These meatballs add a good dose of iron-rich liver into my family's meal, and they don't even know it's in there. I serve them for lunch with a side of marinara for dipping, or pull out a dozen from the freezer and serve them over a grain-free noodle alternative such as spaghetti squash (see page 197) or zucchini noodles (see page 204) for a quick dinner.

PESTO

⅓ cup toasted pine nuts

3 cups packed fresh
basil leaves

3 cloves garlic, peeled

1 teaspoon freshly squeezed
lemon juice

½ teaspoon fine sea salt

⅓ cup extra-virgin olive oil

12 ounces chicken livers

2 tablespoons ghee

2 pounds ground chicken
(both dark and white meat)

1½ teaspoons fine sea salt

3 tablespoons extra-virgin
olive oil

To make the pesto, place the pine nuts, basil, garlic, lemon juice, and sea salt in a food processor or blender and pulse a few times to finely chop the mixture. With the machine running, slowly drizzle in the oil and process until a pourable paste has formed. Continue to process for 15 seconds more, until smooth. Scrape the pesto into a bowl and set it aside.

Rinse the livers and use kitchen shears to trim them of any fat or connective tissues. Pat them dry with a paper towel. Melt the ghee in a skillet over medium-high heat. Add the livers and cook for 4 to 5 minutes per side, until firm and grayish brown.

Place the cooked livers in a food processor and process until they are ground into a smooth paste, about 30 seconds. Remove the blade and add the ground chicken, the pesto (you'll have about 1½ cups) and the salt. Mix by hand until just combined.

Heat 2 tablespoons of the oil in a large cast-iron pan over medium-high heat. Working in batches, use a small cookie scoop or tablespoon to scoop out meatballs about 1 inch in diameter and add them to the pan. Arrange the meatballs in the pan in a single layer, with a bit of space between them to avoid crowding. Cook until the meatballs are browned on the bottom, about 2 minutes.

CONTINUED

Cover the dish and bake for 15 minutes. Remove the cover and bake for 15 minutes more. Serve immediately.

Store leftovers, covered tightly, in the refrigerator for 5 days. To reheat, bake at 350°F for 15 to 20 minutes, until the casserole is heated through, or warm in a skillet over medium-low heat for 5 minutes.

Make It Ahead: Assemble the casserole minus the plantain topping. Cover tightly with plastic wrap and freeze for 4 months. Defrost in the fridge overnight, then add the topping and bake as directed.

Tidbits: Skip a step and purchase an organic rotisserie chicken, or use 3 cups diced Pressure Cooker Chicken (page 315) in place of the roasted chicken.

To comply with SCD, substitute coarsely ground almond meal for the plantain chips and omit the coconut aminos.

SHEPHERD'S PIE

Serves 6 to 8 • I didn't know what real shepherd's pie was until Ryan and I traveled to the United Kingdom as newlyweds. My mom's version of this classic British dish called for a can of cream of mushroom soup (of course), a tub of sour cream, canned green beans, boxed mashed potatoes, a ton of cheese, and canned fried onion rings. While delicious, that one was a far cry from the traditional version. Ground lamb gives the dish a more authentic flavor (and grass-fed lamb is usually less expensive than grass-fed beef), but you can also use ground beef if you prefer. I use mashed cauliflower in place of the traditional mashed potatoes to keep this light and paleo-friendly.

ROASTED GARLIC MASHED CAULIFLOWER

8 cloves garlic, unpeeled

2 tablespoons extra-virgin olive oil

2 heads cauliflower, cut into florets

⅓ cup Chicken Bone Broth (page 310) or Cashew Milk (page 310)

6 tablespoons melted ghee

Fine sea salt and freshly ground black pepper

FILLING

2 tablespoons ghee or avocado oil

½ cup diced yellow onion

2 cups Beef Bone Broth (page 310)

¼ cup tomato paste

2 teaspoons apple cider vinegar

2 teaspoons unflavored powdered gelatin

1 sprig thyme

1 sprig rosemary

To make the mashed cauliflower, preheat the oven to 425°F.

Put the garlic cloves in a small heatproof dish and drizzle them with the olive oil. Cover and roast the garlic for 15 minutes. Set the garlic aside to cool and decrease the oven temperature to 400°F.

To make the filling, meanwhile, melt 1 tablespoon of the ghee in a skillet over medium-high heat. Add the onion and sauté for 3 to 5 minutes, until fragrant and translucent. Whisk in the beef bone broth, tomato paste, vinegar, gelatin, thyme and rosemary sprigs, allspice, and cloves. Bring to a boil, turn the heat to medium-low, and simmer for 5 minutes, until the sauce thickens slightly. Remove the stems from the herbs, then transfer the sauce to a blender and add the dates. Blend on high speed for 30 seconds, until smooth. (Remove the cap in the blender top and place a kitchen towel over the top to allow steam from the hot liquid to release while you blend.)

Wipe the skillet clean and return it to medium-high heat. Add the remaining 1 tablespoon ghee and the minced garlic to the pan and cook for 30 seconds, until fragrant but not browned. Add the lamb, 2 teaspoons salt, and ½ teaspoon pepper and cook, breaking up the meat with a wooden spoon, until the meat is browned and cooked through, about 10 minutes. Drain the fat from the pan,

CONTINUED

¼ teaspoon ground allspice

¼ teaspoon ground cloves

4 small pitted dates

3 cloves garlic, minced

2 pounds ground lamb

Fine sea salt and freshly ground black pepper

2 large carrots, diced (about 1 cup)

½ cup frozen or fresh English peas

then add the carrots and peas and cook for 5 minutes. Stir the sauce into the meat mixture, then spread it evenly into an 11 by 7-inch baking dish.

To finish the roasted garlic mashed cauliflower, put the cauliflower in a steamer basket set inside a large skillet and add ½ inch of water to the skillet. Place the skillet over medium-high heat and bring the water to a boil. Cover, lower the heat to a simmer, and steam the cauliflower for 10 minutes, just until fork tender. Drain well and transfer the cauliflower to a food processor. Squeeze the roasted garlic cloves out of their papery skins. Add the garlic to the processor along with the chicken bone broth, 5 tablespoons of the melted ghee, 2 teaspoons salt, and ¼ teaspoon pepper. Process for 15 seconds, until smooth and fluffy.

Top the lamb mixture with the mashed cauliflower, spreading the mash to the edges of the dish and smoothing the top with a rubber spatula. Brush the top of the mash with the remaining 1 tablespoon melted ghee. Place the dish on a rimmed baking sheet and bake for 25 minutes, until the sauce is bubbling and the cauliflower mash begins to brown. Transfer the dish to a cooling rack and let it rest for 15 minutes before serving.

Make It Ahead: Cover the cooled casserole tightly with two layers of plastic wrap and freeze for 4 months. Defrost in the fridge overnight, then bake as directed.

Tidbits: To make this NF, use the bone broth option in the mashed cauliflower.

CHICKEN POTPIE

Serves 4 to 6 • Sometimes the craving strikes for a creamy homemade potpie with a crisp pastry topping. But it's not easy to accommodate that yearning at the last minute if you're looking to make filling, gravy, and crust from scratch. So I make two or three of these potpies at a time and freeze the extras so I have one on hand when the need arises. If you enjoy more of a biscuit topping than a pastry crust, try using the dumpling dough from my Chicken 'n' Dumplings Soup (page 173) recipe instead.

To make the crust, combine the almond flour, arrowroot, eggs, cold water, baking powder, and salt in a food processor and pulse 4 or 5 times, until combined. Add the palm shortening in spoonfuls spaced out evenly around the bowl. Pulse 4 or 5 times more, just until the shortening is incorporated and you have pea-size bits of dough. Using your hands, form the dough into a ball, cover it tightly with plastic wrap, and chill it in the freezer for no longer than 30 minutes.

To make the filling, melt 2 tablespoons of the ghee in a 10-inch cast-iron skillet over medium-high heat. Season the chicken generously with salt and pepper. Add the chicken to the skillet and brown the pieces really well on both sides, 8 to 10 minutes total. Add the onions and sauté for 3 to 4 minutes, until they are browned. Pour in the bone broth and bring to a boil. Turn the heat to medium-low and simmer for 15 minutes, flipping the chicken pieces once, until the chicken is mostly cooked through.

Using tongs, transfer the chicken breasts to a plate and let them cool. Simmer the broth for 15 minutes more, until reduced to about 3 cups. Pour the broth and onion mixture into a blender and add the arrowroot. Blend on medium-high speed for 15 to 30 seconds, until smooth. (Remove the cap in the blender top and place a kitchen towel over the top to allow steam from the hot liquid to release while you blend.)

CONTINUED

CRUST

2½ cups blanched almond flour

1 cup arrowroot powder

2 eggs, cold

3 tablespoons cold water

1 teaspoon Grain-Free Baking Powder (page 312)

¾ teaspoon fine sea salt

¼ cup cold palm shortening

1 egg yolk, mixed with 1 tablespoon full-fat coconut milk, for wash

FILLING

4 tablespoons ghee or duck fat

2 pounds chicken breasts, bone-in and skin-on

Fine sea salt and freshly ground black pepper

2 small yellow onions, cut into thick slices

5 cups Chicken Bone Broth (page 310)

1½ tablespoons arrowroot powder

2 cups diced carrots, cut into ¼-inch cubes

Return the skillet to medium-high heat and melt the remaining 2 tablespoons ghee. Add the carrots, potato, celery, and garlic and cook for 5 to 7 minutes, until the vegetables are crisp-tender. Debone the chicken, remove and discard the skin, and cut the chicken into 1-inch cubes. Add the chicken, sauce, parsley, and thyme to the skillet and bring to a boil, then turn the heat to low and simmer for 5 minutes, until the sauce has thickened and coats the back of a spoon. Season with salt and pepper to taste, then remove the pan from the heat.

Preheat the oven to 350°F.

Roll out the dough between two sheets of parchment paper into a 12-inch circle that's ⅛ inch thick. Remove the parchment. Using the rolling pin, carefully lay the dough over the filling in the skillet, tucking the excess edges inside the pan. Cut a small X shape with a knife on the top of the dough for venting. Brush the dough with the egg wash, then bake for 40 minutes, until the crust is golden and the filling is bubbling. Let the pie rest on a wire rack for 15 minutes, then serve.

Make It Ahead: **Prepare the filling and crust dough and store separately, tightly covered, in the refrigerator for 2 days. Or assemble the potpie, without the egg wash, in a ceramic pie pan, cover it tightly with plastic wrap, and freeze, unbaked, for 4 months. Remove the potpie from the freezer 30 minutes before baking. Brush the top with the egg wash, then cover the edges of the dough with a silicone pie shield or foil. Bake at 375°F for 30 minutes. Remove the foil and bake for 15 to 20 minutes more, until the crust is golden brown and the filling is bubbling.**

1 cup peeled and diced sweet potato (preferably Hannah or another white-fleshed variety), cut into ½-inch cubes

¾ cup diced celery, cut into ¼-inch cubes

2 cloves garlic, minced

¼ cup chopped fresh flat-leaf parsley

2 teaspoons fresh thyme leaves

CHICKEN DIVAN

Serves 6 to 8 • This chicken casserole with broccoli and a cheesy sauce was on regular rotation in my childhood home. As a kid, I thought this dish was called "Chicken *Divine*," until my mom gave me a copy of her mom's recipe card for my wedding and I realized my mistake. The original recipe is rich—calling for mayonnaise, canned cream soup, cheese, *and* sour cream—so while my rendition still feels divinely indulgent, it is a much lighter completely dairy-free version.

2 pounds chicken breasts, bone-in and skin-on (see Tidbits)

3 tablespoons extra-virgin olive oil

Fine sea salt and freshly ground black pepper

8 ounces Plantain Chips (page 98; see Tidbits)

2 tablespoons nutritional yeast (see Tidbits)

3 cups chopped broccoli

1¼ cups Condensed Cream of Mushroom Soup (page 271)

¾ cup Mayonnaise (page 314)

½ cup plus 2 tablespoons Cashew Milk (page 310)

1 teaspoon freshly squeezed lemon juice

Make It Ahead: Assemble the casserole minus the plantain topping. Cover it tightly with plastic wrap and freeze for 4 months. Defrost in the fridge overnight, then add the topping and bake as directed.

Preheat the oven to 400°F. Place the chicken breasts on a large rimmed baking sheet, drizzle with the oil, and season generously with salt and pepper. Roast for 20 for 25 minutes, until a thermometer inserted into the thickest part of the chicken reads 165°F. Remove the chicken from the oven and let it cool. Keep the oven on.

Meanwhile, pulse the plantain chips in a food processor until they have the texture of coarse sand. Add the nutritional yeast and ¼ teaspoon salt and pulse until combined.

Remove the chicken from the bones, reserving the bones for Chicken Bone Broth (page 310) and discarding the skin. Cut the chicken into thin strips. Lightly grease the bottom of a 9 by 13-inch casserole dish and place the chicken and broccoli in the bottom.

In a large bowl, combine the soup, mayonnaise, cashew milk, lemon juice, ½ teaspoon salt, and ¼ teaspoon pepper. Pour the soup mixture over the chicken and top with the plantain chip mixture. Bake the casserole for 20 minutes, until it's hot in the center and the sauce is bubbling. Serve immediately.

Tidbits: Skip a step and purchase an organic rotisserie chicken, or use 3 cups sliced Pressure Cooker Chicken (page 315) in place of the roasted chicken.

The nutritional yeast in the topping gives the sauce its cheesy flavor. If you tolerate dairy, replace the yeast with 2 tablespoons raw grass-fed Cheddar.

To comply with SCD, substitute coarsely ground almond meal for the plantain chips.

MINI CORN DOGS

Makes 24 • We always had packaged corn dogs from the Schwan's truck (along with bagel bites and mini pizzas) in the freezer growing up. When I first created these grain-free corn dogs, my sister and I sat at the table reminiscing about our childhood while we devoured the whole batch. I also created a nut-free version on my blog for those with nut allergies, but this almond-flour version is a little tastier and a lot crunchier. You will need 24 lollipop sticks for these; pick some up at your local craft store or order them online.

Line a rimmed baking sheet with paper towels and place a wire rack on top.

In a bowl, whisk together the almond flour, arrowroot, baking powder, and salt. Add the eggs, almond milk, honey, ghee, and vinegar and stir until just combined and smooth. Pour the batter into a jar and refrigerate until well chilled, about 2 hours.

Heat the palm shortening in a deep pot over medium-high heat until it reaches 350°F, then lower the heat slightly to maintain a constant temperature. The shortening should be about 4 inches deep in the pot.

Pat the hot dogs dry with a kitchen towel, then skewer one end of each one with a lollipop stick. Holding the end of the stick, dip a hot dog into the chilled batter to completely cover the hot dog. Carefully place the battered hot dog in the oil while turning the stick gently, then drop it entirely into the oil. Fry each corn dog until golden brown, 2 to 3 minutes. Repeat with the remaining hot dogs, working in batches to maintain an even heat and avoid crowding.

Using tongs, transfer the corn dogs to the wire rack to drain and cool for 10 minutes. Serve warm with ketchup and mustard.

Make It Ahead: Freeze the corn dogs in a single layer on a rimmed baking sheet, tightly covered with plastic wrap, for 4 hours. Place the frozen corn dogs in an airtight container and freeze for 4 months. Reheat on a baking sheet in a 400°F oven for 15 to 20 minutes, flipping once halfway through baking, until warmed through.

1½ cups blanched almond flour

½ cup arrowroot powder

1 teaspoon Grain-Free Baking Powder (page 312)

½ teaspoon fine sea salt

2 eggs, beaten

½ cup Almond Milk (page 308)

2 tablespoons light-colored raw honey

2 tablespoons melted ghee, unsalted grass-fed butter, or olive oil

1 teaspoon apple cider vinegar

4 cups palm shortening, avocado oil, or beef tallow, for frying

12 all-beef hot dogs, cut in half crosswise

Ketchup (page 313) and mustard, for serving (optional)

Tidbits: To reuse your frying oil, see Tidbits on page 127.

FISH STICKS WITH FRIES AND TARTAR SAUCE

Makes 12 • Whether you have a child who enjoys fish sticks, or you're an adult who loves fish and chips, this dish is for you. Prepare these fish sticks and fries and keep them in the freezer to have a delicious meal ready in minutes. While traditional breading for fish sticks includes either white flour or cornmeal, I finely grind plantain chips into a breading of sorts, which gives these a nice crunch and flavor.

TARTAR SAUCE

½ cup Mayonnaise (page 314)

1 tablespoon minced cornichons

1 tablespoon chopped capers

1 teaspoon champagne vinegar

1 teaspoon freshly squeezed lemon juice

1 teaspoon coarse-grain mustard

1 teaspoon chopped fresh flat-leaf parsley

⅛ teaspoon freshly ground black pepper

FRIES

1 large parsnip, peeled

1 white-fleshed sweet potato (such as Hannah), scrubbed but unpeeled

3 tablespoons avocado oil

Kosher salt

FISH STICKS

1 pound haddock or cod fillets

4 ounces Plantain Chips (page 98)

Fine sea salt and freshly ground black pepper

2 egg whites, beaten until frothy

2 teaspoons Dijon mustard

Preheat the oven to 450°F.

To make the tartar sauce, in a small bowl, mix together the mayonnaise, cornichons, capers, vinegar, lemon juice, mustard, parsley, and pepper. Place in the refrigerator to chill while you make the fries and fish sticks, or for up to 3 days.

To make the fries, cut the parsnip and sweet potato into matchstick fries. In a bowl, toss the vegetables with the oil. Spread in a single layer—not touching—on a large rimmed baking sheet. Bake for 20 minutes, turning once during baking, until browned.

To make the fish sticks, meanwhile, cut the haddock into 3 by ½-inch strips. Place a wire rack on top of a clean kitchen towel and brush the rack lightly with avocado oil.

In a food processor, or using a mortar and pestle, pulse the plantain chips a few times until they resemble coarse sand. Pour the ground chips into a shallow bowl and combine with ½ teaspoon sea salt and ¼ teaspoon pepper. In a separate shallow bowl, whisk together the egg whites and mustard.

Pat the fish dry with paper towels and season generously with ¾ teaspoon sea salt and ¼ teaspoon pepper. One at a time, dip the fish strips into the egg mixture and shake gently, allowing any excess to drip back into the bowl, then dip the fish into the plantain chip mixture, turning to coat each strip and shaking off any excess. Place the fish strips on the prepared wire rack.

Remove the baking sheet from the oven and scoot the fries over to one side. Position the rack with the fish sticks on the baking sheet and return to the oven. Bake the fish and fries together for 10 to 12 minutes, until the fish is crisp and cooked through. Season the fries generously with kosher salt. Serve the fish sticks and fries immediately with the tartar sauce on the side.

Make It Ahead: Freeze the baked fish sticks and fries in a single layer on a rimmed baking sheet, tightly covered with plastic wrap, for 1 to 2 hours, until hard. Store the frozen fish sticks in an airtight container for 2 months, and the frozen fries in an airtight container for 4 months. Reheat on a baking sheet in a 450°F oven for 10 to 12 minutes, until heated through.

CHICKEN NUGGETS

Makes 96 • As a new mom, I fell into the trap of buying expensive gluten-free chicken nuggets, but they contained quite a few undesirable ingredients. Next I tried a few homemade recipes, but my picky toddler turned up his nose until I created this version. I knew we had a winner when there wasn't a single complaint at dinnertime! I use these as a fallback meal for the entire family when the day has been hectic, and I hide them from Ryan so he doesn't eat too many from my freezer stash. I also frequently pack them in a warmed thermos for lunches. These nuggets use a somewhat unconventional flour in an effort to keep them tree nut– and coconut-free. This recipe has been a huge reader favorite since I first published it on my blog a few years ago.

4 cups palm shortening, lard, or duck fat, for frying

2 cups garbanzo bean flour (see page 9)

¾ cup arrowroot powder

5 teaspoons fine sea salt

2 teaspoons Grain-Free Baking Powder (page 312)

4 eggs, beaten

2 cups sparkling water

2 pounds ground dark meat chicken

2 pounds ground white meat chicken

½ cup Chicken Bone Broth (page 310)

1 teaspoon dry mustard powder

1 teaspoon garlic powder

Ketchup (page 313), Herb Ranch Dressing (page 92), or BBQ Sauce (page 309), for dipping

Line a rimmed baking sheet with paper towels and place a wire rack on top.

Heat the palm shortening in a deep pot over medium-high heat until it reaches 350°F, then lower the heat slightly to maintain a constant temperature. The shortening should be about 2 inches deep in the pot.

In a wide, shallow dish, whisk together the garbanzo bean flour, arrowroot, 2 teaspoons of the salt, and the baking powder. Add the eggs and sparkling water and stir until just combined and smooth.

In a separate bowl, combine the 4 pounds ground chicken, the bone broth, the remaining 3 teaspoons salt, the mustard powder, and garlic powder and mix with your hands. Roll small portions of the meat mixture between your palms, or use a small cookie scoop to create a nugget shape, then dip the nuggets in the batter. Shake off any excess batter and use a mesh skimmer to gently lower six to eight nuggets into the hot oil at a time.

CONTINUED

Fry for 3 to 4 minutes, until the batter has puffed up and is golden brown, then flip and fry for 3 to 4 minutes more, until golden brown. Transfer the nuggets to the wire rack in a single layer to drain and cool for 10 minutes. Serve warm with your sauce of choice for dipping.

Make It Ahead: Freeze the nuggets in a single layer on a rimmed baking sheet, tightly covered with plastic wrap, for 4 hours. Place the frozen nuggets in an airtight container and freeze for 4 months. Reheat on a baking sheet in a 400°F oven for 15 minutes, flipping once halfway through baking, until warmed through.

Tidbits: This batter also works well for fish, or even tempura veggies.

I used to make only two dozen nuggets at a time, but my family goes through these so quickly that now I make this huge batch once every few months to cut down on the mess.

To reuse your frying oil, see Tidbits on page 127.

To make this NSF, serve with the Herb Ranch Dressing.

PIZZA CRUSTS

Makes 2 thin 10-inch crusts • Frozen pizzas still have a place in a grain-free kitchen. I pull them out for Pizza Fridays, as a backup meal when the kids are melting down, or as an easy heat-and-serve dinner for the babysitter. I've seen a couple of grain-free crusts on the market, but they're pretty pricey and I have yet to find one I really like. There's a pizza crust recipe in all of my cookbooks, but it's a recipe I continue to refine. For this book, I wanted to create a crust that would be the end-all, so while I don't regularly bake much with active dry yeast, I included it here to give this crust the most authentic taste possible. Whenever I'm planning a pizza night, I often prepare extra crusts and sauce. I bake a few pizzas right away for dinner and freeze the rest for later meals. I give you a few options for toppings, but feel free to use whatever you like. Double or triple this recipe to really stock up.

Pour the coconut milk into a small saucepan and warm it over low heat to 110°F.

In a bowl, combine the warmed coconut milk, flaxseeds, yeast, and honey. Let the mixture sit for 4 to 5 minutes, until it begins to foam. Whisk in the eggs, oil, and vinegar. Add the arrowroot, coconut flour, baking powder, and salt and whisk again, until fully incorporated with no visible lumps. Cover the bowl with a kitchen towel and let it sit for 1 hour at room temperature.

Preheat the oven to 500°F and have a pizza stone ready. (If your stone is prone to sticking, place a piece of parchment paper on top or lightly grease it with olive oil.)

Scoop half of the dough onto the prepared stone and use an offset spatula to evenly spread it into a thin 10-inch circle; the outer edge of the dough can be slightly thicker. If any air bubbles or holes appear, just smooth it with the spatula. Bake for 6 minutes, until the crust is crispy and golden brown around the edges. (For a very crisp crust, remove the crust from the stone after 6 minutes, place it directly on the oven rack, and bake for 2 minutes more.) Transfer the crust to a wire rack to cool. Repeat with the remaining dough.

CONTINUED

½ cup full-fat coconut milk

2 tablespoons finely ground golden flaxseeds

5 teaspoons gluten-free active dry yeast (see Tidbits)

1 tablespoon light-colored raw honey

4 eggs

¼ cup extra-virgin olive oil

1 teaspoon apple cider vinegar

1½ cups arrowroot powder

½ cup coconut flour

1½ teaspoons Grain-Free Baking Powder (page 312)

1 teaspoon fine sea salt

Toppings of your choice (ideas follow)

Make It Ahead: Parbake the crusts for 5 minutes, until puffy and dry on the top but still pale. Let cool completely on a wire rack, then top as desired (or freeze the crusts with no toppings). Place the pizzas on a baking sheet and freeze, uncovered, until solid, about 3 hours. Cover the frozen pizzas tightly with plastic wrap, then aluminum foil, and store in the freezer for 3 months. Reheat on a preheated pizza stone, or for a crispier crust bake directly on the oven rack, in a 500°F oven for 8 to 10 minutes, until the crust is golden brown and the toppings are bubbly.

Tidbits: Can't tolerate yeast? Each of my cookbooks has a different pizza crust recipe, one of which may better suit you, or just go ahead and leave the yeast out of this recipe. The crust will have a different flavor and be a bit more dense.

TOPPING IDEAS

Top the cooled crusts with your favorite toppings, then bake directly on the oven rack for 5 minutes, until the toppings are bubbling.

CARNIVORE: ½ cup pizza sauce, 1 teaspoon dried oregano, 4 slices crumbled cooked bacon, 2 ounces salami, 2 ounces cooked mild Italian sausage, 2 ounces chopped ham, and ½ cup Ricotta Cheese (page 316) and ¼ cup Parmesan Cheese (page 315) or 6 ounces mozzarella and ⅓ cup Parmesan Cheese.

PINEAPPLE EXPRESS: ½ cup pizza sauce, 1 teaspoon dried oregano, 3 ounces chopped ham, ¼ cup diced fresh pineapple, ¼ cup diced red bell pepper, and ½ cup Ricotta Cheese (page 316) and ¼ cup Parmesan Cheese (page 315) or 6 ounces mozzarella and ⅓ cup Parmesan Cheese.

BARBECUE CHICKEN: ½ cup BBQ Sauce (page 309), 1 teaspoon dried oregano, ½ cup diced Pressure Cooker Chicken (page 315), ¼ cup thinly sliced red onion, 2 slices chopped cooked bacon, 2 tablespoons fresh cilantro leaves, and ½ cup goat's milk Gouda cheese (optional).

GARLIC NAAN

Makes 12 • Ryan can't eat Indian food without a warm piece of naan (Indian flatbread) to soak up the creamy sauces, so I keep this on hand in the freezer for when I make Indian Butter Chicken (page 203) or we order takeout. These flatbreads are crispy on the outside and have a delicious chewy interior, and the buttery-garlic flavor is just divine.

1 cup full-fat coconut milk, warmed

8 egg whites

½ cup extra-virgin olive oil

2 teaspoons apple cider vinegar

¼ cup finely ground golden flaxseeds

3 cups arrowroot powder

¾ cup coconut flour

1 tablespoon Grain-Free Baking Powder (page 312)

2 teaspoons fine sea salt

4 cloves garlic, minced

¼ cup melted ghee

Preheat the oven to 500°F and place two baking sheets inside.

Place the coconut milk, egg whites, oil, vinegar, and flaxseeds in a blender. Pulse a few times to combine, then let the mixture sit for 2 minutes. Add the arrowroot, coconut flour, baking powder, and salt and blend on high speed until smooth, about 15 seconds. Use a spatula to scrape down the sides, then let the batter rest for 1 minute. Blend again on high speed for 10 seconds.

Carefully remove the hot baking sheets from the oven and place a piece of parchment paper on top of each one. Pour about 3 tablespoons of batter onto the parchment like a pancake, and use a rubber spatula to spread the batter into a thin 4-inch-long oval. Repeat to make three flatbreads on each baking sheet. Sprinkle the tops with garlic and bake for 4 minutes, until the breads are puffed up and golden brown. Flip them over and bake for 4 minutes more. Remove the flatbreads from the oven, brush with the melted ghee, and serve immediately. Repeat with the remaining batter.

Make It Ahead: Let the flatbreads cool completely on a wire rack. Place a piece of parchment paper between each flatbread to prevent sticking, then stack and cover tightly with plastic wrap. Store in an airtight container in the freezer for 6 months. Reheat directly on the oven rack at 400°F for 10 to 12 minutes, until heated through.

CONDENSED CREAM OF MUSHROOM SOUP

Makes 2 "cans," or about 2½ cups • The canned varieties of this soup not only contain dairy, but also additives like MSG, cornstarch, sugar, vegetable oils, wheat, modified food starch, and soy. Keep a few batches of this version in the freezer so throwing together a casserole is as easy as popping open a can, only much healthier. Try it in some of my hot dishes, like Poppy Seed Chicken (page 247) or Chicken Divan (page 256), or use it in your favorite tuna noodle or King Ranch casseroles.

Bring a kettle of water to a boil. Place the cashews in a bowl and add enough boiling water to cover. Soak for 30 minutes.

Meanwhile, melt the ghee in a skillet over medium-high heat. Add the shallots and sauté for 2 to 3 minutes, until fragrant. Add the mushrooms and garlic and cook for 5 to 7 minutes, until the shallots and mushrooms are softened.

Drain the cashews and place them in a blender with the bone broth, sherry, and lemon juice. Blend on high speed for 30 seconds, until very smooth. Scrape down the sides if necessary, then add the mushroom mixture and the salt, pepper, and a pinch of nutmeg. Blend on low speed for 15 seconds, until the mixture is creamy. Transfer the soup back to the skillet over low heat. Simmer gently for 5 minutes, until thickened into a paste.

Use immediately in a recipe, or cool the soup completely, then divide it among two clean 12-ounce jars and store them in the fridge for 1 week, or in the freezer for 6 months. Defrost the soup in the fridge for 24 hours before using.

Variations: To make condensed cream of chicken soup, substitute 6 ounces chopped cooked chicken breasts and thighs for the mushrooms. Add the chicken to the blender just before pureeing.

To eat as a bowl of soup, reconstitute the condensed soup by combining one jar with 1 cup Almond Milk (page 308) and ½ cup Chicken Bone Broth.

1 cup (about 150g) whole raw cashews (see Tidbits, page 310)

½ cup ghee or extra-virgin olive oil

2 shallots, diced (about ½ cup)

12 ounces cremini mushrooms, coarsely chopped

3 cloves garlic, minced

½ cup Chicken Bone Broth (page 310)

¼ cup dry sherry (see Tidbits)

1 teaspoon freshly squeezed lemon juice

1½ teaspoons fine sea salt

¼ teaspoon freshly ground black pepper

Ground nutmeg

Tidbits: Don't have sherry? Use ¼ cup dry white wine or dry vermouth plus ½ teaspoon apple cider vinegar instead.

If you tolerate dairy, Pacific Foods makes an organic condensed mushroom soup that has a relatively clean ingredient list.

CHAPTER 8

SWEETS AND TREATS

COWBOY COOKIES

Makes 12 • These loaded chocolate chip cookies were first featured in *Family Circle* magazine in 2000, the winning recipe in a bake-off between the wives of that year's presidential candidates. This grain-free, dairy-free rendition of Laura Bush's Texas-born cookies has become a winner in our home too. Crispy on the outside with a chewy center, these cookies are made heartier with the addition of toasted coconut flakes, pecans, and a punch of cinnamon.

3 tablespoons boiling water

1 tablespoon finely ground golden flaxseeds (see Tidbits)

½ cup unsweetened coconut flakes

½ cup palm shortening or unsalted grass-fed butter

⅓ cup light-colored raw honey

¼ cup coconut sugar

1 teaspoon pure vanilla extract

1 cup blanched almond flour

¼ cup arrowroot powder

3½ tablespoons coconut flour

2 teaspoons ground cinnamon

¾ teaspoon Grain-Free Baking Powder (page 312)

½ teaspoon baking soda

½ teaspoon fine sea salt

¼ cup chopped dark chocolate (80 percent cacao)

¼ cup dairy-free and soy-free semisweet chocolate chips

¼ cup chopped pecans

Preheat the oven to 350°F and line two baking sheets with parchment paper. In a small bowl, whisk together the boiling water and the flaxseeds; set aside to thicken and cool.

Place the coconut flakes on one of the prepared baking sheets and toast in the oven for 2 minutes, until golden. Set aside to cool. Reline the baking sheet with parchment paper.

In the bowl of a stand mixer fitted with the beater attachment, or using an electric handheld mixer, beat the palm shortening on medium speed for 1 minute, until creamy. Add the flaxseed mixture, the honey, coconut sugar, and vanilla and beat on medium speed for 1 minute, until fluffy. Add the almond flour, arrowroot, coconut flour, cinnamon, baking powder, baking soda, and salt and beat for 1 minute on medium speed, until combined. Add the toasted coconut flakes, dark chocolate, chocolate chips, and pecans and beat on low, just until incorporated.

Form twelve golf ball–size balls of dough and drop them onto the two baking sheets. Space them evenly, as the cookies will spread. Bake one sheet at a time for 10 to 12 minutes, rotating the sheet halfway through baking, until the edges of the cookies are golden brown. Cool the cookies on the sheets for 10 minutes, then transfer them to a wire rack to cool completely.

Store the cooled cookies in an airtight container in the refrigerator for 2 weeks, or in the freezer for 6 months.

Tidbits: Use a clean coffee grinder to finely grind the golden flaxseeds if you're unable to find them preground.

NILLA COOKIES

Makes 32 • You cannot have Banana Pudding (page 303) without Nilla Wafers, those delicious round vanilla cookies that come in a box with the pudding recipe printed on the back. Whether I serve this grain-free version with pudding or as a snack on its own, these vanilla-packed crispy cookies are gone in no time in our house. You might also try sandwiching Chocolate Hazelnut Spread (page 307) between two of these cookies, for a delicious treat.

Preheat the oven to 350°F and line two baking sheets with parchment paper.

In the bowl of a stand mixer fitted with the beater attachment, or using an electric handheld mixer, beat the egg whites, palm shortening, and vanilla on medium speed for 30 seconds, until frothy. Add the maple sugar, arrowroot, coconut flour, baking powder, and salt. Beat on medium speed for 15 seconds to combine, then on high for 15 seconds more, until the dough is fluffy.

Using a teaspoon, scoop out the dough and roll it into small balls the size of gumballs. Space the balls 2 inches apart on the prepared baking sheets and press down gently on the tops to flatten them slightly.

Bake one sheet at a time for 8 to 10 minutes, rotating the sheet halfway through baking, until the cookies are golden brown. Transfer the cookies to a wire rack to cool completely.

Store the cooled cookies in an airtight container in the refrigerator for 2 weeks, or in the freezer for 6 months.

2 egg whites, chilled

¼ cup palm shortening

1 tablespoon pure vanilla extract

½ cup plus 2 tablespoons maple sugar

½ cup arrowroot powder

5½ tablespoons coconut flour

½ teaspoon Grain-Free Baking Powder (page 312)

¼ teaspoon fine sea salt

SNICKERDOODLES

Makes 24 • I've always been partial to a buttery-soft snickerdoodle, with its cracked and crispy surface and cinnamony flavor. Traditionally, a snickerdoodle is a sugar cookie rolled in cinnamon and sugar, but in this version I add more cinnamon to the dough for an extra-spicy punch. These are deliciously thin and chewy, with a crispy edge.

4½ tablespoons maple sugar (see Tidbits)

5 teaspoons ground cinnamon

1¼ cups cashew flour

3 tablespoons coconut flour

2 tablespoons arrowroot powder

¾ teaspoon cream of tartar

½ teaspoon baking soda

⅛ teaspoon fine sea salt

¼ cup pure maple syrup

¼ cup palm shortening

1 teaspoon pure vanilla extract

Preheat the oven to 350°F and line two baking sheets with parchment paper.

In a small bowl, combine 1½ tablespoons of the maple sugar and 3 teaspoons of the cinnamon and set aside.

In a food processor, combine the remaining 3 tablespoons maple sugar, the cashew flour, coconut flour, arrowroot, the remaining 2 teaspoons cinnamon, the cream of tartar, baking soda, and salt and pulse 5 times. Add the maple syrup, palm shortening, and vanilla and process for 15 seconds, until combined. Transfer the processor bowl to the fridge and chill the dough for 1 hour.

Using a tablespoon, scoop out the dough and roll it into balls, then roll the balls in the cinnamon sugar to coat. Place on the prepared baking sheets, spacing them evenly to allow for spreading.

Bake one sheet at a time for 10 to 12 minutes, rotating the sheet halfway through baking, until the cookies are golden brown around the edges. Cool the cookies on the sheets for 10 minutes, then transfer them to a wire rack to cool completely.

Store the cooled cookies in an airtight container in the refrigerator for 2 weeks, or in the freezer for 6 months.

Tidbits: Coconut sugar may be substituted for the maple sugar; however, the cookies will be darker in color and have a different flavor.

MINT SLIMS

Makes 24 • I was never a Girl Scout, but I sure did enjoy their cookies growing up. My family could never say no to ordering a few boxes, and the Thin Mints were always my first choice. My favorite way to eat them was straight out of the freezer, when they were cold and extra crunchy. My version dips a crisp, egg-free chocolate cookie in a mint-chocolate glaze. I guarantee that these will disappear just as quickly from the freezer.

In the bowl of a stand mixer fitted with the beater attachment, or using a food processor, combine the almond flour, coconut flour, cocoa powder, baking soda, salt, and maple sugar and mix thoroughly on medium speed.

In a saucepan, combine the honey, coconut oil, chocolate, and peppermint extract and cook over low heat, stirring until melted. Pour the melted chocolate mixture into the dry ingredients and beat on medium speed until fully combined.

Using your hands, pack the dough firmly into two balls, then flatten each into a thick disk. Roll each disk into a ¼-inch-thick circle on a piece of parchment paper. Stack the pieces (with parchment paper in between) on a baking sheet and refrigerate for at least 1 hour, or up to 2 days. (If chilling for more than 2 hours, cover the top piece of dough with another piece of parchment paper.)

When you're ready to bake the cookies, preheat the oven to 350°F and line two or three baking sheets with parchment paper or silicone baking mats.

Remove one of the dough pieces from the refrigerator. Use a 2-inch-round cookie cutter to cut out circles and place them on a prepared baking sheet. Repeat with the remaining dough, rerolling and cutting circles until all the dough is used.

2 cups blanched almond flour

2 tablespoons coconut flour

½ cup unsweetened cocoa powder

½ teaspoon baking soda

¼ teaspoon fine sea salt

¼ cup maple sugar

¼ cup light-colored raw honey

¼ cup expeller-pressed coconut oil

2 ounces unsweetened chocolate, chopped

½ teaspoon pure peppermint extract

COATING

10 ounces dairy-free and soy-free semisweet chocolate chips

¾ teaspoon expeller-pressed coconut oil

¼ teaspoon pure peppermint extract

CONTINUED

Bake one sheet at a time for 8 minutes, rotating the sheet halfway through baking. Cool the cookies on the sheets for 5 minutes, then transfer them to a wire rack to cool completely.

To make the coating, melt the chocolate chips and oil together in a double boiler or a heatproof bowl set over a saucepan filled with about 1 inch of boiling water. Stir the mixture frequently until the chocolate melts. Stir the peppermint extract into the melted chocolate. Turn off the heat and remove the bowl from the pan.

Dip each cooled cookie completely into the melted chocolate and use a fork to lift it out. Tap the fork gently on the side of the bowl to allow any excess chocolate to drip off. Place the dipped cookies on the prepared baking sheets, then refrigerate the cookies for 1 hour to help the chocolate set. Serve chilled.

Store the cookies in an airtight container in the refrigerator for 2 weeks, or in the freezer for 6 months. Eat straightaway; or, if you prefer, defrost in the fridge overnight.

RICOTTA CHEESECAKE
WITH BLUEBERRY SAUCE

Serves 10 to 12 • Cheesecake was Ryan's favorite dessert when we were dating in high school and college. He will still order it occasionally, and just pick around the crust. To achieve that distinctive flavor of cream cheese and cultured sour cream, I use my own cultured, almond-based ricotta cheese and coconut milk–based sour cream. The probiotics in both of these recipes, in addition to a little apple cider vinegar and lemon zest, give this version a similar zing without the cheese. For a shortcut, buy two containers of Kite Hill ricotta instead of making your own.

To make the crust, preheat the oven to 350°F and cut a circle of parchment paper to fit the bottom of a 9-inch springform pan.

In a small bowl, combine the almond flour, coconut flour, cinnamon, baking soda, and salt. In the bowl of a stand mixer fitted with the beater attachment, or using an electric handheld mixer, beat the oil, honey, egg, and vanilla on medium speed until combined. Add the dry ingredients and beat on high speed until combined.

Remove the parchment from the pan and press the dough evenly into the bottom. Lay the parchment on top of the dough and place pie weights or dried beans on top. Bake the crust for 10 minutes, until golden brown. Transfer the pan to a wire rack to cool; keep the oven on.

To make the filling, place the ricotta cheese, almond flour, and maple sugar in a blender and blend on high speed for 30 seconds, until very smooth. Add the eggs, sour cream, honey, lemon zest and juice, vinegar, vanilla, and salt and blend on low speed for 5 seconds, until well incorporated. Pour the filling into the cooled crust and smooth the top with a spatula.

CRUST

¼ cup blanched almond flour

½ cup plus 2 tablespoons coconut flour

½ teaspoon ground cinnamon

¼ teaspoon baking soda

¼ teaspoon fine sea salt

¼ cup expeller-pressed coconut oil, at room temperature

¼ cup light-colored raw honey

1 egg

1 teaspoon pure vanilla extract

FILLING

2 cups Ricotta Cheese (page 316), or any store-bought dairy-free ricotta

6 tablespoons blanched almond flour

1 cup maple sugar (see Tidbits)

4 eggs

CONTINUED

1 cup Dairy-Free Sour Cream (page 311), or any store-bought dairy-free sour cream (see Tidbits)

¼ cup light-colored raw honey

1 teaspoon finely grated lemon zest

¼ teaspoon freshly squeezed lemon juice

½ teaspoon apple cider vinegar

½ teaspoon pure vanilla extract

¼ teaspoon fine sea salt

BLUEBERRY SAUCE

1 pint (12 ounces) fresh blueberries

2 tablespoons pure maple syrup

¾ teaspoon freshly squeezed lemon juice

Fill a saucepan with 10 cups water and bring to a boil over high heat. Set the springform pan on a large piece of aluminum foil and fold up the sides around the pan. Place the pan in a large roasting pan and add enough boiling water to come about halfway up the sides of the springform pan.

Bake the cheesecake for 40 minutes, until the filling is set but still jiggles in the center. Turn the oven off and let the cake cool in the oven with the door closed for 2 hours; this prevents cracking. Transfer the cake to the fridge to chill for 4 hours before serving.

To make the blueberry sauce, place the blueberries, ¼ cup water, the maple syrup, and lemon juice in a saucepan over medium-high heat. Bring to a boil, then turn the heat to low and simmer for 15 minutes. Remove the pan from the heat and use an immersion blender to blend the sauce slightly, or use a fork to crush some of the berries. Pour the sauce into a bowl and chill it in the fridge until ready to serve.

Loosen the cheesecake from the sides of the pan by running a thin metal spatula around the inside rim. Remove the sides of the pan and transfer the base to a cake plate. Using a spatula, spread a thin layer of the blueberry sauce over the top of the cake. Slice the cheesecake with a thin, nonserrated knife that has been dipped in hot water. Wipe the knife clean after each cut. Serve with extra blueberry sauce on the side.

Tidbits: To comply with SCD, substitute honey for the maple sugar.

If you don't have time to make the sour cream, a good alternative is 1 cup chilled coconut cream mixed with ½ teaspoon freshly squeezed lime juice and ¼ teaspoon fine sea salt. You lose a bit of the cultured "cheese" flavor, but the texture is the same.

APPLE CRISP

Serves 8 to 10 • It seems that most people either like fruit crisps or fruit cobblers, but not both. A crisp has a streusel-like topping, while a cobbler has more of a biscuit top. I am partial to crisps because that's what my grandmother made and I like the crunchy topping. Traditionally, toppings have oats or a flour-sugar mixture, but mine gets a nice crunch from a mix of cashew flour and arrowroot. This is amazing with a spoonful of whipped cream or some store-bought dairy-free vanilla ice cream. If you're a cobbler person, check out my peach cobbler recipe in *Celebrations*.

Preheat the oven to 350°F.

In a large bowl, mix together the cashew flour, coconut flour, arrowroot, maple sugar, coconut sugar, and salt. Mix the ghee into the flour mixture using a pastry blender or two knives, until the mixture has the texture of coarse sand. Add the shredded coconut, and use your hands to toss and squeeze the mixture until large, moist clumps form. Place the bowl in the freezer to chill while you prepare the filling.

Peel and core the apples, then cut them into large wedges. In a 2-quart baking dish, combine the apples with the orange zest, lemon zest, lemon juice, maple syrup, cinnamon, nutmeg, and allspice. Remove the topping from the freezer and scatter it over the apples. Place the baking dish on a baking sheet and bake for 1 hour, until the top is brown and the sauce is bubbling. Serve warm with whipped cream on top.

Tidbits: Pull out your granny's old apple coring and peeling contraption to cut down on prep time.

¾ cup cashew flour

¼ cup coconut flour

3 tablespoons arrowroot powder

¼ cup maple sugar

¼ cup coconut sugar

¼ teaspoon fine sea salt

½ cup chilled ghee, or palm shortening

½ cup shredded unsweetened coconut

3 pounds baking apples (such as McIntosh, Empire, Gala, or Braeburn; see Tidbits)

Finely grated zest of 1 orange

Finely grated zest of 1 lemon

1 teaspoon freshly squeezed lemon juice

¼ cup pure maple syrup

1 teaspoon ground cinnamon

½ teaspoon ground nutmeg

¼ teaspoon ground allspice

Whipped Cream (page 93), for serving (optional)

PINEAPPLE UPSIDE-DOWN CAKE

Serves 8 to 10 • My Grandma Marge makes a pineapple upside-down cake for my grandpa's birthday every year. She says it will always be his favorite cake; she has been making it for him in the same cast-iron skillet for more than sixty years. I brought them both a slice of this version to taste, and it passed my grandpa's test. I hope you love it too. The maraschino cherries need to be made a day in advance, but you could use fresh cherries instead. The cake will just have a slightly more sour flavor.

MARASCHINO CHERRIES

¼ cup pomegranate juice

¼ cup light-colored raw honey

Fine sea salt

1 star anise

Finely grated zest of
1 small orange

8 ounces pitted fresh cherries

2 tablespoons freshly squeezed
lemon juice

2 teaspoons pure
almond extract

1½ tablespoons melted ghee

2 tablespoons maple sugar

1 tablespoon coconut sugar

1 (15-ounce) can pineapple
slices, juice reserved

5 egg whites, at room
temperature

¼ cup palm shortening

To make the maraschino cherries, in a saucepan over medium-high heat, combine the pomegranate juice, ¼ cup water, the honey, and a pinch of salt. Bring to a boil, then turn the heat to low and simmer for 10 minutes, stirring occasionally. Add the star anise and orange zest and continue to simmer for 10 minutes more. Remove the pan from the heat and pour the contents into a large clean jar with a lid. Let the mixture cool to room temperature. Add the cherries, lemon juice, and almond extract and push down the cherries to submerge them completely in the liquid. Secure the lid and refrigerate for 24 hours or up to 2 weeks.

Preheat the oven to 350°F.

Place the ghee in a 9-inch round cake pan. Sprinkle the maple sugar and coconut sugar evenly over the ghee and arrange the pineapple slices in a circular pattern on top of the sugars. Place a maraschino cherry in the center of each pineapple slice, pressing them gently into the sugar.

In the bowl of a stand mixer fitted with the whisk attachment, or using an electric handheld mixer, beat the egg whites on medium-high speed for 3 to 5 minutes, until they have tripled in volume and hold soft peaks when the whisk is pulled out. Scoop the whites into a bowl and set aside.

CONTINUED

¼ cup light-colored raw honey

¼ cup pure maple syrup

1 teaspoon pure vanilla extract

½ teaspoon freshly squeezed lemon juice

1½ cups blanched almond flour

⅓ cup arrowroot powder

3 tablespoons coconut flour

2 teaspoons ground cardamom

½ teaspoon baking soda

Return the bowl to the mixer and switch to the beater attachment. Beat together ¼ cup of the reserved pineapple juice, the palm shortening, honey, maple syrup, vanilla, and lemon juice on medium-high speed for 30 seconds. Add the almond flour, arrowroot, coconut flour, cardamom, and baking soda and beat for 30 seconds, until well incorporated. Gently fold in the beaten egg whites with a rubber spatula until they are fully incorporated and there are no visible ribbons of whites in the batter. Pour the batter over the pineapple slices and cherries and smooth the top gently with a spatula.

Bake for 35 minutes, until a toothpick inserted in the center of the cake comes out clean. Immediately run a knife around the edge of the pan to loosen the cake. Place a heatproof serving plate upside-down onto the pan, then flip the plate and pan over. Let the pan rest on top of the cake for 5 minutes so the sugar topping can drizzle down over the cake. Remove the pan and let the cake cool for 30 minutes more. Serve warm or chilled.

Store the cake, covered, in the refrigerator for 7 days.

KEY LIME PIE

Serves 8 to 10 • After I included a recipe for lemon meringue pie in my first cookbook, I received tons of requests for a Key lime pie. It took quite a few iterations to get the consistency right because the traditional pie gets its structure from sweetened condensed milk. I use coconut cream, egg yolks, and a little gelatin to create a similar texture, and tangy Key lime juice for an authentic flavor (see Tidbits). To top things off and balance the sour lime juice, I utilize the egg whites to make a sweet and billowy meringue.

To make the crust, preheat the oven to 350°F and cut a circle of parchment paper to fit the bottom of a 9-inch pie plate.

In a small bowl, combine the coconut flour, almond flour, baking soda, cinnamon, and salt. In the bowl of a stand mixer fitted with the beater attachment, or using an electric handheld mixer, beat the ghee, honey, egg, and vanilla on medium speed until combined. Add the dry ingredients and beat on medium speed until combined.

Remove the parchment paper from the pie plate and press the dough evenly into the bottom and up the sides of the plate. Lay the parchment on top of the dough and place pie weights or dried beans on top. Bake the crust for 10 minutes, until golden brown. Transfer the pan to a wire rack to cool; keep the oven on.

To make the filling, place the cashew milk in a saucepan and sprinkle the gelatin over the top. Set the pan aside for 5 minutes to allow the gelatin to soak up some of the moisture. Carefully remove the cans of coconut milk from the refrigerator and open the tops. Skim the thick coconut cream from the tops of the cans, until you have 1 cup cream. Discard the thin, cloudy coconut water at the bottom of the can or save it for a smoothie. In a large bowl, whisk together the coconut cream, honey, egg yolks, lime zest, lime juice, and salt.

CRUST

½ cup coconut flour

¼ cup blanched almond flour

¼ teaspoon baking soda

¼ teaspoon ground cinnamon

¼ teaspoon fine sea salt

¼ cup melted ghee

¼ cup light-colored raw honey

1 egg

1 teaspoon pure vanilla extract

FILLING

½ cup Cashew Milk (page 310)

1½ teaspoons unflavored powdered gelatin

2 (13.5-ounce) cans full-fat coconut milk, refrigerated upright for 24 hours

¾ cup light-colored raw honey

6 egg yolks

Finely grated zest of 1 Key lime

CONTINUED

Place the saucepan with the cashew milk and gelatin over medium-high heat. Whisk constantly until the gelatin has dissolved, about 10 seconds. Let the mixture heat for 2 to 3 minutes more, until it is steaming but not boiling. Slowly pour the hot gelatin mixture into the coconut cream mixture, whisking constantly to temper the eggs. Pour the filling into the cooled piecrust.

Bake the pie for 20 minutes. The filling will still be liquidy when removed from the oven. Let the pie cool to room temperature on a wire rack, then refrigerate it until firm, at least 6 hours or overnight.

To make the meringue topping, place the honey in a small saucepan and bring to a boil over medium-high heat. Boil for 2 minutes, then remove it from the heat. Place the egg whites in the bowl of a stand mixer fitted with the whisk attachment and beat on medium-high speed until soft peaks form, 3 to 4 minutes. Alternatively, use an electric handheld mixer to beat the whites.

With the mixer running, pour the boiling honey down the side of the bowl in a slow, steady stream. Add the lemon juice and a pinch of salt and continue beating for 8 to 10 minutes, until the meringue has cooled and doubled in volume.

Spread the meringue over the chilled pie and garnish with the lime zest. Cut into wedges and serve immediately.

Make It Ahead: The meringue is best enjoyed within a few hours, but the pie can be baked in advance and stored, tightly wrapped, in the refrigerator for 5 days. Prepare the meringue and top the pie just before serving.

Tidbits: If you cannot find Key limes, substitute ½ cup freshly squeezed lime juice and 2 tablespoons freshly squeezed lemon juice. Garnish with a bit of lime zest.

½ cup plus 2 tablespoons freshly squeezed Key lime juice (see Tidbits)

¼ teaspoon fine sea salt

MERINGUE TOPPING

⅓ cup light-colored raw honey

3 eggs whites

¼ teaspoon freshly squeezed lemon juice

Fine sea salt

Finely grated zest of 1 Key lime

STRAWBERRY BANANA YOGURT POPS

Makes 12 • When Easton was teething, he loved to suck on anything frozen to help ease the pain on his gums. I wanted to develop a frozen treat with no refined sweeteners and a few health benefits. Sweetened with fresh fruit and honey, and containing gut-friendly yogurt, these strawberry banana pops were the perfect solution. Everyone in the family *still* devours these.

1¼ cups Dairy-Free Yogurt (page 312; see Tidbits), or any store-bought dairy-free yogurt

15 large hulled strawberries, halved

2 ripe bananas, cut into chunks

½ teaspoon freshly squeezed lemon juice

Light-colored raw honey (optional; see Tidbits)

Place the yogurt, strawberries, bananas, and lemon juice in a blender and blend on high speed until smooth, about 1 minute. Scrape down the sides of the blender as needed. Taste and add up to 2 tablespoons honey if the mixture is too sour, then blend again on high speed until smooth.

Pour the mixture into twelve ice pop molds. If the molds have slots for sticks, insert the sticks before freezing. If not, freeze the mixture for 2 hours, put a wooden ice pop stick in the middle of each mold, then freeze for 6 hours more, or overnight. (The pops will be easier to remove if you freeze them overnight.)

Remove the pops from the molds by running the molds under warm water for 30 seconds.

Tidbits: To make this NF, substitute a nut-free dairy-free yogurt like one made from coconut milk.

If you're serving this to children under the age of one year, you may want to omit the honey.

CHOCOLATE "PICKLES" POPS

Makes 12 • No, this is not some weird snack I developed to satisfy a pregnancy craving. There are actually no pickles involved, but Asher referred to these fudge pops as chocolate "pickles" instead of "popsicles" for years. I didn't have the heart to correct him when he was little, so I just let it go and my heart melted every time he asked for one. (One day he ate a real sour pickle and realized the two were very different things!) These melt-in-your-mouth dark chocolate fudge pops taste nothing like a pickle, thankfully, and they're one of my favorite treats on a hot summer day. To make these extra special, dip them in chocolate and coat with sprinkles or chopped nuts.

Place ½ cup of the coconut milk in a glass bowl. Sprinkle the gelatin over the top and set it aside to bloom for 10 minutes.

Heat the remaining coconut milk, the maple syrup, cocoa powder, vanilla, and salt in a saucepan over medium-high heat for 5 minutes, whisking occasionally. Do not let it boil. Whisk the softened gelatin into the coconut milk mixture and continue whisking until the gelatin is fully dissolved, about 2 minutes. Pour the mixture through a fine-mesh sieve into a large glass measuring cup with a spout.

Pour the mixture into twelve ice pop molds. If the molds have slots for sticks, insert the sticks before freezing. If not, freeze the mixture for 2 hours, put a wooden ice pop stick in the middle of each mold, then freeze for 6 hours more, or overnight. (The pops will be easier to remove if you freeze them overnight.)

To make the chocolate coating, melt the chocolate chips and oil together in a double boiler or a heatproof bowl set over a saucepan filled with about 1 inch of boiling water. Stir the mixture frequently until the chocolate melts. Turn off the heat and remove the bowl from the pan.

Place your topping of choice in a shallow bowl. Remove the frozen pops from the molds by running the molds under warm water for 30 seconds. Dip the frozen pops into the melted chocolate, then roll the pops through the topping to coat. Place the coated pops on a baking sheet and return them to the freezer for 15 minutes to set before serving.

2 (13.5-ounce) cans full-fat coconut milk

4 teaspoons unflavored powdered gelatin

1 cup pure maple syrup

½ cup unsweetened cocoa powder

2 teaspoons pure vanilla extract

¼ teaspoon fine sea salt

CHOCOLATE COATING

10 ounces dairy-free and soy-free semisweet chocolate chips

¾ teaspoon expeller-pressed coconut oil

Chopped toasted hazelnuts, Rainbow Sprinkles (page 304), freeze-dried strawberries, or toasted shredded coconut, for topping (optional)

ROCKY ROAD ICE CREAM

Makes 4 cups • We are huge ice cream lovers in my family, which is why you will find a good number of dairy-free ice cream recipes in my first book, *Against All Grain*, as well as on my blog. This recipe is inspired by a Rocky Road bar, my favorite candy bar when I was growing up. My mom and I used to split one as a treat. If you're a chocolate ice cream purist, you can omit the mix-ins, but I highly suggest adding everything to get that beloved Rocky Road flavor.

2½ cups (about 370g) raw cashew pieces (see Tidbits, page 310)

1½ teaspoons unflavored powdered gelatin

1¼ cups pure maple syrup

1½ ounces unsweetened chocolate, chopped

½ cup unsweetened cocoa powder

1 teaspoon pure vanilla extract

¾ teaspoon freshly squeezed lemon juice

¼ teaspoon fine sea salt

½ cup natural marshmallows (see Tidbits), cut into bite-size pieces

¼ cup chopped dairy-free dark chocolate pieces

½ cup chopped pecans

Place a 9 by 5-inch loaf pan, or any standard loaf pan, in the freezer to chill. Bring a kettle of water to a boil. Place the cashews in a bowl and add enough boiling water to cover. Soak for 30 minutes.

Place ¼ cup water in a saucepan. Sprinkle the gelatin over the top and set it aside to bloom for 10 minutes.

Place 1¼ cups water in a blender and add the maple syrup. Drain and rinse the cashews, then add them to the blender. Blend on low speed for 30 seconds, then on high speed for 30 seconds, until the mixture is smooth. Scrape down the sides if necessary and blend again on high until all of the cashew pieces are pureed. Pour the cashew mixture into the saucepan with the gelatin, set the pan over medium heat, and whisk until the gelatin has dissolved completely. Remove the pan from the heat and add the unsweetened chocolate, stirring until the chocolate is fully melted.

Transfer the mixture back to the blender and add the cocoa powder, vanilla, lemon juice, and salt. Blend on high speed for 1 minute. Pour the chocolate custard into the chilled loaf pan and freeze for 1 hour. Fold in the marshmallows, dark chocolate, and pecans. Press a piece of plastic wrap directly on top of the custard and freeze for 6 hours, until firm.

Let the ice cream soften for 15 minutes before scooping.

Tidbits: Sometimes I use a natural, gluten-free brand of marshmallows made by Elyon for ease in this recipe, but they do contain sugar. Try the homemade honey marshmallows from *Celebrations* for a natural, gluten- and sugar-free version.

BANANA PUDDING

Serves 6 to 8 • I went to a lot of church potlucks when I was young. Back then, making banana pudding involved vanilla pudding mix, vanilla wafer cookies, and usually a tub of frozen Cool Whip. I think the bananas were the only thing that wasn't from a package! This is a quintessential retro-style dessert that is so easy to make. I know many of you feel nostalgic about this one and have really missed it. So here you go.

Place the cashew milk in a bowl. Sprinkle the gelatin over the top and set it aside to bloom for 10 minutes.

Cut the vanilla bean in half lengthwise and scrape the seeds into a saucepan. Add the pod and pour in the coconut milk. Bring the mixture to a low simmer over medium heat, but don't let it boil.

Whisk together the egg yolks and honey in a bowl, then quickly add half of the hot coconut milk, whisking constantly to temper the eggs. Add the mixture to the remaining coconut milk in the saucepan and stir over medium-high heat for 4 minutes, until the mixture thickens enough to lightly coat the back of a spoon. Don't let the mixture boil. Add the gelatin mixture and whisk until fully dissolved, about 2 minutes. Pour the custard into a glass bowl, then stir in the vanilla. Place a piece of plastic wrap directly on top of the pudding and refrigerate until set, about 4 hours, or up to 3 days.

Spread a thin layer of pudding in a 1½-quart casserole dish or vessel of your choice. Arrange a layer of cookies on top. Slice the bananas crosswise into ⅛-inch-thick rounds and place a layer of banana rounds over the cookies. Spread one-third of the remaining pudding over the bananas and continue layering cookies, bananas, and pudding. Spread the whipped cream over the top with a spatula, making a few decorative peaks. Crumble a few cookies and the dark chocolate shavings over the top.

Serve immediately, or chill in the fridge for up to 2 hours.

1½ cups Cashew Milk (page 310; see Tidbits)

2 teaspoons unflavored powdered gelatin

1 vanilla bean

½ cup full-fat coconut milk

5 egg yolks

½ cup light-colored raw honey

1 teaspoon pure vanilla extract

15 Nilla Cookies (page 279; see Tidbits), plus more for crumbling

3 or 4 bananas

1 cup Whipped Cream (page 93; optional)

Shaved dark chocolate, for serving

Tidbits: If using store-bought cashew milk, increase the gelatin to 3 teaspoons.

To comply with SCD, substitute any of your favorite SCD-friendly cookies for the Nilla Cookies.

RAINBOW SPRINKLES

Makes 2 cups • Sprinkles are kind of essential in a child's life, but they're usually made from refined sugar and artificial food dyes. This is an easy recipe and they'll last in your cupboard for months, so you'll have them around for dairy-free ice cream sundaes, or to top my Chocolate Sprinkle Doughnuts (page 33). Purchase natural brands of food coloring, like India Tree, that are made from food sources. Piping bags fitted with small round tips work best here, but a resealable plastic bag with the corner cut off can work as well.

1 egg white

½ cup arrowroot powder

½ cup maple sugar

¼ teaspoon pure vanilla extract

Natural liquid food coloring

In the bowl of a stand mixer fitted with the whisk attachment, or using an electric handheld mixer, mix the egg white with the arrowroot, maple sugar, and vanilla on medium-high speed until fully combined. Scrape down the sides and mix again on medium-high speed for 30 seconds.

Divide the mixture among three small cups and color them as you'd like, using 3 or 4 drops of coloring per cup. Spoon the colored mixtures into piping bags fitted with a very small round tip, or into resealable plastic bags with one small corner snipped off.

Place the bags in the freezer for 10 minutes; line two or three baking sheets with parchment paper.

Pipe thin straight lines of the mixture onto the prepared baking sheets. Allow the lines to set overnight at room temperature, then use a sharp knife to cut the lines into small sprinkles.

Store in an airtight container at room temperature for 3 months.

Variations: To make chocolate sprinkles, omit the food coloring and add 2 tablespoons unsweetened cocoa powder to the egg white mixture.

To make a really great royal icing that pipes well onto cookies, add 1 ounce melted cacao butter to the egg white mixture.

CHOCOLATE HAZELNUT SPREAD

Makes 1½ cups • Nutella wasn't something I knew about when I was a kid. I first tasted it on a trip to France. Like most tourists, we bought crepes filled with the gooey chocolate spread and bananas. How delicious! When I started researching the original spread to create this recipe, I was shocked by the ingredients: sugar is listed first, followed by refined palm oil (which is different from the palm shortening I use for baking) and a soy-based emulsifier. You can feel good about how this version is made; go ahead and indulge. I spread this on my Grain-Free Wraps (page 313) and roll them up with sliced bananas, or sandwich the spread between two Nilla Cookies (page 279).

Preheat the oven to 350°F.

Place the hazelnuts on a baking sheet and roast for 10 to 15 minutes, until fragrant and golden brown. Watch them carefully so they don't burn. Pour the nuts onto a clean kitchen towel, wrap them up tightly, and let them steam for 1 minute. Massage the hazelnuts in the towel so most of the skins flake off.

Place the skinned nuts in a food processor and process into a smooth butter, about 2 minutes. Add the maple syrup, coconut milk, and cacao butter and continue to process until very smooth, about 1 minute more. Add the cocoa powder, vanilla, and salt and process again for 1 minute, until thick and creamy. Let cool to room temperature.

Store in a jar with a lid in the fridge for 2 weeks, or in the freezer for 6 months.

1 cup hazelnuts

¾ cup pure maple syrup

2 tablespoons full-fat coconut milk

2 ounces raw cacao butter, melted

¼ cup unsweetened cocoa powder

½ teaspoon pure vanilla extract

⅛ teaspoon fine sea salt

BASICS

There is a reason why my parents used canned soups and packaged containers of sour cream rather than making homemade soup or fermenting cream themselves. It definitely takes some time to make these pantry items and adds quite a few extra steps to any recipe.

If you designate one day on the weekend as a prep day, you can get a lot of steps done in advance, and even store extras in the freezer, which makes those time-consuming dishes more realistic. It isn't always feasible for a busy person to make *all* of these items from scratch, so I have also listed my favorite store-bought versions with some of these recipes as a backup.

ALMOND MILK

EF, **NSF**, **SCD**

Commercial almond milks are pretty pricey, and many are full of additives. Almond milk is so simple to make at home with a blender and some cheesecloth, and homemade tastes much better.

Makes 4 cups

1 cup raw almonds

8 cups filtered water

¼ teaspoon fine sea salt

Put the almonds in a bowl and add 4 cups of the filtered water and ⅛ teaspoon of the salt. Soak at room temperature for at least 10 hours or up to overnight.

Drain and rinse the almonds, then transfer them to a blender and add the remaining 4 cups filtered water and ⅛ teaspoon salt. Blend on low speed for 30 seconds, then on high speed for 1 to 2 minutes, until smooth.

Strain the milk through a fine-mesh sieve, a nut milk bag, or a double layer of cheesecloth. Squeeze to remove all of the liquid. Use immediately, or store in an airtight container in the refrigerator for 5 days. Shake well before using.

Tidbits: **If you plan to drink the almond milk on its own or use it for a sweet dish, add 1 to 3 small pitted dates to the blender to sweeten it naturally.**

Other nuts can be substituted for the almonds to make a variety of nut milks. Try hazelnuts, walnuts, or pecans. For cashew milk, see page 310.

Buy It: Use the unsweetened original version and look for brands with the fewest ingredients and no carrageenan or gums, such as New Barn.

BASIC CAULI RICE

EF, NF, NSF, SCD

Serve this as a substitute for rice. It's great with Thai Yellow Curry (page 194), Indian Butter Chicken (page 203), Sheet-Pan Teriyaki Salmon with Broccoli and Asparagus (page 224), or Beef and Broccoli (page 182).

Makes about 3 cups

1 small head cauliflower, cut into florets

1 tablespoon ghee or extra-virgin olive oil

½ cup diced yellow onion

1 clove garlic, minced

¾ teaspoon fine sea salt

Place the cauliflower in a food processor fitted with the grating attachment, or use the large holes on a box grater, and process the florets into rice-size pieces. Pick out any large fragments that didn't shred and chop them up by hand with a knife or save for another use.

Melt the ghee in a large skillet over medium heat. Add the onion and garlic and sauté for 5 minutes, until the onion has softened. Add the cauliflower rice to the pan and sauté for 5 minutes.

Add ¼ cup water and the salt and increase the heat to medium-high. Cook for 15 minutes, until the cauliflower is tender and the liquid has been absorbed.

Variation: To make a Mexican rice version, substitute Chicken Bone Broth (page 310) for the water and stir in ½ cup chopped tomatoes with their juices, ¼ cup canned chopped green chiles, and ¾ teaspoon ground cumin before cooking for 15 minutes. Top with chopped fresh cilantro.

BBQ SAUCE

EF, NF, SCD

Keep this BBQ sauce in your refrigerator to add a punch of flavor and spice up leftovers.

Makes 3 cups

2 to 4 ounces pitted Deglet Noor dates (12 to 17 small dates)

2 cups tomato puree

½ cup apple cider vinegar

¼ cup tomato paste

2 tablespoons coconut aminos (see Tidbits)

2 teaspoons fish sauce

1½ teaspoons natural liquid smoke

1 teaspoon fine sea salt

1 teaspoon sweet paprika

1 teaspoon chili powder

1 teaspoon Dijon mustard

½ teaspoon cayenne pepper

½ teaspoon minced garlic

½ teaspoon onion powder

½ teaspoon ground allspice

½ teaspoon freshly ground black pepper

Bring a kettle of water to a boil. Place the dates in a small bowl and add enough boiling water to cover. Soak for 15 minutes. Drain the dates and place them in a blender with ¼ cup fresh water and all of the remaining ingredients. Blend on high speed until smooth, about 1 minute. »

Pour the sauce into a pan over medium-high heat and bring to a boil. Turn the heat to low and simmer, uncovered, for 30 minutes, until reduced by about half. Let the sauce cool to room temperature and place in an airtight container.

Store the sauce in the fridge for 2 weeks, or in the freezer for 4 months. Defrost in the refrigerator overnight before using.

Tidbits: To comply with SCD, omit the coconut aminos.

CASHEW MILK

EF, NF, SCD

This is a thick version of cashew milk that works really well to thicken sauces or soups. If you purchase cashew milk, be aware that it usually contains additives to keep the milk thin and may not perform as well in these recipes.

Makes 4 cups

2 cups (about 300g) whole raw cashews (see Tidbits)

¼ teaspoon fine sea salt

Put the cashews in a bowl and add cold water to cover. Cover the bowl with a clean kitchen towel and soak for 4 hours at room temperature.

Drain and rinse the cashews, then transfer them to a blender and add 4 cups filtered water and the salt. Blend on low speed for 30 seconds, then on high speed for 2 minutes, until the mixture is creamy and there are no fragments of cashews. Use immediately, or store in an airtight container in the fridge for 5 days. Shake well before using.

Tidbits: To achieve the proper thickness in cashew milk or sauces that use cashews as a thickener, measure the nuts using the gram weight provided. Do the same to substitute skinless almonds or raw macadamia nuts as the differing nut sizes will measure differently in cups.

CHICKEN, BEEF, OR TURKEY BONE BROTH

EF, NF, NSF, SCD

Homemade bone broth, or stock, not only makes the most delicious soups, it is also wonderful for sipping daily. It is easily digestible, helps heal the lining of your gut, and contains valuable nutrients. The key to getting a good gel to your broth is to *not* fill the pot with too much water; add just enough to cover the bones. I prefer to use filtered water to avoid any chemicals and metals in tap water. This recipe can be used with chicken, beef, or turkey bones. I prefer the flavor of the broth when I've used roasted bones, but raw bones will work too.

Makes 8 to 10 cups

4 pounds mixed bones (see Tidbits)

2 tablespoons extra-virgin olive oil (optional)

Fine sea salt and freshly ground black pepper (optional)

4 carrots, halved crosswise

2 celery stalks (with leaves), halved crosswise

1 large yellow onion, quartered

1 bunch flat-leaf parsley

4 cloves garlic, crushed

1 tablespoon apple cider vinegar

6 to 8 cups filtered water

If the bones are cooked, place them in a stockpot or slow cooker insert. If the bones are raw, place them on a baking sheet, drizzle with the olive oil, and season with salt and pepper. Roast in a 400°F oven for 20 minutes. Transfer the bones and any juices to a slow cooker or electric pressure cooker.

Add the carrots, celery, onion, parsley, garlic, and vinegar to the slow cooker or pressure cooker and add enough filtered water to just barely cover the bones.

If using a slow cooker, cover and cook for 24 hours on low. If using a pressure cooker, secure the lid and turn the pressure valve to sealed. Select the manual setting and set it to high pressure for 80 minutes. Let the pressure release naturally, then remove the lid.

Skim the fat from the broth and pour the broth through a fine-mesh sieve to strain out the bones and other solids.

Allow the broth to cool to room temperature, then store in airtight containers in the refrigerator for 1 week, or freeze in silicone muffin molds and, once frozen, transfer to resealable plastic bags for 6 months. Reheat from frozen in a saucepan over medium-low heat for 15 minutes, until heated through.

Tidbits: Ask your butcher for soup bones. For beef stock, use a mix of bones with a little meat on them, such as oxtail, short ribs, or knucklebones. For poultry, use a mix of backs, legs, and feet.

Buy It: Bonafide and Bare Bones Broth are my favorites. Look for a low- or no-sodium variety to use in my recipes.

DAIRY-FREE SOUR CREAM

EF, NSF, SCD

This dairy-free sour cream is a simple alternative for sour cream when you really want something creamy and slightly sour on your Mexican food or in dips.

Makes 1 cup

2 (13.5-ounce) cans full-fat coconut milk (see Tidbits), refrigerated upright for 24 hours

Contents of 1 (50 billion IU) dairy-free and gluten-free probiotic capsule (discard the capsule casing)

2 tablespoons Almond Milk (page 308) or Cashew Milk (opposite page)

½ teaspoon freshly squeezed lime juice

¼ teaspoon fine sea salt

Carefully remove the cans of coconut milk from the refrigerator and open the tops. Skim the thick cream from the tops of the cans, until you have 1 cup cream. Discard the thin, cloudy water at the bottom of the can or save it for a smoothie. Stir in the probiotic powder and cover the bowl with a clean kitchen towel. Let the bowl sit at room temperature for 36 to 48 hours. The longer you leave it, the more sour it will be.

Stir in the almond milk, lime juice, and salt.

Store, tightly covered, in the refrigerator for 1 week.

Tidbits: You may only need 1 can of coconut milk, but I always refrigerate 2 cans because some cans have less cream than others. Store them upright so the cream can rise to the top.

Buy It: If you tolerate some dairy, Green Valley Organics makes a lactose-free sour cream that is delicious.

DAIRY-FREE YOGURT

EF, NSF, SCD

Although there are a lot of dairy-free yogurts available in stores nowadays, many of them use ingredients I don't tolerate well, like tapioca, cane sugar, and guar or xanthan gums. Making yogurt at home is easier than you think, and because it tastes so much better than store-bought, I make a batch a week for me and the kids. The small amount of maple syrup is essential for the fermentation process, but the yogurt will be sugar-free once the bacteria has used up the sugars. This is a plain, sour yogurt that's delicious on its own, but I've added a variation if you want something sweeter. Note: You will need a yogurt maker, Instant Pot, or dehydrator for this recipe.

Makes 6 servings

1 cup (about 150g) whole raw cashews (see Tidbits, page 310)

2 cups filtered water

1½ teaspoons unflavored powdered gelatin

1½ tablespoons pure maple syrup or light-colored raw honey

Contents of 1 (50 billion IU) dairy-free and gluten-free probiotic capsule (discard the capsule casing)

Bring a kettle of water to a boil. Place the cashews in a bowl and add enough boiling water to cover. Soak for 30 minutes, then drain, rinse, and drain again.

Place ½ cup of the filtered water in a saucepan and sprinkle the gelatin over the top. Set aside to let the gelatin bloom for 10 minutes.

Place the cashews in a blender with the remaining 1½ cups filtered water. Blend on high speed until smooth, about 1 minute. Scrape down the sides if needed and blend again, until very smooth.

Place the saucepan with the gelatin over medium-high heat and bring to a boil, whisking constantly to dissolve the gelatin. Turn the heat to medium and add the cashew liquid. Heat the mixture, whisking constantly, until it reaches 120°F, about 5 minutes; do not let it boil.

Remove the pan from the heat and let cool to 110°F, about 15 minutes. Whisk in the maple syrup and the probiotic powder. Pour the mixture through a fine-mesh sieve into six clean ¼-pint (4-ounce) jars and secure the lids. Place the jars in a yogurt maker or a dehydrator with the trays removed, and set to 110°F; ferment for 12 to 16 hours. The longer you leave the yogurt, the sourer it will become.

Place the jars in the refrigerator for 4 hours, or up to 5 days, to allow the gelatin to set and the yogurt to thicken. Stir the yogurt well for a creamy consistency before eating.

Variation: For fruit-flavored yogurt, stir in 2 tablespoons, per jar, of a fresh fruit puree of your choice before chilling in the refrigerator. My family loves strawberry, peach, blueberry, and banana-mango.

GRAIN-FREE BAKING POWDER

EF, NF, NSF

Most commercial baking powders contain aluminum and cornstarch. This homemade version allows you to control the ingredients, and it's so quick to make.

Makes ¾ cup

½ cup cream of tartar

¼ cup baking soda

2 tablespoons arrowroot powder

Combine the cream of tartar, baking soda, and arrowroot in a small bowl.

Store in an airtight container at room temperature for 6 months.

Tidbits: This can be made starch-free by omitting the arrowroot, but it will clump up in the pantry after a couple of days. Scale the recipe down by half and use it up quickly.

GRAIN-FREE WRAPS

NF, NSF

These wraps are so versatile, they've become a fan favorite for sandwiches, breakfast crepes, enchiladas, and even lasagna. See againstallgrain.com/grain-free-wraps for a video of me making these.

Makes 12

6 eggs, beaten

1 cup Almond Milk (page 308; see Tidbits)

6 tablespoons coconut flour

½ cup arrowroot powder

2 tablespoons melted ghee, plus more for cooking

½ teaspoon fine sea salt

Combine the eggs, almond milk, coconut flour, arrowroot, ghee, and salt in a blender. Blend on low speed for 15 seconds, then let the batter sit for 5 minutes. Blend on high speed for 15 seconds more.

Heat an 8-inch crepe pan or well-seasoned griddle over medium-high heat. Melt a small amount of ghee in the pan and spread it all over. Ladle ¼ cup of the batter onto the hot pan and quickly spread it into a paper-thin 8-inch circle with the back of the ladle or by turning the pan quickly with your wrist. Fill in any holes with a drop of batter. Cook for 45 seconds, until the sides start to lift, then gently flip the wrap using a spatula. Cook for 30 seconds on the other side.

Stack the cooked wraps on a plate. Repeat until all of the batter is used, greasing the pan as needed to prevent sticking. Let the wraps cool.

Store in a resealable plastic bag, with parchment paper between each wrap, in the refrigerator for 5 days, or in the freezer for 6 months. Defrost in the refrigerator for 2 hours before using.

Tidbits: To make this NF, substitute ¾ cup full-fat coconut milk mixed with ¼ cup water for the almond milk.

A shallow well-seasoned crepe pan works best for this recipe, or use a large flat griddle to make multiple wraps at a time. Keep the wraps very thin and do not try to flip them until the sides start to lift.

KETCHUP

EF, NF, SCD

This ketchup is free of added sugars and is simple to make. I prefer the less gritty texture of small Deglet Noor dates for this recipe, plus they're easier to find. You can also use Medjool dates, which are larger, sweeter, and a little softer. If you're using Medjool, follow the ounce measurement, not the number of dates, since the two types differ in size. »

Makes 3 cups

2 to 4 ounces pitted Deglet Noor dates
(12 to 17 small dates)

3 cups tomato puree

¼ cup plus 1 tablespoon white wine vinegar

¼ cup tomato paste

1 clove garlic, peeled

1 teaspoon onion powder

¾ teaspoon fine sea salt

¼ teaspoon dry mustard powder

⅛ teaspoon ground cloves

⅛ teaspoon ground allspice

Bring a kettle of water to a boil. Place the dates in a small bowl and add enough boiling water to cover. Soak for 15 minutes. Drain the dates and place them in a blender with ¼ cup plus 2 tablespoons fresh water and all of the remaining ingredients. Blend on high speed until smooth, about 3 minutes.

Pour the ketchup into a saucepan over medium-high heat and bring to a boil, then turn the heat to low and simmer, uncovered, for 30 minutes, until the ketchup has reduced by about half. Let the ketchup cool to room temperature and place in an airtight container.

Store in the fridge for 2 weeks, or in the freezer for 4 months. Defrost in the refrigerator overnight before using.

Buy It: I have yet to find a paleo-friendly ketchup that my kids will get behind, but they do love the Cucina Antica and Sir Kensington's brands found at most health food stores, or the Trader Joe's organic ketchup. These have the lowest sugar content I have seen in commercial brands.

MAYONNAISE

NF, NSF, SCD

Making mayonnaise is really so simple and can be done in a flash. See againstallgrain.com/mayo for a video of me making this version and for tips on how to fix a broken mayo.

Makes ¾ cup

1 egg yolk

1 teaspoon freshly squeezed lemon juice

1 teaspoon white wine vinegar

½ teaspoon fine sea salt

¼ teaspoon Dijon mustard

¾ cup avocado oil

Combine the egg yolk, lemon juice, vinegar, salt, and mustard in a small blender or mini food processor and blend on low speed until combined. With the blender on low speed, begin adding the oil, a drop at a time. When the mixture begins to thicken, add the remaining oil in a slow, steady stream, until all of the oil has been incorporated. Refrigerate for 2 hours before using.

Store in the refrigerator, tightly covered, for 3 days.

Variation: A small blender or mini food processor is essential for this method. But mayonnaise can also be made by hand. Combine the egg yolk, lemon juice, vinegar, salt, and mustard in a bowl and whisk to combine. Add ¼ cup of the oil, ½ teaspoon at a time, whisking vigorously. Gradually add the remaining ½ cup oil in a slow, steady stream, whisking constantly, for 5 to 7 minutes, until thick. Alternatively, many find that using an immersion blender in a tall, slender container works well too.

Tidbits: You can also use macadamia nut, olive, or almond oil in this recipe.

Buy It: Primal Kitchen makes a delicious avocado oil mayonnaise sold at most health food stores.

PARMESAN CHEESE

EF, NSF

This vegan Parmesan cheese replacement tastes delicious on all of your favorite Italian dishes or even used as a topping for a green salad.

Makes 1 cup

¾ cup (about 105g) whole raw cashews
(see Tidbits, page 310)

2½ tablespoons nutritional yeast

¾ teaspoon fine sea salt

½ teaspoon garlic powder

Place the cashews, nutritional yeast, salt, and garlic powder in a food processor and process until it has the texture of fine sand.

Store in an airtight jar in the refrigerator for 2 weeks.

PRESSURE COOKER CHICKEN

EF, NF, NSF, SCD

Don't expect crispy, juicy skin like you would get if you roasted the bird in the oven for an hour, but this 20-minute chicken is fantastic to make at the beginning of the week to use for lunches or to throw on top of a salad for a quick dinner.

Makes about 6 cups shredded chicken

1 (4- to 5-pound) whole chicken

2 carrots, quartered

2 celery stalks, quartered

1 yellow onion, quartered

2 teaspoons fine sea salt

½ teaspoon freshly ground black pepper

Pour 1 cup water into an electric pressure cooker and add a steamer insert to the bottom of the cooker. Stuff the chicken cavity with as much carrot, celery, and onion as can fit and scatter the rest inside the cooker. Season the outside of the chicken and the inside of the cavity generously with the salt and pepper. Lay the bird on the steamer insert, breast side up. Secure the lid, select the manual button, and cook at high pressure for 18 minutes.

Quick release the pressure and transfer the chicken to a plate or carving board. Tent the cooked bird with aluminum foil and let it rest for 10 minutes. Remove the skin and carve the chicken from the bones. Save the bones for bone broth (see page 310 and Tidbits).

Let the chicken cool to room temperature, then store it in an airtight container in the refrigerator for 5 days.

Tidbits: If you want to make bone broth right away, remove the vegetables from the cavity and place them, along with all of the bones, back into the pressure cooker with the remaining liquid. Add 2 teaspoons apple cider vinegar, 1 carrot cut in half, 1 celery stalk cut in half, 1 yellow onion cut into quarters, and 5 to 7 cups water, just enough to barely cover the bones. Secure the lid, select the manual button, and cook at high pressure for 1½ hours. Strain the solids before serving or drinking. See page 311 for storage tips.

PRESSURE COOKER SWEET POTATOES

EF, NF, NSF

Sweet potatoes can take upward of 45 minutes to roast, depending on their size, and make a syrupy mess of a baking sheet if you're not careful. When you're running short on time, this method gives you perfectly tender potatoes in less than 20 minutes.

Serves 4

4 sweet potatoes

1 tablespoon avocado oil

1 teaspoon fine sea salt

Scrub the sweet potatoes well, then rub them all over with the oil. Sprinkle with the salt, patting the potatoes with your hands to get the salt to adhere to the skins.

Pour 1 cup water into an electric pressure cooker and add a steamer insert to the bottom of the cooker. Place the sweet potatoes on the steamer insert. Secure the lid, select the manual button, and cook at high pressure for 15 minutes.

Quick release the pressure, then test the potatoes with a fork for doneness. If the potatoes are on the large side and are still too firm, cook at high pressure for 1 to 3 minutes.

Let the potatoes cool to room temperature, then store them in an airtight container in the refrigerator for 1 week. Reheat in a 400°F oven for 15 minutes, until heated through.

Tidbits: If you prefer roasted sweet potatoes for the crispy skin, try the method on page 186.

RICOTTA CHEESE

EF, NSF, SCD

I use this dairy-free version of my favorite creamy Italian cheese in lasagna (see page 220), on pizzas (see page 265), and even in pancakes (see page 23).

Makes 2½ cups

2 cups skinless slivered almonds

Filtered water

Contents of 1 (50 billion IU) dairy-free and gluten-free probiotic capsule (discard the capsule casing)

¼ to ½ cup Almond Milk (page 308)

¾ teaspoon fine sea salt

Place the almonds in a bowl and add enough filtered water to cover. Add the probiotic powder, then cover the bowl with a clean kitchen towel. Let the bowl sit at room temperature for 36 to 48 hours.

Drain the almonds and place them in a food processor with ¼ cup of the almond milk and the salt. Process until the mixture is very smooth and resembles creamy ricotta cheese. If it is too thick, add a little more almond milk, 1 tablespoon at a time, to thin it out.

Store, tightly covered, in the refrigerator for 1 week, or in the freezer for 4 months. Defrost in the refrigerator for 24 hours before using.

Buy It: Kite Hill makes a dairy-free almond-based ricotta cheese sold at most health food stores.

SANDWICH ROLLS

NSF, SCD

After an easy blender–bread recipe appeared in my last cookbook, readers began to bake the batter into muffins and rolls, which inspired this recipe. I use English muffin rings, but the rings of mason jars would also work well to form the rolls.

Makes 12

8 eggs

½ cup Almond Milk (page 308)

4 teaspoons apple cider vinegar

3 cups (about 450g) whole raw cashews (see Tidbits, page 310)

½ cup coconut flour

2 teaspoons baking soda

1 teaspoon fine sea salt

Place a heatproof dish filled with 2 inches of water on the bottom rack of the oven. Preheat the oven to 325°F. Lightly grease the insides of twelve 3-inch English muffin rings with ghee and place them on a baking sheet lined with parchment paper.

Place the eggs, almond milk, vinegar, and cashews in a blender and process on low speed for 15 seconds. Scrape down the sides and process again on high speed for 30 to 60 seconds, until very smooth. Scrape down the sides once more, then add the coconut flour, baking soda, and salt and blend again on high until fully incorporated, 15 to 30 seconds. Fill each ring halfway with batter.

Bake for 20 minutes, until a toothpick inserted into the center of each roll comes out clean.

Allow the rolls to cool on the baking sheet for 15 minutes, then gently press them out of the rings from the bottom. Cool completely on a wire rack before slicing and using.

Store the rolls, tightly wrapped, at room temperature for 4 days, or in the fridge for 2 weeks.

Freeze the rolls in an airtight container or a resealable plastic freezer bag for 4 months. Defrost at room temperature for 15 minutes before slicing and toasting, or in the refrigerator overnight to serve them untoasted.

ACKNOWLEDGMENTS

As the saying goes, "it takes a village," and I cannot express enough gratitude to my village.

To my husband, Ryan, and our beautiful children, you are what I live for daily.

To our parents, for your taste-testing, dishwashing, cheerleading, and babysitting.

To Maria, for loving our children like your own and caring for them so well while we work.

To my AAG A-team, Sydney, Christina, and Barb, thank you for all of the assistance you provide with the day-to-day tasks of running my life: recipe testing, website, social media sites, and books. I quite literally could not do it without you!

To Julie Bennett, for having grace as I learn the ins and outs of "real" publishing, and for helping to streamline my often disorganized and overambitious ideas.

To Ashley Lima and all of the Ten Speed Press team, thank you for your continued support of my work and for working tirelessly to make this book beautiful, errorless, and just what my fans have been asking for.

To my photography team, Aubrie, Lillian, Besma, and Veronica, you'd think spending almost three weeks straight with strangers would be taxing, but it was the most fun I had all year! Your positive energy, early-morning smiles, and late-afternoon patience was inspiring and made every photo-shoot day so enjoyable. Your work is impeccable, and I can't wait to get the gang back together for whatever the next book may be.

To Kari, for guiding me through the unfamiliar waters of publishing, being my bad-guy even though you're one of the nicest people I know, and for believing in my mission.

To my fabulous recipe testers, thank you for all of your feedback, constructive criticism, and praise. A special thank-you to Rob and his family, who have been trusted recipe testers for all four books now.

And to you, my readers. Whether you own one of my cookbooks, read my blog, or follow me on social media, I wouldn't be writing these books if it weren't for your fervent requests for recipes and stories about finding healing through food. I look forward to releasing a book because it means getting to travel, to meet you all face to face, hear your stories, and give you a hug. Thank you for your continued support. If you keep those recipe requests coming, I will continue writing for you.

RESOURCES

See and shop these brands and my up-to-date favorite brands at againstallgrain.com/shop. Also see my preferred snack brands on page 78.

BAKING AND PANTRY STAPLES

ALMOND FLOUR Wellbee's, Honeyville, Yupik (Canada)

ARROWROOT POWDER Starwest Botanicals, Bob's Red Mill

BAKING POWDER (GRAIN-FREE) Hain Pure Foods

CASHEW FLOUR Wellbee's

CHOCOLATE (BARS, CHIPS, PIECES) Enjoy Life, Guittard, Hu Kitchen

CHOCOLATE (UNSWEETENED BAKING) Guittard

COCOA POWDER Equal Exchange, Navitas Organics

COCONUT FLOUR Tropical Traditions, Nutiva

COCONUT MILK Native Forest, Natural Value, 365

COCONUT OIL Nutiva, Tropical Traditions, Artisana

COCONUT SUGAR Nutiva, Madhava Sweeteners

GELATIN POWDER AND COLLAGEN PEPTIDES (GRASS-FED UNFLAVORED) Vital Proteins

GLUTEN-FREE DRY ACTIVE YEAST Bob's Red Mill

MAPLE SUGAR AND MAPLE SYRUP Coombs Family Farms, A and A Maple

NUTS AND SEEDS Trader Joe's, Nuts.com, Costco

SPICES Simply Organic, Frontier Co-op, Starwest Botanicals, Primal Palate

FATS, OILS, SAUCES, AND CONDIMENTS

AVOCADO OIL MAYONNAISE Primal Kitchen

COCONUT AMINOS Big Tree Farms, Coconut Secret, Thrive Market

FISH SAUCE Red Boat Fish Sauce

GHEE Organic Valley or Pure Indian Foods

GRASS-FED BEEF TALLOW, PASTURED PORK LARD, AND DUCK FAT Fatworks or Epic

KETCHUP Sir Kensington's, Cucina Antica, Trader Joe's Organic

PALM SHORTENING Tropical Traditions

TOMATO PRODUCTS Bionaturae, Yellow Barn, Pomi, Cucina Antica

MEAT AND PROTEINS

Check out EatWild.com for local grass-fed and pasture-raised meats or check your grocery store for these brands:

GRASS-FED BEEF Panorama Meats, U.S. Wellness Meats, Butcher Box

GRASS-FED ORGANIC HOT DOGS AND SAUSAGES Applegate, Fork in the Road, Wellshire

ORGANIC DELI MEATS Diestel, Fork in the Road, True Story, Applegate, Wellshire

ORGANIC EGGS FROM PASTURED HENS Vital Farms, Alexandre Family Farms

ORGANIC, NITRATE-FREE, AND SUGAR-FREE BACON Applegate, Wellshire Farms, Pederson's Natural Farms

PASTURE-RAISED POULTRY U.S. Wellness Meats

PHOTO RECIPE INDEX

BREAKFAST

Lemon Ricotta
Pancakes 23

Crustless Quiche
to Go 24

Biscuits and Sausage
Gravy 26

Banana-Chocolate-
Hazelnut French
Toast 29

Shrimp and Grits with
Bacon Collards 30

Chocolate Sprinkle
Doughnuts 33

Millionaire's Bacon 36

Banana Bread 39

Everything Bagels 40

Açai Berry–Chia
Pudding Parfaits 43

**PACKED
LUNCHES**

Nut-Free Lunchbox
Bread 48

Millionaire's AB&J 53

Deviled Egg Salad
Sandwich 54

AAGwich 57

California Hand
Rolls 60

Meatball Sub 63

Dill Chicken Salad 64

Seven-Layer Bean
Dip Cups 67

Barbecue Chicken
Salad with Peach
Power Slaw 68

Chicken Gyro Wrap 71

Pizza Pockets 72

320

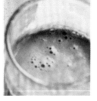

Classic Pickles,
Two Ways 128

Savory Sweet Potato
Mash 130

White Wine
Garlic Spinach and
Mushrooms 133

Cauli Couscous 134

Onion Rings 137

Pesto Squash
Noodles 138

SALADS,
SOUPS, AND
STEWS

Sesame-Crusted
Seared Ahi Salad 145

Thai Crunch with
Steak 146

Italian Chopped
Salad with Red Wine
Vinaigrette 148

Grilled Chicken
Caesar 151

Steak Salad with Roasted
Sweet Potatoes and
Caramelized Onions 152

Grilled Shrimp
Summer Harvest
Salad with Basil
Vinaigrette 155

Chef's Salad 156

French Onion
Soup 159

Loaded Baked Potato
Soup 160

Creamy Broccoli
Soup 163

Tomato Soup with
Zesty Croutons 164

Healing Chicken
Soup 167

Chili Cornbread
Pie 170

Chicken 'N'
Dumplings Soup 173

Betty's Beef Stew 175

QUICK AND
EASY MEALS

Beef and Broccoli 182

Chicken Piccata
with Artichokes and
Spinach 185

Buffalo-Stuffed
Sweet Potatoes 186

Fried Chicken 188

Sloppy Joes 190

Shrimp Fried Rice 193

Thai Yellow Curry 194

No-Mato Bolognese with Spaghetti Squash 197

Crab Cakes with Remoulade Sauce 200

Indian Butter Chicken 203

Spaghetti and Meatballs 204

Pulled Pork with Slaw 206

Shrimp and Sausage Jambalaya 209

Moroccan Chicken Sheet-Pan Supper 210

Honey-Mustard Sheet-Pan Salmon 213

Chicken Parmesan with Roasted Spaghetti Squash 214

French Dip Sandwiches 217

Sausage-Spinach Skillet Lasagna 220

Sheet-Pan Steak Fajitas 223

Sheet-Pan Teriyaki Salmon with Broccoli and Asparagus 224

One-Pan Deconstructed Turkey Dinner 226

MAKE IT AHEAD

Breakfast "Hamburgers" 233

Chocolate-Zucchini Muffins 234

Crispy Nut-Free Waffles 237

Morning Glory Muffins 238

Smoothie Packets 240

Honey-Mustard Chicken 243

Pesto Power Meatballs 244

Poppy Seed Chicken 247

Shepherd's Pie 250

Chicken Potpie 253

Chicken Divan 256

Mini Corn Dogs 259

Fish Sticks with Fries and Tartar Sauce 260

Chicken Nuggets 262

Pizza Crusts 265

Garlic Naan 268

Condensed Cream of Mushroom Soup 271

SWEETS AND TREATS

Cowboy Cookies 276

Nilla Cookies 279

Snickerdoodles 280

Mint Slims 283

Ricotta Cheesecake with Blueberry Sauce 285

Apple Crisp 289

Pineapple Upside-Down Cake 290

Key Lime Pie 293

Strawberry Banana Yogurt Pops 296

Chocolate "Pickles" Pops 299

Rocky Road Ice Cream 300

Banana Pudding 303

Rainbow Sprinkles 304

Chocolate Hazelnut Spread 307

INDEX

Text copyright © 2018 by Simple Writing Holdings, LLC
Photographs copyright © 2018 by Aubrie Pick

Library of Congress Cataloging-in-Publication Data
  Names: Walker, Danielle (Chef), author.
  Title: Danielle Walker's Eat what you love: everyday comfort food you crave; gluten-free, dairy-free, and
    paleo recipes
  Description: First edition. | California : Ten Speed Press, [2018] | Includes
    bibliographical references and indexes.
  Identifiers: LCCN 2017053030
  Subjects: LCSH: Cooking, American. | Comfort food. | Gluten-free
    diet—Recipes. | Egg-free diet—Recipes. | Milk-free diet—Recipes. |
    High-protein diet—Recipes. | Cooking (Natural foods) | LCGFT: Cookbooks.
  Classification: LCC TX715 .W1823 2018 | DDC 641.3—dc23
    LC record available at https://lccn.loc.gov/2017053030

Hardcover ISBN: 978-1-60774-944-8
eBook ISBN: 978-1-60774-945-5

Printed in China

Design by Ashley Lima
Food styling by Lillian Kang
Food styling assistance by Veronica Laramie
Prop styling by Claire Mack
Photography assistance by Bessma Khalaf
Hair and makeup by Lindsay Skog
Wardrobe by Jenn Bonnet

10 9 8 7 6 5 4 3 2 1

First Edition